**ODYSSEY BOOKS & GUIDES**

**Odyssey Books & Guides is a division of Airphoto International Ltd.**
903, Seaview Commercial Building
21–24 Connaught Road West
Sheung Wan, Hong Kong
Tel: (852) 2856 3896; Fax: (852) 2565 8004
E-mail: sales@odysseypublications.com; www.odysseypublications.com

**Distribution in the USA by W.W. Norton & Company, Inc.**
**500 Fifth Avenue, New York, NY 10110, USA**
**Tel: 800-233-4830; Fax: 800-458-6515**
**www.wwnorton.com**

**Distribution in the UK and Europe by Cordee Books and Maps**
**3a De Montfort St. Leicester, UK, LE1 7HD, UK**
**Tel: 0116-254-3579; Fax: 0116-247-1176**
**www.cordee.co.uk**

*The Bund Shanghai: China Faces West*, First Edition
**ISBN: 978-962-217-772-7**
Library of Congress Catalog Card Number has been requested.
Copyright © Peter Hibbard 2007

Front cover illustration by Schiff, North China Daily News, 1940
Other cover illustrations: Palace Hotel and Astor House Hotel
luggage stickers, courtesy 'Picture This Gallery', Hong Kong;
Bund photographs, courtesy Dennis George Crow

(Every effort has been made to trace copyright holders of pictures and
text. We apologize for any errors or omissions in the credits and would be
grateful to be notified of any corrections that should be incorporated in
any future editions.)

Designer: Alex Ng Kin Man
Index: Don Brech, Records Management International Limited Hong Kong
Production by Twin Age Ltd, Hong Kong
E-mail: twinage@netvigator.com
Manufactured in Hong Kong

# THE BUND

SHANGHAI

Sketch by Schiff, 1940

## Acknowledgements

Peter Hibbard would like to thank the staff of the following libraries and archives who made this book possible—Beijing University, Hongkong and Shanghai Hotels Ltd., Hong Kong University, HSBC Group archives, Imperial War Museum London, National Library of China, Public Records Office Kew, Shanghai Bibliotheca, Shanghai Municipal Archives, Royal Commonwealth Society Cambridge, RIBA Library, SOAS London, Thomas Cook. A special note of thanks must be made to Pan Yanming, Sheng Jilin and Wang Renfang, who opened many closed doors.

He would also like to thank the following for making this book a reality—Bruno van der Berg, Bryan Brown, Nick Burns, Amber Chen, Shiatzy Chen, Chen Xueyi, Christopher Choa, Filippo Gabbiani, Michelle Garnaut, Bi Ji Gen, Mark Jared, Kate Kelly, Kelly and Walsh, Malcolm Y. S. Lai, Sylvia Lee, William Leung, Edward Liang, Kathy Lou, Ma Yongzhang, Ted Marr, Lyndon Neri, Eric Niderost, Helen Northey, Eric Politzer, Remo Riva, Ivy Soonthornsima, David Sung, Vivien Shen, Douglas Webster, Amy Wood, Ben Wood, Simon Ye, Delphine Yip. Thanks to Don Brech for highlighting my grammatical idiocies and compiling the index, and to Alex Ng for his talent and dedication in designing this book. A very special thank you must go to Magnus Bartlett and Robert Bickers for their friendship and guidance, and most importantly, I would like to thank my wife, Li Huishan, my daughter, Li Shasha, and my son Caspar Hibbard-Short for their patience and loving support.

Photographs and images by Peter Hibbard, as well as—AIG, American Express, Astor House Hotel, Magnus Bartlett, Robert Bickers, Adrian Bradshaw, 6 Bund, Bund 18, Shiatzy Chen, China Minsheng Banking Corporation, Chinese Museum Collection, Melbourne—Mellerick album (MEL 022, 023, 031, 032, 042), Filippo Gabbiani, Michelle Garnaut, Hongkong and Shanghai Hotels Ltd., HSBC, Donald Insall Associates, Ma Yongzhang (Peace Hotel), Lyndon Neri, Eric Niderost, P&T Group, Eric Politzer, RIBA, Royal Commonwealth Society, Shanghai Construction Archives, Shanghai Municipal Archives (SMA), South China Morning Post, John Swire and Sons, John Warner Publications, Wattis Fine Art, Ben Wood and Delphine Yip, (ben wood STUDIOSHANGHAI), Three on the Bund, Tongji University, Wang Gangfeng, Yang Peiming. With a special thank you to Dennis George Crow for images from his extensive and magnificent collection of rare historic photographs (www.dennisgeorgecrow.com) and to Christopher Bailey, *Picture This Gallery* Hong Kong, for images from his collection, including those from Kelly and Walsh's *So This is Shanghai* (1935) and *Shanghai Today* (1928) (www.picturethiscollection.com).

With so few original photos surviving from the early 20th century, the author has reproduced images from printed sources, including those from the *China Architect's and Builder's Compendium, The China Press, The China Journal, The Far Eastern Review, The Illustrated London News, The North China Daily News, The North China Sunday News Magazine, Shanghai Evening Post & Mercury, The Shanghai Times, SMC Annual Report, Social Shanghai* and *Twentieth-century Impressions of Hong Kong, Shanghai and Other Treaty Ports of China* by Arnold Wright.

### A Note on Spellings

For the sake of simplicity and modern-day reference, pinyin Romanisation has been used as far as possible throughout the text. A special note must be made of the word 'Yangtsze.' As such a spelling was applied to the river (Yangzi in current Pinyin transliteration), to the Bund, and was used as a company name by foreigners in old Shanghai, it has been left in its old form throughout this book.

# THE BUND
# SHANGHAI
## CHINA FACES WEST

### PETER HIBBARD

# INTRODUCTION

In Shanghai, but of the world, the Bund is a remarkable survival of a pre-communist internationalised China. In many ways it used to be China's front door, as ship passengers alighted at the Customs jetty from abroad and entered China for the first time. Memoirs and contemporary reports comment often on the sight that greeted those arriving. Its modernity puzzled them, and sometimes disappointed—for it did not look like the China that many expected. There was not a pagoda to be seen amongst the towers.

That foreign-seeming modernity was a source of pride for many. This was no willow-pattern China, but a real city hooked into global trade and finance. It was also a physically internationalised site—tons of stone came from Hong Kong, marble from Italy and from England, foundations involved thousands of Oregon pines, and finishes involved bronzework from Somerset, mosaics crafted in Venice, and on the Custom House, bells from Loughborough in England.

The Bund was an icon before 1949, sitting on letterheads, the subject of postcards, reverie and fond memoir, and the site as Peter Hibbard shows in this book, of intense competition amongst those building there. It was also an icon thereafter, and the Bund skyline graces the Shanghai room in the Great Hall of the People at Beijing, and was the subject of a poster I bought in a Lhasa bookshop, of all places, in 1993. China reclaimed the Bund after 1949 from its foreign owners, and it also reclaimed the image of the Bund for its own devices.

Peter is the man I would choose to take along on a walk along the Bund. I have had the lucky chance to do so in person, and investigated some of its private places in his company, crawling over the former Cathay Hotel in the early 1990s. I follow his routes when taking friends along myself, and now we have his carefully and comprehensively researched guide to take along as well.

The roar of traffic might distract, and the heights of Pudong's new skyscrapers beckon, but if you take your time, and your guide, this survivor of the world of the griffin, the taipan and the compradore, will come alive again as you wander slowly along.

Robert Bickers, Bristol.

**Author's note**. In so far as the Bund, and its neighbourhood, is a work in progress, so is this book. Prior to the release of our next edition, readers will be able to keep up to date with developments by visiting my website— www.gingergriffin.com. The author would also be delighted to hear from those with past associations of the Bund.

**The Ginger Griffin**
**Telling The Shanghai Story**

# CONTENTS

## CHAPTERS

# Features

# PASSING BY THE BUND

When I took my first steps on the Bund on a grey, drizzly February morning in 1986 it was the people and not the buildings that struck me most. I was surrounded by a slow moving procession of passing figures on their way to somewhere else. They were much more interested in me than in the architectural glories, half-baked in grime and neglect, which seemed to stand as an incidental feature to the routines of everyday life. Apart from those who worked in the buildings' moribund state-run offices, only those who could afford the crude luxuries contained within the two buildings of the Peace Hotel would find

*Sketch by Austrian cartoonist Schiff, 1940*

a way past the licentious guards who watched over every entrance. The former 'Wall Street of Asia' had been cast aside as a remnant of an imperialist past—a past that many Shanghai citizens would have liked to forget. Its buildings also told the tale of a period of chastisement and deprivation that had left the city in a state of innocent hibernation since the late 1940s. Still, despite the removal of most forms of Western ornament from their mistreated faces, they stood as a ghostly reflection of the city's former might in a far-off, but not so distant, age when the world order was of a totally different complexion.

*Cuban 'friendship' visitor on the Bund, 1950s*

*Mass-produced silk-weaving of the Bund, 1950s*

I was living in Shanghai four years later when the new seeds of change began to blow in and the city unashamedly announced its aim to restore its former status as Asia's foremost centre of trade, finance and commerce. The frenzy of activity that followed was reminiscent of the heady, speculative years of the 1920s and 1930s when the 'Paris of the Orient' came of age. Even in those days there was public outcry over the modern apartment blocks and high-rise buildings that were springing up all over the city. Suddenly those historical legacies themselves were under threat as block upon block were turned to ashes from which modern-day skyscrapers were to arise at a hungry speed. The new Oriental Pearl TV Tower, opposite the Bund, climbed ever skywards as the symbol of Shanghai's new ambitions.

The city's rapid modernisation cast a shadow over the future of the Bund. Its buildings were further distanced from public view when an expansive highway, part of Shanghai's inner ring road system, was rolled out along its length in the early 1990s. Visitors thronged to the city's new, elevated walkway to view its 'gallery of world architecture' and to gaze

on the rise of the new Shanghai shining in the face of the old across the river. Emblazoned with a vignette of illuminations, the Bund had become a 'Disneyesque' attraction to parade by at night. During the same period a government plan was hatched to 'sell off the Bund,' and its former occupants from the glory days were invited to move back into their old premises. Many of its loss-making, state-owned enterprises were shunted out as the Bund was earmarked to become the city's premier financial and commercial centre yet again. Even the Shanghai Municipal

*Icons of 1930s and 1990s modernity–the tower of the former Cathay Hotel and the Oriental TV Tower, 1995*

Government, which was behind the scheme and had occupied the palatial premises of the Hongkong and Shanghai Bank since the 1950s, found itself another home.

Things, however, didn't exactly go to plan and in the end only a handful of the old-timers moved back in. Prospective tenants were confronted with a host of insurmountable problems

*View from the Peace Hotel across the Bund and Huangpu River, 1978*

ranging from the political and the bureaucratic, to the titanic financial costs of renting and restoring the decrepit structures. Commentators had been pointing out the unsuitability of the buildings for modern business use as far back as the late 1930s,

*The Bund, 1990s*

and a major stumbling block for would-be residents was the absence of any room for expansion. Moreover, while the Bund wallowed in uncertainty, many multinationals and international banks, including HSBC, were lured by financial incentives to locate across the river to the high-rise towers of Lujiazui—an area which is now firmly established as the city's key financial district. Meanwhile, a handful of state-run banks quietly moved into the vacant premises along the Bund.

1930s poster

Anti-imperialist march on the Bund, early 1960s

Perhaps the planners were asking too much. The task of restoring historical ties proved to be much more of a challenge than the restoration of the buildings themselves. As a commentator noted in 1882, 'here we transact the business of the port in buying and selling and banking, and the costliness of the establishments which line the Bund are sufficient proof of the lucrative nature of the transactions therein despatched.' The buildings were both a symbolic and a physical expression of their owners' success—a link with the past that was lost when they were taken over by the state after 1949. When the buildings were again offered for occupation, prestige and physical

National Day celebrations, 1954

SMA

suitability held sway over sentimentality. The incoming occupants were, understandably, most interested in forging a new identity rather than reliving the past. It is interesting to note, however, that AIG, with a vested heritage in a building they occupied in the 1920s, went to considerable efforts to restore certain features which would otherwise have been lost and the proprietors of a later development at Bund 18 set out to celebrate, rather than eradicate the past.

At the end of the 1990s the Bund was ensnared in an identity crisis and many of its buildings, which were still vacant or occupied by ill-suited tenants, faced an indeterminate future. Spurred on by the glittering prize of hosting the World Expo in

*Commerce on the Bund, 1940*

2010, government planners partly shifted their vision of the Bund away from its predisposition as a financial centre to that of its potential as a world-class showcase for the arts, gastronomy, leisure and retail activity. M on the Bund, the first independently operated eatery to establish itself there, opened in 1999. A host of investors, many with Chinese roots, began to take a fresh, hard and cautious look at the buildings that remained up for grabs.

The blemished face of the Bund began slowly to take on a distinctly Western look as stylishly chic, cosmopolitan restaurants and international fashion houses took up residence. Unsurprisingly, most ordinary citizens continued to walk on by.

*Bund promenade, around 1910*

The city fathers had, perhaps, learned something from the lessons of history. Going back to the latter half of the 19th century the Bund was much more than a mere centre of trade and finance—it was the very core of foreign, and in particular British, life in Shanghai. The top floors of its buildings housed the highest and most spacious apartments fitted out with the latest luxuries and amenities, and its elite wined and dined at the Shanghai Club. Everything from York hams to New Zealand potatoes, cheeses, wines and spirits as well as Hartlepool coal could be had. The town band played classics in its English-style garden, whilst the nearby Lyceum Theatre hosted Gilbert and Sullivan and home-grown British farces. A British court, prison, museum, library and church were all to be found on the doorstep. During the early 20th century the hotels on the Bund housed the finest restaurants, bars and ballrooms, and the latest Paris fashions were on parade at the Sassoon House arcade. The Union Jack flew high above most of the buildings, the Custom House clock played the Westminster chimes, and British merchant

*Local newspaper fashion page, 1930*

*Flying the flag, 2006*

and military vessels lined the shore. Physically, the Bund marked the boundary of a foreign controlled area from which all else emanated westwards.

Not only did the Bund provide the comforts of home, it also looked like home. It presented a Western face to visitors who

*The harbour, 1934*

were usually in some part surprised, bemused, exhilarated or disappointed by its appearance, and usually evoked analogies with European or American cities. An 1897 visitor compared it to the Promenade des Anglais in Nice, whilst Noel Coward, on his 1929 visit, viewed the face of Shanghai as a 'cross between Huddersfield and Brussels.' Philosopher Bertrand Russell saw the Bund as an example of 'ugliness and efficiency.' Fickle in identity, the interiors of its ostentatious banks could be confused with those of a grand hotel or a Monte Carlo casino by those unaccustomed to

Flying the flag, 1934

Cathay Hotel advert, 1938

The sketch of the Chartered Bank's entrance hall in 1922 looks more like a contemporary rendering in its role as Bund 18

*Left: The Bund looking north, 1860s   Right: The Bund looking south, around 1870*

the style in which business had to be seen to be done on the Bund. The same charge of capriciousness may be alleged against some of the renovated buildings on the Bund today.

With some cognisance of their history, many buildings on the Bund, and indeed around the city, bear heritage plaques issued by the Shanghai Municipal Government. Despite the fact that the buildings were listed as a Modern Heritage Site at a UNESCO experts meeting in Chandigargh in 2003, the heritage protection status of all the buildings on the Bund, with a few exceptions, is only skin deep. Many renovations to date have either entirely defrocked the interiors of their historical character or have inappropriately reinvented them in inferior fabric and style. Shanghai's overpowering desire for modernity and internationalism pays scant respect to the past. As a case in point, the Bank of China, intent on removing the building's original marble, consulted a leading restoration architect on how the new marble could be made to look old. He, of course, was shocked. Moreover, swathes of the buildings' granite faces have been lastingly disfigured by unbefitting treatments.

Concerns and debates over historical conservation and restoration are becoming more poignant as development on the

Dennis George Crow

Bund proceeds. However, those preservationists bent on restoring an original interior look can sometimes deny the history of the buildings themselves. All of the buildings' interiors were modified and renewed at various times during their history in response to evolving societal and practical needs, ranging from those of visiting tourists to their occupation by Japanese and American armed forces, regardless of the negligence and maltreatment they were dealt with during and after the 1950s. Time doesn't stand still and historical misconceptions are hardly helped by the fact that most of the heritage plaques on the buildings are in some way or another factually incorrect.

In the following pages I hope to allow readers some insight and appreciation of the development of the waterfront and its

*The Bund, 1950s*                                                SMA

buildings as a living creation that has evolved, and continues to evolve, over time. Its physical features are a reflection of the social relations that defined its past and are redefining its future.

Special consideration is given to the Bund's two most iconic structures—the former buildings of the Hongkong and Shanghai Bank and the Cathay Hotel. Although the buildings differ in terms of their recent restoration and reinvention, their

P&T Group

decorative riches render an ultimate narrative and a corporeal embodiment of the spirit of a bygone age. The bank's palatial interior has been thoughtfully restored and its owners are proud to show it off to the public—even outside of normal banking hours. Whilst the ground floor of the hotel was victim to a soulless and imitative modernisation in

*Artist Cyril Fairey's rendering of the Hongkong & Shanghai Bank*

the early 1990s, many highly evocative original features have survived on its upper floors. Its former grandeur, hopefully, is set to be restored with a multi-million dollar facelift. This book also highlights the significance of many other fine symbolic and decorative features found along the Bund which would generally not be evident to the passer-by.

The Bund continues in a transitional state and its destiny over the coming years remains far from certain. Undoubtedly additional elite service establishments will find their place in those buildings still open to outside investment, and more are likely to follow when the state-run banks, its stop-gap tenants, find more fitting ground or cyber-space. The future of the Bund crucially depends on its revival as a centre for social life rather than as a lifestyle showcase. Whilst the face of the

Bund symbolises the city's past glories and its future aspirations, Shanghai's development as a multi-centred megalopolis threatens to relegate it to the periphery of common experience. On the Bund itself, the massive highway, which bisects its public spaces, is as much a social as a physical barrier. The two sides of the road may as well be continents apart, as

*The redesigned waterfront, 1990s*

inexpensive fast-food outlets and tacky souvenir shops inhabit the waterside area, whilst world-class restaurants and international designer emporia parade their riches on the other side. A new middle ground is unlikely to be established as the Bund's historical predilection as home to the wealthy and successful is reasserted.

A highly impressive major redevelopment project, which is now underway at the northern end of the Bund in the 'Waitanyuan' area, holds the key to success for the Bund's reinvention. Set around parks and dotted with a wealth of historic architectural pleasures, many of which are to be preserved, the scheme carries the prospect of rekindling the spirit of the Bund and bringing its life, energy and style back again. There is no doubt that the Bund area will increasingly attract more passers-by, from all over China and from around the globe, wishing to experience and indulge in the quintessential spirit of the city—even if they can't all afford its finer pleasures. The Bund was built as a spectacle—and that's the way it is to remain.

Peace Hotel

*Cathay Hotel reception, 1930s*

# ILLUMINATING THE BUND

Today the Bund is brightly illuminated with a spectacle of lights guaranteed to attract a swarm of sightseers each and every evening. It was a very different matter back in the 19th century, when illuminations and

*Ulysses S. Grant*

pageants were generally only reserved for special jubilee celebrations. By the end of the century, the Bund had been illuminated on three occasions; in 1887 for Queen Victoria's jubilee and again in 1897 for her diamond jubilee, as well as for Shanghai's own diamond jubilee in 1893. And whilst Shanghai society conjured up costly pageants and illuminations in honour of their far-distant

monarch, it paid little comparable courtesy to its earliest royal visitors. The first British royal visit to Shanghai by the Duke of Edinburgh in 1869 was a sedentary affair, with its highlight appearing to be the making of some new friendships with the fairer sex at a ball and with those of the sterner sex at the bowling alley. Like other royal visitors who had come before him, including those from Germany, Italy and Japan, his presence wasn't celebrated in a blaze of light or fanfare.

Shanghai's first major public display of illuminations was reserved for a regal, rather than a royal personage. It came on the occasion of former US President Ulysses S. Grant's visit in May 1879—which just so happened to coincide with Queen Victoria's birthday. Grant, who was two years into his round-the-world trip with his family, viewed a spectacular torch-lit procession along the Bund from the balcony of the Hongkong and Shanghai Bank. The Settlement was heavily decorated with bunting, and the offices of Jardine, Matheson & Co. alone were decorated with 1,500

*Decorations for the Duke of Connaught's visit, 1890*

Chinese and Japanese candle-lit lanterns. Ships anchored in the Huangpu River set the stage for enormous firework displays. The event was unfortunately marred, as was commonplace on such occasions, by a serious firework accident injuring nine people.

There was only one other man who would have received such a brilliant welcome and that was Prince George, heir to the British throne. So when the Shanghai community learned that he was to visit the city in 1881, they set about arranging a suitable reception, including the use of gas illuminations. Their extensive preparations, however, were disappointingly thwarted as the prince and his brother, who were under the orders of the Captain of their

*Left: First display of electric light, with the Astor House Hotel in the background, 1882*

23

*Coronation Day, June 1911*

man-of-war, were unable attend the pageant. The celebrations were further dampened by heavy rain and a very poor turnout by Shanghai's Chinese residents.

Even though the first trial of electric light in Shanghai took place just days after Ulysses S. Grant departed, it wasn't until 26th July 1882 that the first electric lights, courtesy of the Shanghai Electric Co., were to be seen on the Bund. In order to avoid disappointment, the Chinese were advised to cast aside their preconception that one electric lamp was going to fill the whole city with radiance. They weren't disappointed and thousands gazed on the moon-like lamps with 'evident admiration and complacency.'

The illuminations and celebrations for the next royal visit, that of the Duke and Duchess of Connaught for one

day in April 1890, were the best ever seen in Shanghai and there were no disappointments. A ladder carriage of the fire company, with a huge dragon snorting fire and smoke perched on it, stole the show. Underneath, fiery letters displayed the motto 'say the word and down comes your houses.' Soon after, electric lighting was used for the first time as part of the illuminations to celebrate Shanghai's 50th anniversary as a treaty port in 1893, though yet again the events were spoiled by heavy rain. Furthermore, the events

*Early 1960s illuminations*    Yang Peiming

*Astor House Hotel decorations, June 1911*

*Present-day illuminations*

were also 'spoiled' by the Chinese community refusing to parade as planned.

Perhaps the most magnificent celebrations in Shanghai's concession-era history were staged for the coronation of King George V in June 1911. Ribbons of coloured electric lights transformed the Bund from a business centre into 'a fairy like scene.' Chinese lanterns bearing the Union Jack were hung from all the trees and Chinese characters proclaiming 'God save the King' were hung below the Custom House clock. The British, as well as the Chinese, were out celebrating like never before.

Faint ribbons of light outlining the features of the Bund's buildings and white on red banners, bearing Chinese slogans, set the backdrop for the nationalistic and patriotic rallies and marches that the wide avenue afforded after 1949. That was until one night in September 1989 when, unannounced, the Bund instantly and majestically was brought to life in a blaze of flood lighting. It was a trial run for the upcoming 40th anniversary of the founding of the People's Republic of China. By chance, I happened to be there and the response from the crowds was charged with the same euphoria that must have been evident when the first electric light on the Bund shone well over a century ago.

*National Day, 1954*                    SMA

# NEW KIDS ON THE BUND

Three on the Bund

Three on the Bund

*Exploring the Peace Hotel and Bund 18*

In a charity event, organised by Three on the Bund and the Huangpu District Government in May 2006, and led by myself, a group of local school children were given the opportunity to visit some buildings on the Bund, which hitherto they had only seen from the outside or read about in books. They were in for a few surprises as they explored the upper floors of the Peace Hotel and the dusty and neglected interior of the former Shanghai Club. Adoration and astonishment soon shone on their faces as they played out their adventure in this alien territory. Some of the children compared their journey to that of being aboard a time machine passing through a series of historical porches—as entrances to buildings holding dreamlike stories.

One message that they all came away with was that the importance of the Bund was not only bound up in its history— but also in its future—and for a future happy ending, an appreciation of and respect for the past was indispensable. Wang Kai, a student at Guangming High School, called the Bund 'Shanghai's name card' and declared that 'yesterday's Bund is beautiful, today's Bund is still beautiful, tomorrow's Bund will be even more beautiful.' There is hope that the next generation will have a greater awareness of the importance of Shanghai's unique historical inheritance and of the need for its careful preservation.

# STREETS AND SETTLEMENTS— CHRISTENING THE BUND

The word Bund, often mistaken for a German expression, actually derives from the Hindustani word *band* meaning an artificial causeway or embankment. In the early 1860s there were, in fact, four roads following the waterways surrounding the British Settlement on all its four sides that were also described as 'bunds.'

So what was this British, or English, Settlement? The establishment of British communities on the China coast following the First Opium War of 1839-1842 has been well documented. In short, upon the signing of the Treaty of Nanking in 1842, British residents were given rights to reside and trade in Shanghai and in four other, so-called, treaty ports, which were subsequently imbued with 'extraterritorial' status leaving their foreign residents immune from Chinese sovereign jurisdiction. Similar treaties were granted to the Americans and the French in 1844.

Captain George Balfour, the first British Consul, agreed a set of 'Land Regulations,' which had been drawn up by the local Chinese authorities in 1845, that were to lay the ground rules on how the British inhabited area was to be managed and administered. Balfour wanted to secure an exclusive British zone and regulations were drawn up to define its boundaries and to deal with matters such as building codes and land taxation. In 1846 Balfour had secured 138 acres of British Settlement land running

# STREE

### OF

# English and American

## JANUA

*Map from a Shanghai street and business directory, 1872*

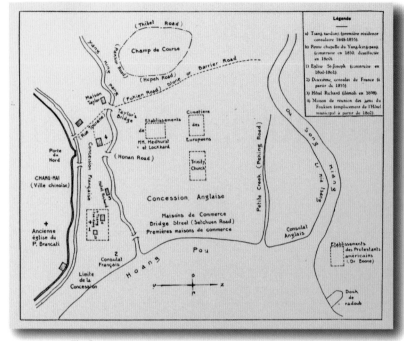

*The Concession areas, 1847 to 1851*

along most of the length of the present-day Bund and three blocks westwards to today's Central Henan Road. His successor, Rutherford Alcock, extended the area to 470 acres in November 1848.

The Settlement then stretched all the way along the Bund, westwards to today's Central Tibet Road (the former West Bund or Defence Creek), northwards to Suzhou Creek (the North Bund) and southwards to East Yan'an Road (the South Bund).

With a familiar, tenacious sagacity the British disposed of their desires to maintain exclusivity and pushed forward new Land Regulations, adopted in 1854, which allowed Chinese to buy and rent land. For the first and not the only time in its history Shanghai had become 'hot' as a safe refuge from China's wars and alarums. During the murderous rage of the Taiping Rebellion (1851–1864) and particularly after the fall of the neighbouring city of Suzhou in 1860, the Settlement was overrun with high-profit yielding Chinese, and Consul Medhurst came up with a scheme to keep everybody content by renaming the thoroughfares within its confines in 1862.

The Bund itself was officially renamed as Yangtsze Road, after Shanghai's life-giving river, and the streets running off it were named after Chinese cities running in alphabetical order from south to north. The South Gate Street became known as Canton Road, Mission Road as Foochow Road, Custom House Road as Hankow Road, Ropewalk Road as Hangchow Road (changed to Kiukiang Road in 1864), Park Lane to Nanking Road and Consulate Road to Peking Road. Later, and with no regard for the order, Jinkee Road, appeared between Nanking and Peking Road. The Chinese chose to adopt a numerical rather than an alphabetical order, with Nanking Road being designated as the Great (or number one) Maloo (horse road) and the four roads running south of it known as the second to the fifth Maloo—the latter being today's Guangdong Road.

The street names in their modern Chinese versions, though slightly disruptive of the original alphabetical order, survive to this

SMA

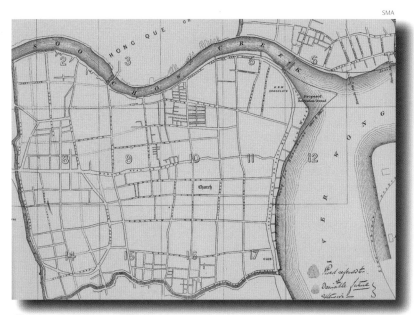

*SMC map showing the four bunds, 1863*

*Present-day street sign*

day—as does the use of the Maloo assignations by some Shanghai residents. It appears that the use of Yangtsze Road, in place of the Bund, was never commonly adopted by foreigners or Chinese. The assignation 'The Bund or Yangtsze Road' had disappeared from most foreign maps by the end of the 19th century. Similarly, despite its official designation as Zhongshan Road No. 1 (E.) in December 1945 (First Zhongshan Road (E.) today), the area continues to be known by its old familiar name of the 'Waitan' (meaning outer shore) to the Chinese and as the Bund to foreigners.

In much the same vein, the area of the 1848 British Settlement was still referred to as such well into the early 20th century despite the fact that it had been amalgamated with the American Settlement to become the International Settlement in 1863. In 1899 the International Settlement was extended to form an area of 8.3 square miles. The early Land Regulations had laid the basis for the formation of the Shanghai Municipal Council in 1854 (referred to as SMC hereafter) which was to govern and administer this area. The SMC, that was largely representative of big British business interests, had no less than five and no more than nine members until 1928. Prior to the election of the first three Chinese members in that year the British held five seats and the US and Japan each had two.

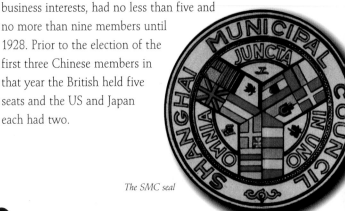

*The SMC seal*

Consul Medhurst left another legacy to Shanghai. He suggested that all thoroughfares be called roads, as the Chinese pronunciation of the word road was similar to its Chinese name. To this day very few 'streets' are found in the city and the present-day Shanghai Municipal Government has been in a quandary over how to present a consistent Romanised version of Shanghai's road names that are intelligible to a vastly expanding and profitable foreign public. As part of a larger campaign on street naming matters, city bureaucrats have recently raised concerns over properties using the Bund as a street address, as in days of old. However, it is far from likely that this signature historic area will ever be popularly associated with its cumbersome Chinese street name by foreigners. In this book I refer to the buildings by the name of their original owner or occupier, alongside their respective old Bund addresses—which still correspond to the present-day street addresses.

*The Shanghai Municipal Council, 1940, with Tony Keswick in the chairman's seat*

John Swire and Sons

# OFFICIAL STREET JUSTICE

The entire area of land comprised within the British limits having now come into the possession of foreigners, either by purchase or pre-emption, the time has come for the adoption of a useful and uniform nomenclature for the streets and roads, as well those which are now open, as those of which the line has only been laid down. The former are already provided with names, both the foreign and native population, having severally adopted such designations, as the practical disposition of the one, or the grotesque fantasy of the other, has suggested. But it is obvious that the municipal and social needs of so large a community of two peoples, who are daily being brought into more and more intimate contact one with the other, cannot be satisfied so long as the streets they inhabit are differently named by both, neither party being able to pronounce or comprehend the term adopted by the other.

The foreigners being the dominant portion of the community and charged with the order and security of the Settlement, while the Chinese are but recent immigrants, who have swarmed in for their own conveniences and safety, it follows, that, if either has the right to enforce on the other a system of nomenclature as near as possible adapted to the necessities of both, the foreigners possess that right: and it is one which must be exercised, or the Chinese part of the population, with their usual sagacity for mutual combination, will ever long make the entire settlement a Chinese city, and we shall find such names as, if translated would read, "Virtue and Benevolence Street", "Painted Silk Lane," "Justice and Harmony Road" intruding themselves in flaming characters alongside the less modest appellations the Municipal Council has already posted up.

This is no imagination, but a most probable contingency, as any one may judge of, who will take the trouble to walk the back streets, and read for himself, presuming him to be acquainted with the Chinese character.

Granting then that the foreign portion of the community is entitled to decide on the system of nomenclature best adapted to both, it is I think due to the Chinese and a matter of public utility, that such terms as they are more familiar with, and can pronounce, should be adopted if possible, and this may be done by taking the names of their own Provinces, Cities and Rivers, which are equally well known to ourselves, and this is the scheme I have to recommend to the acceptance of the Municipal Council.

*Part of a handwritten 'Memorandum on Naming of the Shanghae Streets, Consul Medhurst, British Consulate, 5 May 1862'*

# North-China Sunday News

## MAGAZINE SUPPLEMENT

Vol. I, No. 23              SHANGHAI, SUNDAY, APRIL 27, 1930              GR

# The Bund in the 'Sixties

THE BUND LOOKING NORTH

THE VIEW SOUTHWARD ALONG THE FRONT

These two old photographs give an excellent idea how the Shanghai Bund looked in the 1860's, and of the tremendous development which has taken place since. Very few of the buildings here shown are still in existence. The upper view, looking north from the vicinity of what is now Nanking Road, shows the Soochow Creek and the Bund Gardens. In the lower picture the view is southward from near the same spot, showing the bridge over the Yang King Pang which joined the International Settlement and the French Concession. The Chinese-style building, part of which is seen in the foreground, was the Custom House—a marked contrast to the imposing building which now stands on the same site.

# YAWNS, LAWNS AND DREAMS— THE MAKING OF THE BUND

I t's hard to imagine that the Bund as it is today, with its 11-lane highway and elevated walkway overlooking the Huangpu River, was little more than a muddy towpath in the 1840s. A road, 30 feet wide, was originally planned in front of the properties of the Bund's earliest foreign inhabitants but, in 1856, the incipient SMC decided that a further 50 feet should be reclaimed to make an 80-foot-wide esplanade. Several of the Bund's occupants objected and the plan was revised to allow for an esplanade, with a granite facing, just 60 feet wide. The result of the work which was quickly undertaken, perhaps too quickly, was far from attractive. When exposed at low tide the flotsam and stench of the sloping muddy shoreline, which was steadily expanding as silt accrued, infested the fine 'hongs,' as the foreign companies and their premises were known, along the Bund. Despite proposals, in 1860, to turn the Bund into a proper esplanade with an inner part reserved for vehicles and the conversion of the ugly muddy foreshore into a fine promenade with gardens, it wasn't until three long decades later that such a vision became a reality.

The first concrete proposals, in 1869, to create a protected river bank with an attractive curvature, or Bund line, came to nothing. The SMC finally began its 'bunding' or filling in of the foreshore, in the 1880s. Along with the new waterfront came modern amenities including the introduction of the first

*The Public Garden bandstand with its electric light on top, 1886*

telephones in 1881 and electric lighting in June 1883. The bandstand in the Bund's Public Gardens was the venue for the first public demonstration of electric light in Shanghai almost exactly one year earlier.

I n May 1886 grass lawns extending from the Public Gardens to the north of the Bund to just south of the present-day Hankou Road were opened to the public. In July 1888, the lawns were extended to Yangjingbang Creek (today's East Yan'an Road), on

the southern boundary of the International Settlement with the French Concession. An 1889 SMC order allowing 'respectable and decently dressed natives' to use the lawns was shortly afterwards revoked as so many Chinese

*The Bund looking north with the Shanghai Club to the left, late 1870s*

*The newly created lawns, with the Central Hotel on the Nanjing Road corner to the left, 1886*

*Cutting the lawns, 1880s*

SMA

*The new lawns at the southern of the end of the Bund, late 1880s*

were using the seats to slumber on. Work on completing the new Bund line continued until 1896. Around that time, the French and Chinese administered bunds to the south were also paved following a large fire in 1894 when many wretched waterfront buildings were destroyed. However, as an 1896 commentator noted, 'passing the Shanghai Club the Bund crosses a bridge to the French Settlement, where it ceases to be interesting to the traveller, and loses itself in regions where English feet seldom tread.'

Following a hectic couple of years of building on the Bund and the introduction of tramways, which necessitated the laying of wood block paving, the SMC again seriously considered a widening scheme, over a one-year period, in 1908. Although that proposal was rejected on account of cost, the SMC had little choice but to further reclaim and widen the Bund some ten years later as the demands of modern motor transport made their impression. Just as in recent times, a sudden explosion of vehicle numbers was threatening to bring gridlock to the city's streets. A massive increase in the number of large trucks on the streets brought about by the city's rapid industrialisation was particularly alarming. The number of trucks in the International Settlement rose from around 80 in 1919 to over 700 in 1926, whilst the number of cars increased from around 1,200 to 3,500 over the same period. By 1929 there were around 5,400 cars and 1,500 trucks registered.

YELLY FOODY OFSAW TEE !

*Cartoon by Sapajou, March 1924*

It was not just motor transport that was causing havoc, however, as the streets of Shanghai were littered with rickshaws, primitive wooden wheelbarrows and all manner of slow-moving homemade conveyances. A report from the late 19th century commented that 'the Bund is crowded at all hours of the day by foot passengers and vehicles. Neat broughams, victorias, dog carts, drawn by sleek Chinese ponies, and driven by Celestial coachmen in strange liveries, pass and repass; flocks of jinricshas, some running swiftly and smoothly along on spider wheels,

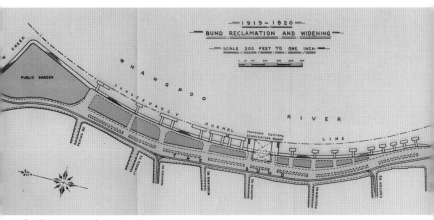

*Bund improvement scheme, 1919-1920*

hand-carts pushed by panting coolies, and the celebrated vehicle of China, the only one not imported by the foreigner—the passenger barrow, with seats arranged over the wheel like those of an Irish jaunting car, on which sometimes a whole family sits and is whirled gaily along by a muscular coolie.' Despite certain restrictions, the sight of wheelbarrows carrying anything from tubes and timber, to teddy bears and toddlers is not uncommon today. Shanghai's streets are also still lumbered with three-wheeled cycle rickshaws, a prototype of which was introduced to the city in 1924, capable of carrying the load of a small van.

The SMC's plan to widen the Bund to 120 feet, which was put forward in March 1919, aroused a hitherto unheard of level of conflict and debate amongst Shanghai's foreign community. Most of the widening work, which involved a 55-foot

*The Public Gardens before they were remodelled, 1919*

*The Bund's new lawns, 1921*

carriageway for trams and fast traffic and one 30 feet wide for slow traffic as well as car parking ranks, and laying of new lawns, was completed by the end of 1920. As part of the scheme an extra 25 benches, marked 'reserved for foreigners' were ordered for the Bund and the Public Gardens. Higher railings were also placed around the Public Gardens as many 'vagrants and drunken sea-men' were in the habit of spending the night there. Work on the most contentious aspect of the scheme, which involved shaving off 60 feet from the Public Gardens and the destruction of many historic trees, was left to last.

Work was suspended for a couple of weeks in late June 1921 while the SMC went through the motions of reviewing two petitions it had received. The Shanghai Civic League, which purported to represent all foreign residents, had gathered together over 200 names of those against any attempt to widen the road at the expense of the garden. They felt that the widening or the rebuilding of the Garden Bridge was required. The names of two of the city's leading architects, R. A. Curry and Arthur Dallas, were on the list. Another petition received in favour of the scheme included the names of M. H. Logan of Palmer and Turner, and G. H. Stitt, manager of the Hongkong and Shanghai Bank.

There was little doubt as to who would triumph as the final decision on such matters lay in the hands of a relatively small quorum of the Settlement's wealthiest foreigner ratepayers. The scheme was approved at a ratepayers' meeting on 6th July even though only 100 of the 1,800 eligible to vote were in attendance. In its defence the SMC pointed out that the gardens were actually to be enlarged as part of the reclamation scheme, and sent a letter to the Civic League pointing out that, although 1,700 ratepayers were absent, it by no means inferred that they were in sympathy with the organisation's aims. The League was also informed that,

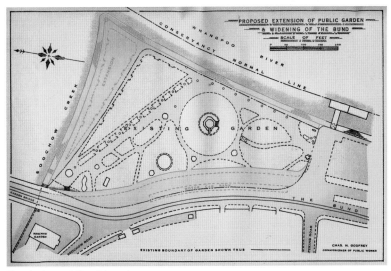

*Plans for the remodelling of the garden*

*The Public Gardens before and after reclamation work in 1905*

whilst residents were entitled to sign petitions, they had no entitlement to an 'authoritative mandate.' Not only were Chinese excluded from having a say in the running of the International Settlement, but the majority of foreigners were as well. In 1920 the Settlement population comprised 759,839 Chinese and 23,307 foreigners.

A similar scheme to enlarge the garden, involving the bunding of the northern shore of the Suzhou Creek, which was drawn up in 1882, was initially deferred on account of cost but ultimately denied by the Chinese authorities. However, a strip of land on its western perimeter was shaved off to widen the adjoining road in 1905, as part of a scheme which considerably enlarged the garden. On that occasion there were no protests.

The work on widening the road outside the gardens, involving the introduction of car parking spaces and the planting of magnolia trees, was finished by the end of 1921. However, even the Commissioner of Public Works, in a letter to the Secretary of the SMC in 1923, had to concede that 'the Bund had become ugly since widening as the removal of the old trees in the garden had brought into very great prominence all the poles carrying overhead cables.' The newly planted magnolia trees had also all died.

It wasn't long before the competing interests of recreational amenity and motor traffic were to reach even greater heights when the question of opening the foreshore to the Chinese was raised. As pressure was mounting on the SMC to throw open the neighbouring Public Gardens to the Chinese in 1926, the

Commissioner of Police, Edward Ivo Medhurst Barrett, took a pragmatic stance in telling the Council that he was personally in favour of opening the path along the river bank and the lawns to the Chinese. At that point the Bund lawns were guarded by chain railings, which would only be removed for the convenience of foreigners in the summer. Barrett noted that it was proving almost impossible to restrict Chinese wearing foreign dress from walking along the footpath near the river.

Perhaps the British public viewpoint could be summed up in the words of an angry resident who, in a letter of March 1925 to the *North China Daily News*, questioned whether the stretch was for foreigners or not after spotting five Chinese using the seats marked 'reserved for foreigners only.' He called for the return of foreign policing in the form of a big Scottish officer who had kept matters under control in years gone by.

However the lawns, like the Public Gardens, were opened to the Chinese in June 1928. The Chinese could now rest a little more comfortably—at least for a while. The upkeep of the lawns was proving difficult after they were opened to everyone and, in 1930, the SMC considered turning them all into flower beds with paved walkways. The plan was abandoned soon after in favour of turning all the five lawns south of Jiujiang Road into parking lots. The surviving lawns then became even more crowded,

*Policing the Bund, early 20th century*

and when they were re-laid in 1932 police were given instructions to 'restrict the use of lawns as far as possible within their discretion.' Their powers of discretion, however, were annulled by the power of the masses. An SMC survey of the Bund lawns between Jiujiang Road and Beijing Road in July 1936 found that 70% of the 4,500 people using them were asleep at any given hour between 9.00 a.m. and 1.00 p.m.

Following the new, relaxed regulations in 1928 more hawkers, who were generally seen as harmless in small doses, and beggars, who were generally accused of spoiling Shanghai's foreign show street, were to be found on the Bund. The 130 members of the SMC Police, all but six of them Chinese, who held responsibility for the Bund in early 1940, were kept very busy. They were making around 4,500 arrests monthly for obstruction and 350 arrests for loitering, which invoked a jail sentence of four to ten days. Of the other nuisances, arrests for hawking totalled around 700, whilst those for begging were fewer than 30 a month.

On the traffic front, two major road projects, which were to temporarily ease congestion in the Settlement, had been completed before the widening of the Bund in the early 1920s. The Yangjingbang Creek, which in its early days had been designated as the South Bund, was filled in during 1914 and 1915 and converted to a 90-foot-wide road. Controversy between the French and the British over whether it should be filled in had gone on for over 50 years. However the SMC's suggestion to name it as Avenue Edward VII, after it was culverted, was agreed by the French Council in a desire 'to perpetuate the local memory of the illustrious sovereign.' Naturally the street was known as Avenue Edouard VII on its southern side.

The avenue became a playground for the Chinese who could taunt the opposing French and International Settlement police forces on each of its sides with impunity, but was considered by many to be too wide. The SMC retorted to its critics in 1920 saying that 'perhaps twenty years hence this road will not be considered any too wide and the foresight shown in providing such a road will be commended.' In a connected scheme, work on filling in the Tibet Road Creek, the Settlement's earlier West Bund, to help ease north-south traffic flow and pressure on the Bund was completed with the opening of a new 80-foot-wide road in 1920.

Strong Chinese protestations over the building of a regular tramway network in the early 1880s gave way to a call for building some form of overhead railway system in the city. The suggestion found favour with the editor of the *North China Daily News* in January 1882 when he pointed out that 'Chinese coolies and the other classes who crowd our streets are eminently terrestrial bodies, and an elevated tramway would not interfere with their pursuits or recreation.' The idea was picked up again in June 1921 when a British resident suggested in a letter to the *North China Daily News* that an end to the traffic woes of Shanghai could be solved by building an overhead, light electric railway along Avenue Edward VII, westwards to the Hongqiao district. The idea was rejected by local professionals who considered it impossible to make foundations for the supports that would be necessary for such a scheme.

Avenue Edward VII from the Bund to Tibet Road, however, was remodelled in 1928 with a 28-foot-wide central section being resurfaced to provide a motor vehicle only thoroughfare. Shanghai's, if not China's, first urban highway had been created. Known locally as the 'Speedway,' four Chinese pedestrians who had loitered within its perimeter were killed, being their own fault of course, before the road was officially opened at the end of that year. The numbers of those killed and injured in traffic accidents in the Settlement rose from 53 and 1,005 respectively in 1920 to 142 and 10,973 in 1930. The SMC reported that 'the majority of accidents were due to the carelessness and indifference of pedestrians and their lack of traffic sense.'

Cover of a book by Ellen Thorbecke, 1940, with illustrations by Schiff

*Drawing of the proposed elevated railway along the Bund, November 1932*

Even with all the road improvements the traffic situation on the Bund had become so chronic by 1933 that the SMC was considering measures including staggered lunch hours for firms in order to reduce midday congestion. The idea of an elevated

*Mr. Sidney J. Powell*

railway, traversing the Bund and extending far into the Shanghai suburbs, was raised again in 1932 by Sidney J. Powell, a respected professional engineer and architect based in the city. Powell envisaged the use of silent rubber-tyred vehicles crossing the city 20 feet above ground level on tracks supported by arches at intervals of 100 feet. He promised journey times of ten minutes from the Bund to the furthermost western reaches of the International Settlement or to the new civic centre of the Chinese controlled Greater Shanghai Municipal Government to the northeast of the city at Jiangwan. In 1935, the scheme was looked on favourably by all the relevant administrations across the city, but was ultimately thwarted by its ambition to cross too many political and administrative barriers, as well as by the extensive destruction of the northern part of the city caused by the 1937 hostilities.

A final solution to relieve overcrowding and congestion by the construction of a bridge across or a tunnel under the Huangpu River and the development of the Pudong area on the other side had been seriously talked about since the late 1920s. At that time the only way to cross the river was by passenger ferry, and the SMC thwarted plans by the Greater Shanghai Municipal Government to introduce vehicle ferries landing near the Bund in the 1930s. Passengers arriving from Pudong had no choice but to pick up their hire cars at designated points along the Bund. Coincident with further ill-timed plans to develop the Shanghai civic centre, plans for a bridge were announced by Mayor Wu in 1936. It wasn't until after the Second World War that plans for a tunnel or bridge were again seriously considered by the new Shanghai City Council which finally approved a plan to build a bridge in 1947 using a massive loan from the American government. The substantial austerity and uncertainty of the times, however, left the scheme high and dry.

*The heart of the International Settlement and the Huangpu River, around 1930*

Many dreams lost in the somnolence of Shanghai's years of abandon have been uncannily reawakened in the 1990s. The Nanpu Bridge, the first to cross the Huangpu River, was completed in 1991. The first elevated section of the city highway, albeit carrying cars and not trains, was completed along the former Avenue Edward VII and Avenue Foch, now Yan'an Road, to Hongqiao in 1995. An elevated, light railway line, although not running along the Bund but still terminating at the same point envisaged in the 1930s, opened in 2000. The Bund, which was yet again widened in the early 1990s has been criticised by some as being too wide and traffic planners have been dreaming up schemes to rid it of its hordes of motorised pests. Some have suggested submerging the vehicles in the river alongside the Bund,

some have insensitively mooted the idea of building an elevated highway along the Bund, and others have talked about bringing back the trams. It will be necessary to pedestrianise the area if the Bund is really going to come back to life in the future.

The recent widening of Central Tibet Road is again seen as key to relieving congestion on the Bund. With a similar aim, there is talk of converting the only direct tunnel link between the Bund

*Fairground entrance to the Bund Sightseeing Tunnel, 2006*

and the foreshore on the other side of the Huangpu River in Lujiazui, which in typical Shanghai fashion was opened as an expensive tourist attraction featuring a sound and light show in 2001, into a much needed regular means of commuter transport.

A most astounding proposal to relieve the Bund of its traffic woes, and to enhance its commercial viability, was announced in early 2006. Raymond Shaw, a Beijing-born engineer now resident in the USA, wants to raise the buildings along the Bund using hydraulic jacks to allow the creation of more than 200,000 square metres of prime shopping and entertainment space below. In so doing the Bund promenade could be restored and the traffic concealed below. Despite past experience in such affairs, including shifting the historic Nanking Theatre in Shanghai some 70 metres from its original location in 2003, Shaw admits that the huge scale of the project might not receive official consideration before 2014. Sceptics there may be many, but it would be well to bear in mind the lessons of history, even if the scheme is not realised for yet another Cycle of Cathay, or 60 years hence.

For the present, the Bund's promenade, which was reinvented as an elevated walkway in an effort to shore up the city's flood defences in the early 1990s, will stand high as a barricade between the buildings and the riverside. As in times past, the promenade is perpetually overcrowded, and even though there are caged plots of flower beds and foliage alongside, real lawns are nowhere to be seen. And even if they were reintroduced to the Bund area there is no doubt, as elsewhere throughout the city, that everybody would be barred entry—apart from the odd itinerant dog.

*Will's Bridge, 1875*

John Warner Publications

# BRIDGES AND BLUNDERS

The Garden Bridge, that crosses Suzhou Creek to the north of the Bund, was expected to have a life span of around 40 years when it was completed in 1908. Even though its British engineers admitted that it was by no means an ornamental structure it has continued to carry traffic to and fro to the present-day. Its predecessors didn't fare so well.

The first bridge to cross the Suzhou Creek was erected by the Soochow Creek Bridge Company in 1857. Wills Bridge, named after its advocate, was a wooden draw-bridge funded by foreign merchants who were soon handsomely rewarded from the proceeds of its costly toll fees. Before that time the only way across was by ferry, and few foreigners made the trip. As soon as the bridge was completed the shores on its northern side were reported to 'have become the favourite resort of constitutional walkers.' The advent of the bridge allowed the foreign settlement, which was becoming crowded around the Bund, to spread across the creek to an area that was then unofficially designated as the American Settlement. It also bestowed civilising influences on a lawless area, often compared to America's Wild West, which was renowned for the rough antics of its 'floating' drunken seafarer population.

Wills had a great incentive to build the bridge, as he and others were to benefit from a faster connection to a dock where opium vessels discharged their valuable cargoes. He also owned land across the bridge, including a lot that he sold at a huge profit for the building of the Astor House Hotel, which was completed in 1858 (see page 212). However, by the end of the 1860s the foreign population, which had grown from around 300 when the bridge was completed to over 1,600, were becoming tired of paying their annual fees—as were the Chinese who were forced to pay in cash every time they crossed.

The Suzhou Creek Bridge Company set about the construction of the first iron bridge across the creek in 1871. The SMC's plans to purchase it came to nothing when the half-completed structure fell apart and sank into the water in May that year. What was left of it was

later sold off as scrap. The SMC now took matters into their own hands and erected the first Garden Bridge, made of wood, in 1873.

*Construction of the Garden Bridge, 1907*

*Tram crossing the bridge, 1950s*   SMA

The bridge proved costly to maintain and in 1888 the SMC was looking to replace it with a more permanent iron or steel structure. However, none of the 31 plans submitted was approved by the Council on account of their high cost and what the Council called their 'unsuitability.' It wasn't made

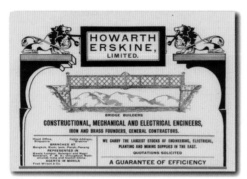

*Advert, 1905*

30-foot tall girders at the centre. All the steelwork was manufactured by the Cleveland Bridge Company in Darlington, England. The bridge, with its wood-block paving, was opened to traffic on 20th January 1908.

plain to the public that all of the designs would have proved failures had they been built as the Council's engineer had failed to provide the companies concerned with adequate technical information. Yet another engineering blunder had been made. In 1890 the Council decided on repairing the Garden Bridge so that it could continue to function for a further ten years.

In fact, more than ten years had passed when the absolute necessity of replacing it with a steel bridge arose in 1906 when the tramway system was being introduced to the city. The new Garden Bridge, designed by the Municipal Engineer's Department and constructed by Messrs. Howarth, Erskine Ltd. of Singapore, had two equal spans of just over 171 feet, with

There were strong calls from a civic lobby to enlarge or rebuild the bridge when the Bund was being widened in the early 1920s. On that occasion the Council disagreed, and if it weren't for the events of the Pacific War the bridge might have disappeared long ago. The Council put forward proposals to eventually replace it with a new bridge no less than 80 feet wide in 1933, with the expectation that a 'centenary memorial bridge' would be completed in 1942 or 1943. Following the outbreak of Sino-Japanese hostilities in 1937 the bridge was manned by Japanese army sentries to the north and by their British counterparts to the south. The tram service over the bridge, which was suspended in August of that year, wasn't restored until June 1942.

NO DOGS AND HARDLY ANY CHINESE FEATURE

# NO DOGS AND HARDLY ANY CHINESE

The origins of the anomalously assigned Public Gardens go back in legend to 1860 when silt began to build up around a sunken ship on the shores fronting the British Consulate at the northern end of the Bund. In 1864, demands were made for the unsightly Consular mud-flats, as they were called, to be filled in and converted into a botanical garden. The SMC had planned to get the preliminary work done by the end of 1865 using mud from the Yangjingbang Creek at the southern end of the Bund. But, as usual, things went more slowly than expected and one of Shanghai's first British architects, Henry Lester, was reprimanded for his unsatisfactory building work. By 1868, however, all was well and the garden was completed, fenced and thrown open to the public.

However the definition of public that was used largely excluded those of local origin, the SMC having made it clear in 1871

*The Public Gardens, early 1880s*

SMA

*Entrance to the gardens, 1880s*

ASTOR HOUSE

DOGS ARE NOT ALLOWED
TO ENTER THE GARDEN
UNLESS LED.

*Gardens under heavy snow, 1880s*

that 'the garden was to be invested with the atmosphere of a quiet English park.' From its earliest days the garden was barred to most Chinese, although police were originally given orders to admit respectable and well-dressed Chinese and those accompanied by, and in the service of, foreigners. Even so, there were incessant complaints by foreigners over the numbers of Chinese in the park despite further measures to restrict entry.

Matters came to a head in the 1880s as 'Chinese Gentlemen, of high character and intelligence' who had lost their right to enter the grounds made their views heard. An editorial in the *North China Daily News* of November 1885 put forward the case for keeping the garden beyond the bounds of Chinese patronage. It insisted that 'all reasonable persons will acknowledge the great obstacle of opening the gates of the Garden indiscriminately. The little enclosure would swarm with Chinese to such an extent as to render it unavailable as a foreign promenade; the air would resound with the strident yells which pass among the natives for conversation, foreign ears and stomachs would be offended by sights and sounds inseparable from a code of etiquette which

does not insist upon the use of pocket handkerchiefs or forbid stentorian cleaning of the throat and grass, flowers and shrubs would soon show signs of hopeless deterioration. All this is undeniable.' The editor did, however, suggest that a ticket system be introduced to allow entry to those Chinese conversant with foreign ways so as not to confront good taste. The editor's conciliatory tone changed just a few months later when he proclaimed 'the affairs of this Settlement bristle with anomalies. Chinese rentpayers who are clamouring now for equal rights, have no voice whatsoever in the Government of the place, and no place at the meeting of voters. The garden, moreover, is laid out exclusively after foreign taste, and was notoriously designed for foreign use.' The 'better class' of Chinese found further affront in that other Asiatics, including Japanese and Koreans, some of whom were far from respectable, as well as dogs on leashes were permitted entry to the gardens at that time.

The SMC resolved to set up a separate Chinese Public Garden, between Huqiu Road and Sichuan Road on Suzhou Creek, which, in 1890, was opened to all without prejudice.

The senior Chinese official in Shanghai named the garden as 'China and all the Nations Rejoice Together.' However, few of the well-dressed Chinese elite, or foreigners—apart from those who had their houseboats moored alongside—ventured past its gates where members of the lower classes of Chinese society would congregate in their multitude. The respectable Chinese classes were thereafter barred from the Public Gardens. They did, however, have recourse to their own far grander pleasure gardens to the west of the International Settlement.

Even with the new regulations, complaints by foreigners about the nuisances caused by those Chinese still permitted to enter the Public Gardens continued in abundance. Many

*Chinese admitted to the Public Gardens for the first, and only time, on the occasion of the coronation of King George V, 1911*

*Breaking the rules—seated amahs during a band performance, early 20th century*    SMA

were directed at the 'amahs,' or nannies, who were often accused of letting foreign children in their charge run riot, spoiling flower beds and causing havoc during musical performances. Other recurrent objections were raised as to why dogs were sometimes permitted to enter.

The Public Gardens Regulations which were posted next to the entrance gate were very clear on these matters. And even though the infamous phrase 'Dogs and Chinese Not Admitted' was never found amongst them, there were separate regulations with regard to dogs, the control of children, the use of seats and rights of entry. It is interesting to note that whilst the 1903 regulations

stated that 'no Chinese are admitted except servants in attendance upon foreigners,' the 1917 regulations (reprinted on page 63), took a more neutral approach and made no mention of the Chinese whatsoever. No doubt this was a move to defuse growing resentment and friction with the local community. However, in the latter regulations, which were operative until the gardens were opened to all, the Chinese seem to be denied any existence at all and are demoted to the category of 'others.'

Regardless of the taxonomy, the message and the greater insult was clear to those that sought it. Dogs and Chinese were accorded equal status. The association of a dog, itself a term of debasement in Chinese culture, coalesced in popular consciousness to become a potent epithet for the wrongs of foreign imperialism in China. Many Chinese were educated to believe, and still believe, that a sign containing the term 'no dogs and Chinese' actually did exist.

Serious consideration of the admission of Chinese to the Public Gardens, and indeed to all the other foreign parks in the Settlement, began in 1926 when three members of the Chinese Chamber of Commerce started discussions with the Parks Committee. But British officialdom would not accept any resolution until the period of severe unrest and anti-foreignism, which was sweeping China, came to an end. It wasn't until the beginning of June 1928 that the gates were finally opened to all. Well, they were not actually open to all as a ten copper cent admission charge was imposed. The expense, equivalent to half a day's labour or more, effectively kept out the poorer class of Chinese, as well as the less advantaged elements of the foreign community, including the stateless White Russians. Dogs were still not admitted.

Even a reporter from the *North China Daily News* had to

*The gardens in 1900*   Dennis George Crow

*The gardens in 1934*

admit that the park had an atmosphere of normality, despite the overwhelming number of Chinese visitors, after it opened. However he couldn't refrain from pointing out that a small number of Chinese youths were sprawled full length on the benches. Again, complaints,

*Some habits never die, Huangpu Park, 2006*

largely relating to overcrowding, began to be heard. The pricing policy certainly restricted visitor numbers, but with a city population of well over three million it was normal for around 1,800 entrance tickets to be sold on an average day in 1933!

Special use of the garden was granted free of charge to members of the Japanese Army Water Police and the Japanese Gendarmerie for their early morning exercises in 1939 and 1940, and they insisted on taking their dogs with them. As a sign of the changing times, little heed was taken of the advice by British members of the SMC that dogs were not allowed. Following the retrocession of the International Settlement on 1st August 1943, the collaborationist City Government opened the gardens with free entry to all just two days later. They also simultaneously set about eradicating all Anglo-American

signs and street names from around the city.

Today the former grounds of the Public Gardens are largely covered with paving and known as the Huangpu Park. The park houses the Bund Historical Museum, which is located at the base of the early 1990s Monument to the People's Heroes, and has a collection of photographs chronicling Shanghai's modern history and a copy of the SMC's records reporting the admission of the Chinese to its confines. The former grounds of the Chinese Public Garden have recently been transformed into an attractive recreational area.

*Statue of a People's Hero in the Huangpu Park*

## Public and Reserve Gardens

# REGULATIONS

1. The Gardens are reserved for the Foreign Community.

2. The Gardens are opened daily to the public from 6 a.m. and will be closed half an hour after midnight.

3. No persons are admitted unless respectably dressed.

4. Dogs and bicycles are not admitted.

5. Perambulators must be confined to the paths.

6. Birdnesting, plucking flowers, climbing trees or damaging the trees, shrubs, or grass is strictly prohibited; visitors and others in charge of children are requested to aid in preventing such mischief.

7. No person is allowed within the band stand enclosure.

8. Amahs in charge of children are not permitted to occupy the seats and chairs during band performances.

9. Children unaccompanied by foreigners are not allowed in Reserve Garden.

10. The police have instructions to enforce these regulations.

By Order.
N. O. Liddell.
Secretary.
Council Room. Shanghai. Sept. 13th. 1917

## 外滩风景区管理通告

外滩是上海重要的风景游览区，为保证外滩的环境整洁和良好社会秩序，根据有关法规，特通告如下：

一、外滩风景区系指北至外白渡桥、南至新开河的中山东一路、中山东二路的沿江地区，包括人行天桥和地下人行通道。

二、任何单位和个人在外滩都要自觉地遵纪守法、文明游览，维护社会秩序尊重社会公德。

三、保证环境卫生，爱护公共设施和绿化，禁止随地吐痰和乱扔杂物，不准损折花木和践踏草坪花坛。

四、未经外滩风景区管理办公室批准，辖区内不准举办公共活动，不准设摊设亭从事经营活动。

五、禁止任何扰乱社会秩序和有碍市容观瞻的活动和行为。

六、任何单位和个人都要自觉遵守本通告的规定、服从执勤人员的管理，违者由有关部门视情节轻重予以批评教育或依法处理。

### 上海市黄浦区人民政府一九九五年一月

THE BUND SIGHTSEEING AREA NOTICE

The Bund sightseeing area is a major scenic spot in shanghai.To guarantee clean and tidy surroundings and peaceful social order,We hereby give a public notice of regulations as the following:
1)The Bund sightseeing area refers to the river-side zhongshan Road(E.1)and zhongshan Road(E.2) ranging from the north Garden Bridge to the south xinkaihe,including overpasses and underground passageways.
2)Any person or organization visiting the Bund should conscientiously observe the law maintain good manners follow social order and abide by social morals.
3)To keep the environment clean and protect public facilities and greenery,spitting,littering,picking flowers,ruining trees and walking on lawns and flower beds is prohibited in the area.
4)Any person if without the licence given by the Administrative of the Bund sightseeing Area is not allowed to carry any social activities.This also applies to commercial activities such as setting up stands or booths in the area for trading or offering service.
5)Any activity or action against social order or repugnant to the eye is prohibited.
6)Any person or organization in the area should abide by regulations in this notice and follow the instructions of patrols in the area.Any one who violates the regulations will be dealt with according to the seriousness of his or her case.

SHANGHAI HUANGPU DISTRICT PEOPLE'S GOVE
199

*Present-day regulations*

*The Bund looking south, 1860s*

*The Bund looking north, 1880s*

# SETTLING DOWN—
# THE ARCHITECTS OF
# THE BUND

The architectural profession enjoyed modest esteem in 19th century Shanghai as landowners generally saw little need for their skills or expense. As demonstrated by the early development of the Bund, direct dealings with Chinese contractors to supervise construction often produced practical, if not particularly successful, results. Such arrangements didn't bode well for the professional practitioner. Little money from the huge cost of building the Shanghai Club in the early 1860s found its way into the pocket of Charles St. George Cleverly, the Colonial Surveyor of Hong Kong, for his design work. Other more modest pioneering Bund residents, including W. R. Adamson, decided to design and build their premises themselves.

A Scotsman, Mr. Strachan, was the first professional architect accredited to work in the city after his arrival in 1849. Apart from the fact that he employed Ningbo craftsmen and produced Greek-styled buildings, little is known of his work and certainly none of it survives. William Kidner, who came to Shanghai to supervise the construction of the Holy Trinity Church (later cathedral) near the Bund from 1866–1869, was the first British architect of any importance to work in the city. During his three-year sojourn, amongst other buildings, he completed the British Consulate prison on the Bund and the nearby Lyceum Theatre in 1867. He paid several return visits to Asia and his Shanghai practice passed into the hands of his British partner, J. M. Cory, soon after he had designed the Hongkong and Shanghai Bank building on the Bund in 1877. Nothing of his work on the Bund survives, but the

*Hongkong and Shanghai Bank's first building on the Bund*

cathedral does. The last sign of Cory's work on the Bund, the second generation Custom House, was demolished in 1924. He assisted Mr. J. Chambers in the design of the building and died during the course of its construction in 1893.

The most enduring and financially successful British architect in Shanghai, Henry Lester, arrived in 1863 to carry out a survey of the International Settlement for the SMC. Lester, a London-trained architect and land surveyor, had set up his own practice by 1872 and went on to construct many buildings around the Settlement. However, his main activity was in land dealing and by the time of his death in 1926 he was probably the largest landowner in Shanghai with an estate valued at three million pounds. His company, which combined architectural services with land and property dealings, set a precedent which was to be followed by many others up to the 1940s. And today many foreign architectural practices in the city are following the same path yet again.

Shanghai's architectural fraternity began to grow and take on new importance towards the end of the 19th century as the demand for larger and more advanced buildings required their professional services, as well as those of professional engineers. In 1890 there were just three professional architectural practices in the city. By 1900 there were seven and in 1910 a total of 15. In

1925 this number had risen to 46 and in 1937 there were 54, predominantly foreign, offices in the city.

The Shanghai Society of Engineers and Architects, which had been founded in January 1901 by Mr. Gabriel James Morrison to 'promote the science and practice of Engineering and Architecture in all their branches,' had attracted over 100 members by 1904. At that time only around a third of its members had any form of professional qualification. An Institute of Architects in China was established in the city soon after and was incorporated in Hong Kong, with the approval of the Royal Institute of British Architects, in 1907. However on its home ground the Institute, which represented most of Shanghai's leading architects, had no luck in securing their desire for an obligatory registration of professional architects in the city. Even though the Institute was recognised by the SMC in 1907, Shanghai's consular officials decided in 1909 that they 'did not find sufficient reason for the registration of architects and conceived that by so doing it would give them a monopoly of business.' On the same day the decision was reported, a letter to the *North China Daily News* expressed the view that 'the best built houses are built without the help of architects using a Chinese contractor.' That such a view, and lack of regulation, still prevailed and, indeed, continued to prevail over the following decades is in part why Shanghai's historic architecture is so unusually eclectic. And, of course, money was a major consideration as architects would expect a seven percent commission on the total cost of a new building.

The early builders and architects of the Bund had no notion of what engineering difficulties were to confront their 20th century successors. In the 1920s boreholes were sunk to nearly 1,000 feet in depth without the discovery of any bedrock. The Shanghai soil, or to be more precise its alluvial silt with a fifty percent water content, presented new challenges to those seeking to build high. Mr. Sidney J. Powell, quoted in 1920, asserted that 'Shanghai can only stand six floors, London sixty floors, New York and Hong Kong any number.' George Leopold Wilson, the architect of many of the Bund's large surviving structures remarked that 'there are few other cities in the world, if any, which present such difficulties regarding the foundations for buildings of any magnitude...even though the weight is spread over the whole site, it is usual for a building to sink about six inches, and sometimes more. So long as it settles evenly there is nothing to worry about, but when the settlement is uneven the architect and engineer have a few sleepless nights.'

The buildings on the Bund are effectively floating on a sea of mud. It was, of course, usual to estimate beforehand what the settlement would be. In designing buildings for the Hongkong and Shanghai Bank, the Chartered Bank and the Yokohama Specie Bank, the ground floor was set 12 inches above where it was expected to rest. Temporary steps were erected from the street and removed one at a time. The settling process could take several years and, to compound matters, the footpaths in front of the buildings were themselves raised on occasions—notably in the early 1920s and the early 1930s.

The major buildings on the Bund are resting on huge concrete rafts underpinned by wooden piles up to 100 feet in length. Huge quantities of imported Oregon pine (Douglas Fir) were used for this purpose. Some 1,600 piles were used in the construction of Sassoon House and over 2,600 piles supported the huge mass of the Hongkong and Shanghai Bank.

Peace Hotel

*Piling operations underway at Sassoon House, 1926*

And it wasn't just the piles that were imported. Amazingly, the bulk of the materials used for the construction and decoration of the Bund's buildings were too. That included tons of rare Italian marble, granite from Hong Kong and Japan, and just about everything from pre-fabricated structural steel to Crittall metal windows, and from pre-moulded ceilings to Shanks sanitary ware from England.

*Construction of the new Hongkong and Shanghai Bank, 1923*

Modern equipment was rarely used in the construction of buildings before the arrival of the London contractors, Messrs. Trollope & Colls on the Bund in 1921. Before that time heavy materials were raised by block and tackle and mechanisation was viewed in terms of how many cheap Chinese labourers were on hand. Trollope and Colls introduced modern construction methods and imported the first tower cranes ever to be seen in China. It wasn't, however, until around 1930 that the widespread use of electric cement mixers was adopted.

The Bund's architects were drawn from a small number of foreign architectural practices in the city. In the first decade of the 20th century when the first major buildings appeared, Atkinson & Dallas stood out as the city's leading architects and civil engineers. Mr. Brenan Atkinson, who had been practising as an architect in the city since the early 1890s, was joined by the former Assistant Municipal Engineer, Mr. Arthur Dallas, to form the partnership in 1897. Mr. Atkinson died in 1907 just before the completion of their Great Northern Telegraph Company Building on the Bund, after which his brother took his place in the firm. They went on to design the Banque de L'Indo-Chine, which was completed six years later.

*Buildings on the northern section of the Bund, mid-1920s*

Other architects of this period included the Munich educated Mr. Heinrich Becker who designed the Russo-Chinese Bank, the German-Asiatic Bank (rebuilt in 1948) and the Club Concordia (demolished in 1935), and the British firm of Scott & Carter who designed the Palace Hotel. The latter partnership ended when Mr. Carter died during the course of its construction.

But it was the firm of Palmer and Turner which, soon after their arrival in 1912, went on to dominate the architectural nomenclature of the Bund. They designed nine landmark buildings, commencing with the Union Building in 1915 and concluding with the Bank of China, which they had direct involvement with until 1939 when their Shanghai office closed. In the intervening years they designed magnificent buildings for the Yangtsze Insurance Association, the Glen Line, the Chartered Bank, the Hongkong and Shanghai Bank, the Yokohama Specie Bank, the Chinese Maritime Customs and Sassoon House, incorporating the Cathay Hotel. They also presided over a major conversion of the Palace Hotel in the mid-1920s and were consulting architects for the monumental Broadway Mansions just to the north of the Bund on Suzhou Creek.

Other major British architectural firms were to claim few spoils on the Bund. However, Messrs. Stewardson & Spence designed the Jardine Matheson & Co. Building and the McBain Building—whilst Lester, Johnson & Morriss were to erect three buildings in the early 1920s. Although Henry Lester retired in 1915, he was still alive to see his company's achievements in the form of the NKK Building, the Bank of Taiwan and the North China Daily News Building. The firm was established in 1913 when the businesses of Mr. Lester and Mr. George A. Johnson were amalgamated and Mr. Gordon Morriss was taken into partnership. Messrs. Lester and Morriss were also directors of the *North China Daily News.*

Henry Lester was often mimicked as being one of the most miserly members of the British community. Despite his wealth, he lived in modest accommodations and was reported to use public trams to get around the city. In his early Shanghai days he kept residences at a number of Bund addresses including the Masonic Lodge and the Shanghai Club. He was renowned for his daily stroll along the Bund and, although he was the oldest member of the Shanghai Club, he was said to never go into its bar except on Christmas Eve when the boys of the club treated the members to cake and wine. Although he had made many bequests unbeknown to the public before his death, his fortune was posthumously passed on to a trust, which, among numerous worthy causes, built grand educational institutes in the city, including the Lester Institute of Technical Education which offered courses in engineering and architecture.

# PALMER AND TURNER— STANDING THE TEST OF TIME

In his 1985 book *Tall Stories* Malcolm Purvis, a former partner of Palmer and Turner, traced the company's long and illustrious history to 1868 when its progenitor, Englishman William Salway, arrived in Hong Kong. Salway formed a partnership with Wilberforce Wilson that was joined by Lieutenant Sotheby Godfrey Bird in 1878, after which Salway announced his retirement. Wilson retired soon after new arrival Clement Palmer, a remarkably talented 23-year-old British architect, had drawn up plans for the hugely successful new premises of the Hongkong and Shanghai Bank in 1883. The project secured the fortunes of the Bird and Palmer partnership and a host of other landmark buildings in Hong Kong followed. Sadly, virtually nothing is left of these today. Little is known about Arthur Turner, who joined Palmer and Bird to act as structural engineer, but following Bird's retirement, the company took on the name of Palmer and Turner in 1891.

The Bird family link with Palmer and Turner, however, was to endure over three generations, with G. V. Bird becoming a partner at the Shanghai office in 1937 shortly before its closure at the outbreak of the Second World War. Following the events of 1937, things were desperate for the firm and George Leopold Wilson, the company's doyen architect and senior partner, was considering closing it down. He was largely talked out of it by the manager of the Hongkong and Shanghai Bank. The bank had enjoyed a long and close relationship with the firm and Wilson had designed their landmark buildings in Hong Kong and Shanghai.

In a letter to a retired partner in 1938 Wilson states 'I have never been so worried, struggling to keep the firm after paying out so much in capital and goodwill during the past few years and having no partners with any cash and anyone with their money tied up in property in Shanghai does not know whether they have a bean in the world today ... I do not expect there will be building work of any magnitude in Shanghai for at least two years so I propose cutting down the staff to a man and a boy.' (Reprinted from *Tall Stories*)

Their Shanghai office closed in 1939 and the Hong Kong office followed in 1941. Whilst the Hong Kong office reopened following the War, Palmer and Turner's long overdue return to Shanghai didn't take place until July 1990. Although Palmer and Turner reformed its corporate structure to become the P&T Group in 1982, establishing it as not only the oldest but also the largest architectural engineering practice in South East Asia, most people in Shanghai just refer to the company by its old familiar name, one that is engraved on the finest historic buildings in the city. The P&T Group today is occupied with major projects in Shanghai and throughout China. On the Bund the Group was involved with proposals for

*Mr. Clement Palmer, partner 1884-1909*

the enlargement of their own former Hongkong and Shanghai Bank building. However, HSBC decided not to reoccupy the building. They also put together proposals for the Peninsula Hotel Group in the same building, which is now occupied by the Pudong Development Bank. A new Peninsula hotel is now being established further up the Bund.

# TUG WILSON—MASTER ARCHITECT AND MAN OF MORES

*Mr. George Leopold Wilson and Mrs. Wilson*

George Leopold Wilson had a long and distinguished career in the Far East. Born on 1st November 1880 and educated in London, he began his career when he was articled to H. W. Peck Architects in 1898. During his time as assistant to E. B. J. Cluson from 1901–1908 he made frequent trips to France and Italy. His love of new places and challenges saw him leave England's shores in 1908 to take up an assistant's post with Palmer and Turner in Hong Kong.

Wilson accompanied Lt. Col. M. H. Logan to Shanghai in 1912 to open a branch office where they both became partners in

A.

RIBA

[FELLOW.]

CANDIDATE'S SEPARATE STATEMENT.

Every Candidate desirous of being admitted a Fellow of the Royal Institute of British Architects must furnish the Council with information suggested in the items hereinbelow printed.

*Wilson's application to become a fellow of the Royal Institute of British Architects, 1926*

1914. They took up offices in the Union Building, at No. 3, after they had completed it in the following year. Wilson personally designed, or assisted in the design, of six of the nine Palmer and Turner buildings on the Bund. Wilson spoke of good architecture as 'creative expression inspired by the beauty of the past.' His ideal combination of proportion, mass and form with simple interior decoration, colour and lighting was epitomised in the creation of Sassoon House and the Cathay Hotel (now the north wing of the Peace Hotel). His other landmark buildings in the vicinity of the Bund—the Metropole Hotel, Hamilton House and the Royal Asiatic Society buildings—still stand today as testament to the inimitable and progressive nature of the city in the early 1930s. Whilst on vacation in Europe and America in 1931, Wilson wrote in a letter that 'there is not a great deal which Shanghai can today learn from elsewhere which would be in the direction of improving practice here.'

Tug Wilson was unusually civic minded. He was an active council member of the Royal Asiatic Society and largely responsible for the collection of funds to build its premises. He was also president of the Union Club of China for many years. The Club was an adventurous undertaking when it opened in 1919 in that it 'promoted social intercourse between Chinese and foreign members of the business world.' Originally only open to British, Americans and Chinese nationals, it later was open to all

Early Architecture in Shanghai

Written by the late Thomas W. Kingsmill about twenty years ago

**Roads in the Forties**

IN the early days of Shanghai the main requirement of a house in China was then supposed to be a wide verandah with round brick pillars running round, or at least on three sides, and this was the type generally adopted. In some cases architectural aid was procured from the Southern colony, but the greater number of the houses were of the type referred to. A characteristic specimen of this style survived till within a few years ago in the

house inhabited by the firm of Shaw, Ripley & Co. at the junction of the Rope-walk Road, now the Kiukiang Road, and the Bund. As land was cheap an open space generally surrounded these primitive houses, and the compounds were planted with trees, mostly willows. As the growth of a city was not contemplated the passage-ways were never denominated streets but were called simply roads, and of these the first laid out were the Consulate, now the Peking Road; Park Lane, now the Nanking

PHOTO TAKEN IN THE SEVENTIES OF THE ORIENTAL BANK—NOW THE CHARTERED BANK OF INDIA, AUSTRALIA AND CHINA—AND THE CENTRAL HOTEL, FORMERLY OCCUPIED BY THE HONGKONG AND SHANGHAI BANK

*Article from Social Shanghai magazine, 1911*

and by the time it was closed in 1934 Wilson noted that it had 'fulfilled its purpose.' He was a member of most clubs in Shanghai, Hong Kong and Singapore, played polo and adored steeple-chasing. His charming wife, with whom he had one son, was also notable as one of Shanghai's great socialites.

At the outbreak of the Second World War he had managed to get his wife safely out of Shanghai. On his attempt to return England, though, he was less fortunate. His ship was bombed and he found himself shipwrecked on a small island near Sumatra. Surviving the incident, he spent the war years in England as a volunteer with the Ministry of Works, before returning to Hong Kong to rehabilitate the Colony. He returned to England following his retirement as senior partner of Palmer and Turner in 1952.

Wilson's plans for his retirement home were started whilst he was in Shanghai. He purchased Hatch Farm at Lindford, in the English county of Hampshire, in 1934, and drew up plans for its conversion. Short periods away from Shanghai were spent visiting the house, and the renovation and decoration work was completed during his retirement. Paintings by Le Meyeur, the Belgian artist, hung on the walls and treasures from the Far East were to be found in abundance. Wilson died there in September 1967.

# SHANGHAI MUD, SHANGHAI GOLD— BUILDING THE BUND

In the early years land was cheap on the Bund and it wasn't long before the first crude, rambling houses of foreign 'hongs,' or firms, began to spread haphazardly along the waterfront. The earliest buildings on the Bund, including those of the first lot holders, Jardine Matheson & Co and the Oriental Bank, were based on designs from the 'south' featuring wide verandas with round brick or wooden columns on all four sides. In 'compradoric style' they would feature large grounds populated with willow trees. The first major building contractor to establish his presence on the Bund was a Cantonese gentleman who employed a staff of Cantonese workmen, and was known to his foreign clients as 'Chop Dollar.'

In the early 1860s Shanghai was experiencing a most extraordinary land and property boom as up to 700,000 Chinese citizens flooded into the British and American Settlements to escape the atrocities of the Taiping rebels raging outside the city. Huge profits were being made by the British in providing accommodation for the new population, and drinking champagne by the case was the order of the day. Many extravagant plans were laid, including those for the Shanghai Club on the Bund. That building, and others to follow, represented a new ostentation indicative of the times and featured three floors, overly thick brick walls and Chinese roof tiles. Chop Dollar began work on the Shanghai Club in 1861. However, by the time of its completion in 1864 many defects had appeared and its top

*The Shanghai Club, 1886*

veranda collapsed. It was described by Club officials 'as a stately structure, which in spite of all the scientific abuse lavished on its architectural peculiarities takes up so much room on the Bund.' But it wasn't only physical defects that afflicted the building. Like many others built during that period it was soon in deep debt as land values on the Bund plummeted and businesses were turned upside down following the departure of around 500,000 Chinese after the troubles were quelled in 1864. Some reports put the number of Chinese in the area as just 80,000 in the following year.

The good times were over, at least for a short while. Other grand edifices were, however, soon to follow—including the Hongkong and Shanghai's Bank's second premises on the Bund, which, after its demolition in the 1920s, was described by the Bank's chief as 'a very pretentious building,' that was 'too large.' Many smaller buildings, in the old compradoric style managed to survive alongside until the end of the 19th century and beyond. The last such building, belonging to Dent & Co. on the corner of Jiujiang Road and the Bund, was torn down in 1915.

On adjacent Nanjing Road some of the hastily built three-storey structures, which were designed to accommodate refugees from the Taiping Rebellion, survived until 1901. The Chinese had generally never felt comfortable in these elevated structures and after the Rebellion their top floors were chopped off.

Again, it was an increasing influx of Chinese into the protectorate of the International Settlement towards the end of the 19th century that resulted in a tremendous increase in land values in the city. The actual cost of lots along the Bund went up over tenfold between 1890 and 1911. This, in turn, had a tremendous effect on the nature of building activity along the Bund. Investors were thinking big and tall and the construction of the city's highest building (at 94 feet), the Palace Hotel, was underway in 1906, as were huge new premises for the Great Northern Telegraph Offices and the Club Concordia (the German Club) nearby. The Palace Hotel was the

*Artist's impression of the new Palace Hotel*

*The Dodwell & Co. premises, 1908*

first in a long line of buildings on the Bund to seize the accolade as the tallest building in Shanghai, and barring Chinese pagoda structures and the odd cathedral spire, the tallest in China.

In 1904, the year that plans were drawn up for the Palace Hotel, an even more ambitious scheme was submitted to the SMC by Dodwell & Co., a major British merchant house engaged in importing, exporting and shipping which had its premises on the present site of No. 3 the Bund. Their proposal to build a 115-foot, steel-framed structure was well received by Mr. Mayne, the SMC Engineer and Surveyor. In a letter dated 7th January 1905 to J.O.P. Bland, the Secretary of the SMC, he wrote that 'when a firm is willing to sink such a large sum of money in an enterprise of this kind, I think it should be encouraged, provided the public rights are not interfered with.' He went on to say that such a building 'will undoubtedly be an object lesson to the Chinese in rapid and scientific building construction—a lesson badly needed—it will furnish excellent office accommodation in a very central location and will add a very fine building—designed by one of the best firms in America—to our Bund frontage.' The Council accepted the proposal, but only on the condition that the plans were modified to allow the neighbouring street to be widened by ten feet. Dodwell & Co. were forced to abandon their ideas owing to the extra expense involved. It wasn't long, however, before new plans were drawn up for the company by Moorhead & Halse, Engineers and Architects, for an even taller building. Their plans for a nine-storey, 123-foot-high structure which were submitted in June 1910 were again approved with conditions, but Dodwell & Co. yet again decided not to go ahead on account of the additional costs involved.

*The old premises of the Hongkong and Shanghai Bank, 1908*

*Bund panorama, late 1924*

In 1910, an even more extraordinary proposal for an entertainment centre housed in a 300-foot pagoda-style building near the Bund was endorsed by Mr. Mayne's successor, Mr. Godfrey. Godfrey said 'the whole question of the erection of tall buildings in Shanghai rests upon the present application.' He foresaw the day when Shanghai would become a city of skyscrapers and decided to leave it to the community to decide if 'Shanghai would be better served by tall buildings with more open spaces, than low buildings with little, or nothing, but narrow roads.' The scheme was duly passed by Shanghai's foreign ratepayers. Even though it was never built, it affirmed that the foreign public who had the power to change the face of the city were in favour of modernisation and that engineering difficulties involved with such a project could be challenged. Mr. Godfrey has turned out to be something of a futurist as his vision of Shanghai is only comprehensively taking shape today.

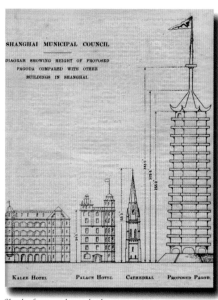

As in times of uncertainty and turmoil in the past, the years following the overthrow of the Qing dynasty in 1911 saw a large influx of well-to-do Chinese to the city. Shanghai experienced a period of unprecedented growth and its rapid industrialisation also attracted a large number of Chinese workers and Japanese

*Sketch of proposed pagoda skyscraper, 1910*

nationals to the city. The construction industry was booming and, despite a temporary lull in foreign building activities on account of the First World War, three large buildings were completed on the Bund between 1915 and 1918, including the Union Building at the present-day No. 3—which eventually claimed its title as the tallest in the city.

Business confidence was also booming after the war—as was the city's foreign population. In the International Settlement this had more than doubled to over 23,000 between 1910 and 1920, with the American community seeing a particularly large increase from 940 to 2,264. Meanwhile, the Chinese population in the Settlement had risen by more than 150,000 to over 750,000 in the same period. It was no surprise that a host of prestigious companies along the Bund announced grand plans to rebuild their outdated premises around 1920.

Despite the SMC's earlier recognition that the Shanghai skyline was set to rise higher, there was some debate over the new proposals for buildings along the Bund. The SMC was concerned that such a large concentration of tall buildings along the limited frontage of the Bund would have an adverse effect on the amenity of the streets that ran off it. There were inadequate regulations in place when the Union Building was built and its height along the adjoining Guangdong Road was the same as its Bund frontage.

Whilst no restrictions were placed on the height of the buildings facing the Bund, regulations were shortly after drawn up to restrict building height on the adjoining and comparatively narrow streets. Buildings were only allowed to maintain the height of their Bund frontage for a maximum of 80 feet along the

*A period of great change on the Bund, 1924*

Picture This

adjoining streets. However, all the proposals or statements of intent submitted to the SMC in 1919, including those for Jardine, Matheson & Co, Nisshin Kisen Kaisha and the Bank of Taiwan, required at least a 160-foot frontage. Fortunately the Council made special concessions based on the rather weak assertion that the roads opened on to 'unlimited space' and 'enjoyed an extra amount of light and air.' If it weren't for the SMC's flexibility the major buildings that we see along the Bund today might have looked totally different to what they do now.

Between 1921 and 1925 no less than seven new buildings were erected on the Bund. Despite the tumultuous events in the city, commencing with the May 30th Massacre in 1925 and the strikes, boycotts and anti-foreign demonstrations that followed, to the killing of thousands of suspected Communists by Nationalist troops and Green Gang members in April 1927, it didn't take long for business to return to normal. Indeed it was the scions of Chinese big business that supported, voluntarily or not, the new Nationalist Government. The Bank of Taiwan and the new Custom House were completed on the Bund in 1927.

In the late 1920s everything was booming again. Foreign and Chinese money was flooding into the city. Sir Victor Sassoon spearheaded the foreign crusade by transferring vast amounts of his fortune from Bombay to Shanghai. The price of land on which his Sassoon House and Cathay Hotel was being built on the Bund doubled over the course of its construction from 1926 to 1929. The last was by far the most outstanding year in terms of land values and property transactions in Shanghai's history, and the old saying of 'Shanghai Mud, Shanghai Gold' had never rung so true.

Yet the sounds of war were never far away. The Sino-Japanese hostilities in Zhabei district, to the north of Suzhou Creek, during the first five months of 1932 served as a wake-up call and delayed major building projects around the city. The impact of the events was compounded by a rapid depreciation in the value of silver soon after. Whilst there were no building projects underway on the Bund in 1932, some buildings behind the northern section of the Bund, in what is now known as the 'Waitanyuan' area, were affected. The more devastating events of 1937, however, delayed the completion of the Bund's last pre-war building, the Bank of China, and stalled plans for the Art Deco form of the Commercial Bank of China, which weren't fully realised until 1948.

# THE END OF AN ERA—
# BOMBS ON THE BUND

*Carnage on the doorstep of the Cathay Hotel*

The first signs of renewed Sino-Japanese hostilities around Shanghai appeared following the Japanese occupation of Beijing and the commencement of the Sino-Japanese War in July 1937. Following a series of scurrilous minor skirmishes, local fighting broke out to the north of the city on 13th August, and on the morning of 14th August the Chinese commenced bombing from the air. The Japanese flagship *Idzumo*, which was moored some distance away

from the Bund off the shore to the east of the Garden Bridge, was their main objective that morning.

In the late afternoon, bombs from two different Chinese bombers were haplessly dispatched into the heart of foreign Shanghai. Two bombs fell on the corner of the present-day East Yan'an Road and Central Tibet Road. Two others hit both buildings of the present-day Peace Hotel (see page 240) on the corner of East Nanjing Road and the Bund. The incidents left over 1,200 people dead and hundreds more injured. The Chinese reported that the bombs had released themselves onto their unintended targets as the planes' bomb racks had been damaged by Japanese fire. It was more likely, however, that the 'accident' had been ruthlessly contrived, amongst other reasons, to draw international attention to the conflict.

Bloody Saturday, as it became known, was a day Shanghai was never to recover from. No amount of sandbags could provide a defence against the massive body blow with which Shanghai had been so cruelly punished. The siege lasted until November, after which the Japanese occupied the Chinese city and districts to the north of the International Settlement. In early December, following Chiang Kai-shek's withdrawal from Shanghai, the Japanese marched through the International Settlement in a victory parade.

The incident marked the beginning of a spiralling downturn in the fortunes of the city. The economy faltered, inflation propelled prices beyond people's means, and the control by the West filtered away as the days went by. Foreign trade on the Yangtsze River, Shanghai's principal *raison d'être*, had been driven away and the great port city languished in idleness.

Although Shanghai appeared almost as normal in the dying months of 1937, the audible signals of war grew incessantly louder. The mighty grip of the Japanese tightened to throttle Shanghai. However, the former status of the International Settlement, though increasingly impoverished, was preserved right up until the Japanese attack on Pearl Harbour on 8th December (Shanghai time) 1941.

*The final chapter, cover of a 1941 guidebook*

# FINDING THE RIGHT BUND ADDRESS

## No. 1 The McBain Building

The McBain Building was more familiarly known in old Shanghai as the Shell or Asiatic Petroleum Company Building. The Shell International Petroleum Company, which had established its presence in Shanghai in 1907, continued to operate in the building right up until the dawn of the Cultural Revolution in 1966. Nien Cheng, assistant to the British general manager at that time, recounts her story of the following years in her best-selling book *Life and Death in Shanghai*. Her British-educated husband had been general manger of the office prior to his death in 1957.

The building itself was owned by the George McBain Company. Its founder, George McBain, who arrived in the Far East in the 1870s to work for a bank in Hong Kong, soon diverted his interests to shipping on the Yangtsze River. In addition he developed tobacco and oil-producing businesses in Sumatra. Lord Kadoorie recounted to Harriet Sergeant in her book *Shanghai* how McBain had fallen in love with the daughter of the sampan woman who made deliveries and cleaned his ship. They had nine children and when the family travelled back to Europe on the Trans-Siberian railway they had their own private carriage and retinue of servants.

The family lived in great style. Their stately mansion on Bubbling Well Road, set in ten acres of grounds, was one of the finest in the city. Following its sale in 1924, the estate was converted into the legendary Majestic Hotel, which was sadly demolished in 1933. George McBain died at the relatively young age of 57 in February 1904. A glowing tribute was paid to him in

*No. 1, still open to offers in 2006*

*The McBain Building, 1931*

the *North China Daily News*—'no man has ever amassed a fortune in China with a more rigid observance of the nicest honour and strictest integrity than George McBain. No ship owner was ever more beloved by his employees or treated them with more kindness and consideration.'

When work on the building started in June 1913 one of George's sons, William Robert Brown McBain, who became the senior partner in the business, had quite a battle with the SMC over the appropriate installation of sanitary fittings. The seven-storey Renaissance-style building designed by Moorhead and Halse, which was completed in 1915, contained a series of flats on its top floor reserved for Shell executives. An eighth floor was added in 1939.

Cambridge-educated William, a squadron commander in the First World War, was decorated with the Military Cross and the Air Force Cross. One of the building's earliest occupants, the British Chamber of Commerce, was born of the same conflict. Established in 1915 to promote Britain against the enemy, its chairman and SMC member, John Johnstone, remarked at a meeting in the building in 1916 that 'we are more determined than ever that military Germany shall be crushed and that commercially she shall no longer enjoy the advantage which we have hitherto allowed her.' The organisation moved its offices to No. 17 the Bund in the 1920s, and was in residence at No. 27 the Bund when the tables were turned by the Japanese in 1941.

William McBain cut a flamboyant figure and was the owner of Shanghai's first private aircraft. His beloved Armstrong Whitworth two-seater first took off from a muddy field in Hongqiao in May 1920. On his inaugural flight William was accompanied by a Japanese engineer, but he promised his friends that they would all get their turn. He was also a member of the SMC and the chairman of the Greyhound Racing Club in the 1920s. Despite his pedigree, he turned out to be one of the loudest opponents of the SMC's plans to banish greyhound racing from the International Settlement. On that occasion, in 1931, the Council won.

The back part of the building now hosts a variety of companies, including AIA, whilst the front part, with its Bund entrance, awaits new tenants. All that is left of the past are two bronze plaques bearing the Shell logo, which are now housed in the Shanghai Municipal History Museum.

*Advert, 1936*

# No. 2 **The Shanghai Club**

Membership of the Shanghai Race Club and the Shanghai Club were prerequisites for respectability in the British business community. The Shanghai Club proudly stood as a bastion of civility and manners for Shanghai's British elite. In the words of the *North China Daily News* it was 'a microcosm *par excellence* of the Settlement.' Affiliated to gentlemen's clubs in India and other parts of the Empire, it was an exclusive domain ministered by strict codes of social and personal conduct.

# THE LONGEST BAR IN THE WORLD

Dennis George Crow

*The Club, 1890s*

The first Shanghai Club, equipped with 12 residential rooms, was built on a lot formerly occupied by Hiram Fogg's provisions store and opened in May 1864. It was far too lavish and poorly managed for its means of support and was forced to close for several months in 1867. Even with changes in ownership and management, beginning in 1870, its reputation as the local sphinx of finance was hard to cast off. Despite extensive alterations in 1886, by the end of the 19th century physical demands on the Club's premises were becoming so intense that calls were made for a new home. Its membership had shot up from 290 in 1880 to 551 in 1893, and to nearly 1,000 in 1900, whilst its library had grown from 2,763 volumes in 1878 to over 13,000 in 1900. The passing of the old Club was much lamented by its senior members who, together with younger associates, took up temporary premises on Dianchi Road and were afforded club privileges by the Club Concordia (see page 275) on the Bund, whilst building work was underway.

The new Club, which opened on 6th January 1911, was famed for its 'Long Bar'—and it was long—stretching 110 feet 7 inches along the south face of the building. The established taipans, or big bosses, would gather at the end of the bar near the waterfront whilst newcomers to Shanghai, known as 'griffins,' would be relegated to the murky depths of the tavern. According to Shanghai tradition newcomers remaining in the city were griffins for one year, one month, one week, one day, one hour, one minute and one second after their arrival. After that they became fully fledged 'Shanghailanders.' The term griffin was otherwise used to refer to wild Mongolian ponies that had been tamed over a period of time. American media man, Carl Crow, jocularly described a griffin as 'a pony which has not yet won a race and a foreigner whose first employment contract has not yet been renewed.' The bar acted as a barometer of social progress as those who fared well in the climate would advance ever closer to the sunlight and success afforded by a position near its windows. Jay Denby in his humorous *Letters of a Shanghai Griffin*, published in 1910, remarked that success was plain to see—'a taipan, let me explain, is a red-faced man

(the redder the face, the taipanner the taipan) who has either
sufficient brains or bluff to make others work for him and yet
retain the kudos and the bulk of the spoil himself.'

*The Long Bar*

The Club was Shanghai's
unofficial business exchange and
its oak-panelled, Jacobean-style
bar was at its busiest at
lunchtimes when customary
deals were thrashed out over a
scotch or pink gin. Crow noted
that 'there were probably few
places in the world where per
capita consumption of alcoholic
drinks was greater than at the
Shanghai Club during the tiffin
hour nor few places that presented a more perfect picture of
decorous conviviality.' Its walls were festooned with a large
collection of animal heads initiated by Mr. Arthur de Carle
Sowerby, big-game hunter, founder of the *China Journal*–
Shanghai's own scientific and literary monthly—and director of the
Shanghai Museum. Such trophies of members' hunting trips also
adorned the Domino Room and came from far-flung places such
as Indo-China and Kenya.

Other members of the club were more occupied with
shooting billiard balls than boars' heads. Shanghai's most
prestigious tournaments, the Shanghai Club Cup and the Shanghai
Amateur Billiard Association Cup were played out on ten of the
finest billiard tables to be found in the Far East. And on one
occasion, in July 1924, the Club was faced with the loss, rather
than the acquisition, of some of its prized trophies. Both of the
competition cups disappeared on the night of 22nd July 1924.
The Shanghai Club Cup bore the name of Mr. Gordon Morriss,
Club champion and a leading British personage with interests in
the *North China Daily News* and the architectural firm of Lester,
Johnson and Morriss. Two days later the enterprising thief found
himself before the magistrate of the Mixed Court, a Shanghai

institution set up to try cases involving Chinese charged by foreigners, after he had been turned in by a local pawnbroker. Eddie Lolo as he liked to be known, or Bar boy No. 18 as he was known to all at the Club, gave himself away rather too easily as he was the only bar boy to wear Western dress. The *China Press*, a local newspaper, described him as a dapper chap, 'a Beau Brummel and a factor among the gals.' Many members on the other side of the bar would surely have thought of themselves in similar terms.

The club's brand of respectable hospitality was far from open to all. When Club chairman, W. A. C. Platt, opened the new building he asserted that it was to be run on the principle of 'the greatest happiness of the greatest number.' Non-establishment sticklers and dissenters would find no place within its confines. Membership was hugely expensive and subject to a members' ballot where four out of five had to be in agreement. It was also the only Club in the city to expressly deny membership to the Chinese. However the Club excluded many members of its own nationality as it did the Chinese. Visiting millionaire Thomas Lipton, rich, but still a grocer, was not granted Club courtesies.

Women, of course, were not permitted to enter and were only admitted on very rare occasions throughout the Club's history. Shortly after the opening of the new Club on

*Celebrating the coronation of King George V in 1911*

19th January 1911 there was a 'ladies reception day' and there were very few ladies of Shanghai who were not there. Another special event at which women were allowed to partake of cocktails and observe their men in their secondary home was in March 1927 for the Club's Diamond Jubilee. A bust of King

George V was unveiled to mark the occasion, and, as the *North China Daily News* remarked, it was only the second time that ladies had been invited to the Club in recent years. In the 1930s the Club held an annual ladies' night, which took the form of 'a hospitable dance ball held in the main dining hall.' In 1933 it attracted 600 members and their spouses who danced through the night. Unlike the nearby American Club, which opened a special section for lady members in 1937, admittedly more in response to financial needs than egalitarian principles, the Shanghai Club's doors remained firmly closed to members of the fairer sex.

One of the most famous anecdotes concerning the club's exclusivity is sometimes recounted as taking place at the time of the Japanese occupation in 1941, although it actually took place in May 1949 as the Communists were fighting for Shanghai. Noel Barber in his book, *The Fall of Shanghai*, reports on how Eldon Cook found the closest shelter from gunfire at the door of the Club. His boss, who caught sight of him from the Long Bar, went to the door and remarked 'you can't come in here! You're not a member.' Apparently he had second thoughts. 'Wait a moment,' he cried and vanished inside to reappear with another elderly member. 'Come inside,' he beckoned Cook. 'I'll propose you and my friend will second you for temporary membership - so you can come in now.'

Fleeting visitors came away with differing impressions of the Long Bar. Noel Coward remarked that 'one could see the curvature of the earth along it,' whilst Christopher Isherwood and W. H. Auden commented 'needless to say, it proved to be far shorter than we had expected.' In fact, by the time of their visit in 1938, an establishment on the site of the old Belmont Hotel at 42nd Street and Park Avenue in New York boasted a bar nearly 30 feet longer than the one at the Club.

*A surviving dwarf billiard table*

*Opening ceremony, January 1911*

*Commemorative key used*
*to open the building*

The membership, although predominantly British, included some Japanese in the 1930s and it was on 12th December 1941 that a Japanese member, accompanied by a Japanese Naval officer, gave the final orders for all to leave the club at lunchtime. The building was then taken over by the Japanese Naval Landing Party. The Long Bar itself is often reported to have been sawn in half and shipped to Japan during those years. In reality it was only after the building was converted into the International Seaman's Club in 1956 that part of the bar was chopped off and moved upstairs. However, the Japanese did cut away the lower section of the billiards tables' legs to allow them to play the game in comfort. Following the War the tables rested on wooden platforms and when the building closed down many stunted tables were cocooned inside.

L ike its predecessor, the new Club building was more
extravagant than could be afforded, and was 50 percent over
budget at the time of its formal opening by the British Consul,
General Sir Pelham Warren. Warren had laid the foundation stone
less than two years earlier on 20th February 1909, following the
demolition of the old building at the end of 1908. A guard of
honour composed of armed Sikhs and bluejackets from HMS
*Flora* lined both sides of the Bund and the Town Band struck up
*'Land of Hope and Glory'* as the doors to Shanghai's societal
sanctum were thrown open.

The appearance of the building in an interpreted English
Renaissance style also came under fire for its ill-suited windows
and roof. The Club committee admitted that they chose the
design on the basis of its plan, rather than its front elevation.
Such peculiarities also had something to do with the fact that
Bertram Tarrant's original designs had been altered by Mr. A. G.
Bray following Tarrant's death during the course of construction.
However, Bray, whose company had originally come third in the
competition to design the building, did a better job in modelling
the interior. The centrepiece was a grand hall covered by a
barrelled glass ceiling with Italian marble columns rising to the
height of its two floors.

*Artist's impression of the Club, 1909*

The Club was replete with all the amenities a gentleman could ask for. Its basement contained two bowling alleys, an oyster bar, barber's shop and two wine cellars. On the ground floor, apart from the Long Bar, there was a commodious news room, a smoking room, a billiards room and a domino room. A huge

*Where one of the royal portraits once hung, 2006*

dining room, richly decorated in warm reds, was reached by way of fine, white Sicilian marble stairs extending along the entire Bund frontage of the first floor. Life-size portraits of King Edward VII and Queen Alexandra, painted partly by, and partly under the supervision of, the Royal artist Sir Samuel Luke Fildes, were hung over the large open fireplaces. They were gifts of the Eastern Extension Telegraph Company and the Great Northern Telegraph Company, which had premises a few doors away. There were three other dining rooms on the first floor, as well as a library and reading room, another billiards room and a card room.

The two floors above housed 40 en-suite bedrooms each with a fireplace and a hot water radiator. Their fine ornamental ironwork, fire grates and stained glass were imported from Birmingham and their velvet-pile carpets from Yorkshire. A thoroughly British breakfast of kedgeree, bacon and eggs, porridge, toast and Oxford marmalade came with a copy of the *North China Daily News* or *The Times* of London.

*No. 1 in 2006*

The portraits of Chairman Mao and Zhou Enlai that had been hung on the walls in the 1950s had long gone by the time the face of Colonel Sanders appeared in the building in 1990. During most of the 1990s, Shanghai's first KFC outlet occupied the formerly sacred grounds of the famous Long Bar. Sanders' figure stood just a few yards away from where a life-size plaster statue of Chairman Mao used to greet visitors and where banners proclaiming 'Proletarians of the World Unite' were transmogrified under the slogan 'finger likin' good.' Upstairs, the bar of the International Seaman's Club had become a sleazy and dimly lit setting for Shanghai's nefarious pleasures, and the rooms above were under the undistinguished management of the East Wind Hotel. At the time of the building's closure in 2000 the past symbol of British propriety was lifelessly filled with a hodgepodge of outdated and ill-fitting commercial activity. Since then the building has occasionally been used by film crews requiring a period setting—although one crew obviously felt it was too attractive and smothered the marble work in paint.

Fortunately, although rampantly rundown, many of the building's fine original features were to survive, and its architectural value, if not its historic valour, has been recognised by the highest level of government. Potential new investors were advised that, as part of any redevelopment scheme, the interiors within the first three floors of the building would have to be preserved intact. A number of interested parties have looked at the building with an eye to converting it into a hotel, so it may not be that long before luxuries, like those of old, will be found on the premises again.

# PEARL HARBOR—AND SHANGHAI

IT WAS HALF PAST FOUR in the morning of December 8, 1941—December 7, Pearl Harbor time. I was asleep in my room on the top floor of the Shanghai Club on the Bund, overlooking the Whangpoo River.

Suddenly I was awakened by explosions, like heavy firing. Half awake, I thought Moscow had fallen, and was sufficiently conscious to feel unhappy about it; for surely the Japanese were celebrating a German victory. In the morning we should see their captive victory balloons up over the city with long streamers proclaiming in Chinese the Axis success.

But the firing was too heavy. I ran to the window.

There on the river stretch just before the club was a vivid scene of war. Along the Bund just under the window were brilliant explosions as field pieces fired and shells struck their target up the river. Reddish streaks made by tracer bullets chased one another in low curves. Then came bursts of flame from the target.

From further downstream, at the bend of the river, flashes marked the firing of the Japanese flagship *Idzumo*.

Amazed and stunned, we on the top floor got together and watched.

We knew they were firing at the British gunboat *Petrel*. Quickly she burst into flames, was battered to pieces. She sank. Her lifeboats drifted away, afire, and floated downstream. True to British Navy tradition, the *Petrel* went down fighting. Her hopeless resistance was the only defense Shanghai was to know.

The heavy field pieces and ammunition wagons rumbled away. All was silence again.

...Immediately we thought of internment, quickly dressed in our warmest clothes, gathered up a few necessaries. We went down to the lobby. Men were standing around, waiting, expecting a visit of importance. Six o'clock came, but the heavy iron gates at the club entrance remained closed for the first time in many decades.

Presently a Japanese officer appeared and informed the Sikh watchman that the club might open as usual. So we drifted into the dining room to an uninteresting breakfast.

The day was bleak and cold, and the sun did not shine.

...No one could imagine what the day would bring; but, as required by proclamation, men went to their places of business. Some Americans, British, and other enemies found their offices already sealed tight under Japanese guard.

...While the doors of such banks as the National City, the Chase, the Hong Kong and Shanghai, and the Chartered remained closed, plastered with proclamations, inside was activity. During several months the Japanese required the services of the British, American, and Dutch staffs to assist in liquidation. Then they took over the bank assets and moved their own banks bodily into the premises.

Japanese censorship, well known to Shanghai, was extended to cover *all* newspapers. The *North China Daily News*, British, was stopped at once; the *Shanghai Times*, British in registry, continued as a Japanese organ; the *Shanghai Evening Post and Mercury*, American, controlled by C. V. Starr of Shanghai and New York, was taken by the Japanese as an afternoon newspaper for propaganda.

In the famous Cathay Hotel, owned by the Sassoon interests, all seemed as usual; but Japanese sat in the manager's office. And so it was with all enemy-owned hotels.

...We in the Shanghai Club were spared four days, receiving notice on December 12 to vacate in two hours; the Japanese Navy needed that. ...Think of the Shanghai Club, with its longest bar in the world crowded three deep during the tiffin hour, where men talked business and exchange, hunting and ponies, and the races. Think of Empire Day and the King's Birthday and the turnout of the old guard; of Ladies' Night and Royalty, the colorful gathering of Army and Navy and officialdom. That fine old sanctum of the Empire, now the home of the Japanese Navy.

Excerpt from:
Edna Lee Booker, *Flight from China*, The Macmillan Company, New York. 1945.

# No. 3 The Union Building

The groundbreaking design of the Union Building, which was the first building in Shanghai to employ a full skeletal steel framework, set a new standard for buildings on the Bund. The steel structure allowed the graceful lines of the building to extend upwards to the top of the 105-foot roof and also allowed the architects to dispense with the need for internal structural walls. In essence it was China's first open-plan office building, its tenants deciding on the internal layout of their offices according to their desires. Palmer and Turner's first building on the Bund marked their arrival, housed their offices, and set the pattern for a series of other groundbreaking buildings that were to follow.

The building, in free Renaissance style, with its corner tower topped by a golden argosy weather vane 150 feet above the ground, contained three sections. The front section contained six spacious storeys, whilst to the rear there was a ten-storey section for servants' quarters as well as storage rooms for the office tenants who occupied all but the top floor. The top floor was devoted to residential flats.

*Three on the Bund, 2006*

The Union Insurance Society of Canton Limited occupied an office on the ground floor that extended almost the full depth of the building, constituting by far the largest open office space in the city. It had windows on three sides, with a large lantern overhead. This hugely profitable company, established by a group of pioneer British merchants in 1835, had opened branches in London, Singapore, Yokohama, Melbourne and Shanghai between 1895 and 1899. In 1906 the company merged with the China Traders' Insurance Company (later known as the British Traders Insurance Company) and additional branches were set up across the US, Canada, China, Japan, New Zealand and Brazil. The company later merged with the China Fire Insurance Company in 1915 and with the Yangtsze Insurance Association, at No. 26 the Bund, in 1926.

Despite the assertion on the heritage plaque outside the building that it was originally occupied by the Mercantile Bank of India, they didn't actually move into the building until June 1935. The bank took ownership of the building from the Union Insurance Society of Canton in July 1941 at a cost of £80,000. Most properties at that time were being taken over by Japanese interests, and the *North China Daily News* flew the fading British flag by announcing that the purchase was 'indicative of British confidence in Shanghai as a commercial centre.' The bank's business was acquired by the Hongkong and Shanghai Banking Corporation in 1959.

Fully owned by a Singapore-based family through the GITI Group, the building set new standards yet again when it opened as Three on the Bund in 2004. Many talents were drawn upon including Handel Lee, in the early stages of the creation of this upmarket centre for the arts, culture and cuisine—incorporating the Shanghai Gallery of Art, fine restaurants, including Jean Georges, the Whampoa Club, Laris and New Heights, as well as the Giorgio Armani flagship store and the Evian Spa by Three. It is also the only entirely foreign-owned building on the Bund today.

# THE MICHAEL GRAVES VISION

A representative of Handel Lee initially approached Lyndon Neri whilst he and Michael Graves were staying in Hong Kong. Initially, Lyndon was too embarrassed to present the project to Mr. Graves and they twice turned it down before a ten-page dispatch from Mr. Lee convinced them otherwise. With an art gallery at its core, they found the concept 'interesting and special' and one that took matters 'to a different level of abstraction.' Around eight months later, in 1999, they took their first steps into the dilapidated confines of No. 3 The Bund. There was 'hanging plaster everywhere.'

The design process, which started in 2000, took two years to complete. Graves and Neri designed most of the interior spaces, although some 'heavy-hitters,' including Claudio Silverstein and Massimiliano Fuksas executed the designs for Giorgio Armani and Emporio Armani, as others did for the Whampoa Club and Evian Spa. It was important to bring the vibrancy and energy that was

*Awaiting a new life as Three on the Bund*

evident in the interactions of people and commerce along the Bund, and the Huangpu River, into the building. Mirrors were placed in the restaurants to allow people to react to the visual presence of water within the structure.

The 'whole idea of welcoming' was also a very important design element. The building belonged to a time when classicist ideas of architecture clearly defined a hierarchy of social position and space. There were grand public entrances and

*The entrance lobby before renovation*

*The space from which the atrium was created*

cavernous spaces for the privileged, whilst the serving classes would enter their cramped quarters from concealed back doors. Graves and Neri attempted to break down such barriers by creating a non-forbidding environment that welcomed everybody, even if they couldn't afford to buy an Armani suit. The building was also infused with elements of Chinese surprise, where 'moments of architecture' could

be captured on a journey through its interior.

After a year of construction work on the building, which was not without its critics, Three on the Bund opened in early 2004. There were 'loud Western voices challenging us, asking why we didn't keep the old part of it. In reality there was hardly anything to keep.' However, among other features, the cornices on the third floor gallery were preserved, as were eight fireplaces; while the floor design in the Jean Georges restaurant was taken from an original pattern, and the entry lobby was replicated. Many presumed that the core building was destroyed to create the huge atrium running up from its third floor. The architects were adamant in taking a 'spatial historical point of view' and, in

*Jean Georges restaurant*

fact, inserted new architecture into what was an empty space in the original design that had only haphazardly been filled in over the passing years.

Although Neri is supportive of the government's intent to ensure that renovations are properly executed on the Bund, he is very wary of the city's predilection to 'replicate something just for the sake of replicating it.' He asserts that most of the renovation on the Bund is 'bastardised' and is critical of the newly arrived self-proclaimed 'experts' who haven't done their research and lack a proper understanding of architecture, planning and history. The obsession with physical preservation too often translates into a totally inappropriate replication and a 'Disneyfication' of Shanghai. For

Neri, sincerity, understanding and conceptual clarity are key features of keeping the vital 'essence' of a building alive.

*From an interview with Lyndon Neri. He was Director of Projects in Asia and associate-in-charge for Michael Graves and Associates during the reinvention of Three on the Bund. Following the project he founded the partnership of Neri & Hu Design and Research Office in Shanghai. Images courtesy of Lyndon Neri.*

*The atrium*

# THE C.M.L.I. BUILDING—
# IT SHOULD HAVE BEEN ON THE BUND

*Artist's impression of the building, 1910*

**M**ore than a few guests at the opening ceremony of the premises of the China Mutual Life Insurance Company Ld. (C.M.L.I.) in June 1910 expressed regret that Shanghai's new 'show building' was not on the Bund itself. They had to console themselves with the thought that the building's location, one block away from the waterfront on Guangdong Road, represented an expression of the outward growth of commercial success beyond the Bund. There would have been regrets of a much graver magnitude if the elegantly designed building had been demolished, as was anticipated in the 1930s; or if its extravagant interior decoration had been destroyed, as would have been expected during the

Cultural Revolution. Somehow, defeating the odds, the building still stands as a singular example of the pomp and artistry of a forgotten era. It is also one which many people continue to pass on by, oblivious to its wealth of interior riches.

*Decorated on the occasion of the coronation of King George V, 1911*

The C.M.L.I. was founded in 1898 by James Alexander Wattie, a Canadian of Scottish descent, who had come to Shanghai a few years earlier as an insurance man with the Sun Life Insurance Company of Canada. Wattie, a veritable financial wizard, pioneered the opening up of the insurance market for the Chinese and realised huge returns for his enterprise. His company's assets

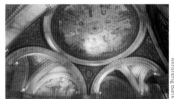

Minsheng Bank

had multiplied twentyfold by 1904 and in the year the building opened profits shot up by 16 percent. In September 1906 the company decided to erect a new building on the site opposite their rented offices, which had previously been occupied by the German Club since 1881.

*Mr. Wattie in his office, 1910*

Minsheng Bank

*The present-day entrance vestibule*

Their new, English Renaissance-style building, faced in Qingdao granite, was designed by Mr. F. G. Drewitt of Atkinson & Dallas, and its fabulous marble interior was created by Paolo Triscornia di Ferdinando of Carrara in Italy. The building's entrance vestibule, which is still largely intact, features quadruple panels of Paonazzo marble in avant-garde fashion, translucent green Mexican onyx columns, a colourful geometrical patterned marble floor and a spectacular domed ceiling inlaid with Salviati gold mosaic. Its original stained-glass windows, made by R. E. Pearce & Company in London and depicting the 'Virtues', have

also miraculously survived. Two groups of allegorical, carved marble figures, portraying aspects of the insurance business, are still found over the entrance to the main hall—one depicting the spinning and cutting of the thread of life and the other representing youth relieving old age. Now occupied by the China Minsheng Banking Corporation, China's first privately owned bank, the main hall features 18 rich and ruddy antique marble columns and pilasters. The only loss has been that of a large stained-glass dome, again representing the Virtues, which has been replaced by a plain glass, rectangular-shaped skylight.

*The entrance vestibule featuring the two friezes, 1910*

*Surviving stained glass and marble frieze with figure holding the thread of life*

The building is still plentifully stocked with traces of its C.M.L.I. heritage. The company's distinctive monogram remains, heavily etched, on two of the banking halls' windows, as well as on one window in the bank's ATM lobby, with its entrance on Guangdong Road. It is also evident on the wooden stair panels leading off the other entrance on Guangdong Road, and the company's initials (C.M.L.I.C. Lᴅ) are visible in the stained glass above the main entrance. Wattie's personal presence, however, wasn't so enduring, as following an injury sustained in a polo accident before the building opened, he was forced to spend many of the following years in England, before finally settling in Australia in 1931. However, his wide-ranging business interests, including rubber and land finance, continued to be represented in the building before, and after, it was sold to his old associates, the

Sun Life Insurance Company of Canada in 1924.

In the following year, the SMC was presented with an opportunity to purchase the building to allow its plans to widen Central Sichuan Road to proceed—plans which would have called for at least the front quarter of the building to be demolished. Prudently they decided to wait—and were encouraged by the sale of the building opposite, formerly occupied by the Standard Oil Co., in 1928. Its new owners had declared their intent to knock it down and build a slimmer and taller structure in its place. The SMC had another opportunity to buy the old C.M.L.I. building in 1930, but again backed off in the expectation that it, too, would be demolished by its new owner. As it became clear that neither of the new owners had any immediate plans to rebuild, the SMC was left with the vain hope that their plans could be realised by 1940. Thankfully they weren't, and the narrow bottleneck at their junction remains a noticeable feature of an otherwise wide road today.

The C.M.L.I. building's new owner, Yu Yaqing (Yu Ya-ching), was one of the most powerful figures in old Shanghai. Renowned for his lavish spending on life's luxuries, including a retinue of a dozen or so concubines, he was also one of the first Chinese members of the

*The C.M.L.I. general office, 1910*

French Municipal Council. He made the building home for his huge shipping business, the San Peh Steam Navigation Co. Rather than knocking the building down, Yu set about making some interesting additions, including that of a rooftop temple in 1931. The Masonic Club, which had been in temporary accommodation following the demolition of its building on the Bund in 1927, moved into Wattie's former apartment at the top of the building in January 1933.

*Yu Yaqing*

The building's heavily pockmarked marble interior tells the tale of how it was boarded up, and put under wraps during the Cultural Revolution. However, the identity of the building's saviour, be it a descendant of the Yu family or that of a sympathetic senior party official, has never been disclosed.

*The intricately carved staircase*

# No. 5 The NKK Building

NKK had inhabited a collection of old buildings on the corner of the Bund and Guangdong Road, formerly used by a Japanese fire insurance company, in 1907. By 1917, the buildings within the compound of the Japanese Nisshin Kisen Kaisha Shipping Co. were, by their own admission, regarded as an eyesore and they commissioned Lester, Johnson and Morriss to design their new Renaissance-style premises. The building was completed in late 1921. NKK's presence on the Bund, alongside other Japanese interests, was indicative of the growing influence of Japan in China following the Sino-Japanese War of 1894-1895. The company was formed in 1907 upon the amalgamation of the Osaka Shosen Kaisha (OSK) and other Japanese shipping lines. Two OSK mail steamers, under contract to the Imperial Japanese Government, were first put into service on the Yangtsze River in 1898—signalling the first threat to Chinese and British dominance on China's most important waterway. Less than 40 years later all British vessels were banished from the river by the Japanese.

One of the earliest applicants for a space in the new building was a Japanese entrepreneur who wished to open a Turkish bath and restaurant in part of the basement. In recent times, the building has again been open to businesses seeking a Bund address in quite a different manner to those of its neighbours. Sections of the building, which is owned by the Shanghai Shipping Company, have been leased on short-term agreements by a few individualistic entrepreneurs. Part of the basement is now occupied by a British-run bar and part of the first floor is occupied by Design Republic, a life-style design showcase established by Lyndon Neri and Rossana Hu. Three on the Bund also have their offices in the building.

It was, however, the transformation of the roof of the building into the now legendary *M on the Bund* in 1999, the Bund's first independently operated eatery in modern times, which set the benchmark for the subsequent development of restaurants and cultural venues that were to follow. M on the Bund expanded its premises in the building with the opening of the Glamour Bar, below the restaurant, in June 2006.

*No. 5 in 2006*

*View from M on the Bund*

# THE MICHELLE GARNAUT VISION

I first came to Shanghai in 1985 and, as some of my friends were there, stayed at the Shanghai Conservatory of Music. I came a couple of times...and we rode around on our bikes and I remember going into the Peace Hotel and being astounded by the sight of all the old hotel furniture stored in one of the ground floor rooms. In those days the antique shops and warehouses were piled high with furniture. I'd get so excited about it all—but didn't have a penny—so just bought a few pieces of old junk and that was the end of that. My first memory of the Bund was of 20-watt light bulbs, everything was so dim and it was all so grey. Shanghai was only grey then.

And then my friend Ted Marr organised the ball at the Peace Hotel in 1991. I came back with Ted as his 'official date' for the next ball in 1992 and we stayed at the Peace Hotel, with its massive rooms, with filthy carpets and disgusting bathrooms. I returned with another friend the next year and kept coming back—because I loved

M. Garnaut

Shanghai. In 1995, in the middle of a whole pile of dramas in Hong Kong, Bruno, my restaurant manager, and I came and stayed at the Peace Hotel. It was Bruno's first visit to the city. He said to me 'I think we should open a restaurant here' and I said *maybe*...but I don't think it's really ready and it's a few years away, at least, in terms of supporting a restaurant like ours.

In September 1996, I was once again back with Ted Marr, who was working on preparations for his Handover Ball. The event was to begin in Beijing, passing through Shanghai, before ending up in Hong Kong on 30th June 1997, the day on which the colony was to be handed back to China. When I met the Peace Hotel management with Ted to discuss the food and beverage arrangements, I just suddenly said 'can I come and cook at this hotel?' Mr. Wang, the general manager, said 'I don't think so, I don't think so...' I said no, really, I'm serious and I talked him into letting me do it. They told me that I had to cook a meal for them and that I also had to sit with them for dinner in the Peace Grill. I phoned the restaurant (M at the Fringe) in Hong Kong and got somebody, in fact a lawyer who worked in Ted's office who I didn't know, to bring the food to Shanghai on the Monday morning to cook that evening. He brought up a pavlova base, salmon, mashed potato, all ready, and everything for me to assemble. So, all dressed up for dinner, I went into the kitchen and I cooked this meal for 12 people, and, sat and talked and was verbose and all of that! At the end of the meal Mr. Wang said 'OK, you can cook for a month and you can come next week.' After telling him things

really didn't work like that, I told him I would come in two months' time and stay for a week.

In the end, five of us came up to Shanghai and we cooked at the Peace Hotel for 11 days. At that time they had between zero and eight people in the restaurant on any given night. So we opened up on the first night with a bit of a party and a press thing. Despite their round-the-world sales trips and all of that, the idea that we would invite people and pay for them was completely alien to the management. They insisted that their big bosses should receive an invitation.

The event was set for six o'clock and, at around a quarter to five, 20 or so of the Jin Jiang bosses came and sat down and snapped their fingers wanting this and that. We'd also invited foreign journalists and some people I knew. The next day they asked where was the money from the night. I told them that there was no money as we didn't charge anybody and they said, 'What?' I retorted, 'you didn't charge the Jin Jiang guys did you?'...'Of course not, it's our hotel, but *you* can't have people that don't pay.' And I thought

*The Peace Hotel grill-room*

that this was off to a bad, bloody start. We ended up entertaining 50 people a night. It was a remarkable experience, but it was horrible and I was just nerve-racked the whole time. They closed the kitchen; they closed the whole place up and they would lock up the bar at 10.30 p.m. while we still had customers there—and we'd be down to our rooms emptying out our mini-bars because there was nothing left to sell. And the people were really critical...it was really expensive, too expensive, for what we were doing and the wine list was of two of this and one of that—and it was all corked anyway. We even had to courier table knives up from Hong Kong.

There are endless stories about working at the Peace Hotel with all the nice rats, being locked out of the kitchen, and all the fridges breaking down. We had all the food for ten days in one fridge, because you couldn't get anything locally, but it was blowing heat. So we broke into the kitchen to rescue the food and, as it was freezing cold outside, some of it ended up wrapped in foil on the window-sills. The management weren't there—they'd left at 4.00 p.m. Friday afternoon for their weekend break. Mr. Wang called me up on Monday morning saying there was a big problem as I'd broken a lock and, despite explaining the situation, I was told I just couldn't do things like that, that I could be arrested... and was given a most terrifying lecture. Still, we only had another week to go.

M. Garnaut

Adrian Bradshaw    *Transformed from an empty shell into the elegant setting of M on the Bund*

In all fairness to the hotel they did pay us. But we didn't care about the money...I wanted to see if there was a market and to meet people outside of a small circle in Shanghai—which was fantastic and that worked.

We nicknamed the whole episode 'M at the Fringe goes to pieces' as it was such a fiasco.

I came back a couple of months later when my partner's wife, a Shanghainese who had stayed until 1974 and hated the city, said that I should come along to Uncle 'Wang's' funeral. As he was a former vice-mayor of Shanghai, she thought I would get the chance to meet some important people...I thought it such madness to use a funeral as a networking platform. Michael, her husband, and I were the only foreigners there and we were pushed up to the front whilst it was being filmed...I had to go and do all sorts of bowing for this man. I had no idea who he was and I was thinking that the crowd might be wondering if he'd had a foreign wife, or something.

It was on that visit in March 1997 that I decided to return and open a restaurant and we met up with a real estate person who said she could get me anything I wanted on the Bund. I looked at a number of buildings...all just offices and all abandoned...it was just a disaster. At that point nobody, but nobody, lived in this area and it used to take half a day to go

*'M' opening night, with Michelle Garnaut in the centre*

M. Garnaut

and buy a loaf of bread from the Hilton Hotel. Everybody said that you couldn't be more than five minutes outside the triangle of the Portman, the Okura Garden and the Hilton hotels, so I sort of shelved the Bund in my head. From then until the end of 1998 I spent at least a week every month in Shanghai looking at old houses. The one we spent the most time working on, for a period of eight months, was another of those disaster stories. The owner, a New York based local, who from the very start was a slime bag, but from a very good family, turned up in Shanghai with a completely different contract to the one we had worked out and told us that

we should sign it. No way. I walked away in tears and arrived back in Hong Kong on Christmas Eve with tears still rolling down my face.

A month later, Alice, the agent who had shown me property on the Bund just after the Peace Hotel show, called up and said 'I've got the most fantastic site and you have to see it.' I felt I was completely over Shanghai and wasn't going to do it, but she said 'you really have to see this' and I asked where it was. She told me, the Bund. I said 'don't be ridiculous— nobody goes to the Bund.' I hadn't been back to the Bund in two years—apart from visits to the Peace Hotel. But the place

*M. Garnaut*

stank, it was horrible and believe me, after having worked in the kitchen, there was no way I would ever eat there. But she said 'no, no, no, you must.' So I called an old Cantonese architect friend and asked him to take a look. He told me I would be mad if I didn't come up to see it.

It was a freezing January day when I arrived. The whole building was blacked out as the Jingdu Company, which was leasing it from the Shanghai Shipping Company, was undertaking work on it. I walked up seven flights of stairs to find what looked like a concrete bunker, with a tiny window and a tiny door. I walked through it onto the terrace and went 'Oh

my god!...Oh my god!' Over the previous two years I'd got really insular about Shanghai... everything was at street level and I felt claustrophobic as there were so few buildings that actually had a vista. Within four months we'd signed the contract! Although it was mostly said behind our backs, everybody thought we were absolutely crazy...She's female, a Westerner, doesn't speak Chinese, doesn't know China and she wants to open a fancy restaurant. And who's going to go to a fancy restaurant and who's going to pay lots of money for a meal in Shanghai and who's going to go to the Bund, particularly who is going to go to the Bund? However, I was lucky

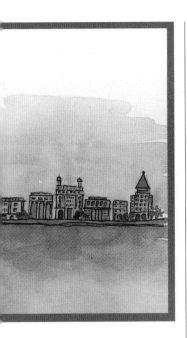

to know some visionary people who knew that the elevated highway was being extended, putting foreigners in the western suburbs back within easy reach of the Bund, and that a new airport was to be opened. At that time Pudong was a massive construction site. Still, despite its extensive areas of empty buildings, we knew it was going to work and that businesses were going to move there—they had to—the government said so! So we thought there was going to be a new middle ground back in the Bund area.

From the day we opened we were pretty full and we've been full ever since. And one of the remarkable things was that everyone thought that the Chinese wouldn't come. We had hundreds of them right from the beginning, especially the old-fashioned cadre types, with their bad haircuts and white socks, who behaved like they owned the place. People would come and ask how I ever got such a fantastic space and I told them you could name your space on the Bund—its all empty. However, it was quite a bit of luck. About six months after we opened, the head of the Jingdu Company was arrested for fraud and their business was closed down. I was really nervous about it and I thought that we were going to lose the restaurant. However, the High Court intervened and, when the whole thing was resolved, we signed a new lease directly with the Shanghai Shipping Company. It's a miracle we survived, and what astounds me is that it took five years for anybody else to open—I couldn't believe that nobody else hadn't opened within a year...I've always had a real pit of nerves in the bottom of my stomach that everything would one day go wrong in China again. But where we are now, we can't complain.

*From an interview with Michelle Garnaut*

*The photographer of this 1886 shot notes that the new building is known as 'Jews Synagogue' on account of its 'uncommon style of architecture'*

Melbourne Chinese Museum Collection

## N̲o̲. 6 The Russell & Co. Building

Although the opening of Dolce & Gabbana's flagship store in July 2006 at No. 6, or 6 Bund as it is now known, marked a new chapter in the building's history, its past still remains shrouded in a lacy veil of mystery. Acknowledged as one of the oldest buildings on the Bund, it is generally documented as being built in 1897 as premises for either the Imperial Bank of China or the Commercial Bank of China. It is actually the case that the Imperial Bank of China, which was later to become the Commercial Bank of China, opened its doors there in May 1897. However, the building itself was completed many years earlier than is generally realised as the new premises for Russell & Co., one of the most illustrious American companies to operate in China in the 19th century. Photographic evidence shows that the building, which was described as new, was there in 1886; whilst the American scholar Eric Politzer dates the building back to

1881. Indeed, it was in that year that the company first appeared as occupying No. 6 The Bund in a locally published Shanghai directory.

Russell & Co. was established in Guangzhou by Samuel Russell in 1824 and its early importance to the civil and commercial life of Shanghai was witnessed by the fact that one of its agents, Henry G. Wolcott, was appointed as the first Acting US Consul in Shanghai in 1845. Another Russell man, Edward Cunningham, became American Vice Consul soon after and was a key figure in the establishment of the first Shanghai Council in 1854. Diplomatic associations continued through the 1870s until 1882 when the Consulate of Sweden and Norway was housed within the Russell compound. Their Consul General, K. B. Forbes, was also a partner in the company. In terms of firsts, Russell & Co. laid the first successful telegraph line in Shanghai in 1866 and established the Shanghai Steam Navigation Company—whose fleet was the first to fly the American flag on the Yangtsze River in 1867.

It was not long after, however, that competition came from the Chinese themselves with the founding of the China Merchants Steam Navigation Company in 1872 on the initiative of one of China's most important statesmen, Li Hongzhang. Their first steamer, the *Aden*, purchased from the P & O Company, was the earliest merchant vessel to fly the Chinese flag out of Shanghai. The beginning of a short but eventful relationship, bound up in twists and turns, between China Merchants and their American competitors started in 1877 when the Chinese company purchased the entire fleet of 17 steamships from the Shanghai Steam Navigation Company. The company's substantial property holdings, including land on the French Bund, were also transferred to the China Merchants. And, as the *North China Daily News* reported, the company added 'steadily if not rapidly' to its property portfolio in the early 1880s.

In the first major turn of events prompted by Sino-French hostilities in Indo-China, China Merchants sold their steamships and property back to Russell & Co. in July 1884. Although there were those who claimed that this was a practical business decision, the real motives became evident as the ships and properties were transferred back into the hands of China Merchants just a year later. As soon as the steamers arrived back in port in August 1885 they were stripped of their Stars and Stripes banners to be yet again replaced by those of the Chinese Dragon. In the same month, Russell & Co. announced themselves as commercial agents for the Viceroy of Chihili, Li Hongzhang's official title, as well as general agents of the China Merchants Steamship Navigation Company for a period of three years.

The China Merchants Steam Navigation Company was reinvigorated after the return of its fleet and Li Hongzhang set about diffusing the cumbersome influence of government officialdom by appointing two new directors to manage the company. The imposing figure of Sheng Xuanhuai, who also held the post as general manager of the Imperial Telegraphs, was appointed director general. He was not afraid of bringing foreigners into the business and Mr. Osborne Middleton, who had previously worked as general manager for Russell's, went on to spend 25 years in the service of China Merchants before his retirement in 1908. During the disquiet of the Boxer uprising in 1900 the company transferred all their property, goods, and several of its ships into his name.

The events of 1884 and 1885 had not only provided China Merchants protection under the American flag, but had also given them an opportunity to shed their bureaucratic shackles and maintain business relations with Russell's. The events also allowed China Merchants to acquire a Bund address in 1885. The company moved from its original premises just off the Bund on Hankou Road in August 1885 and took up residence at No. 9 The Bund shortly after.

*The building, occupied by the Imperial Bank of China, 1900*

The next astonishing chain of events began in the middle of 1891 when, like a shot out of the blue, the formerly omnipotent Russell & Co. was forced into liquidation, and W. S. Jackson was appointed as the underwriter. Jackson was acting secretary of the Yangtsze Insurance Association, to which Russell & Co. had been secretary before their collapse. The building, known as the 'Red Brick House,' was subsequently occupied by a number of companies, including the Shanghai Waterworks Company and the Sun and Standard Insurance Company, as well as being used as a private residence.

Soon after the roof of the building had been destroyed by an intense fire on the morning of 7th April 1893, the property was transferred into the hands of China Merchants. It was registered, rather unusually, at both the American and British Consulates in October 1893. The *North China Daily News* reported that it was, in fact, purchased by Viceroy Li as an investment for his son. Russell's were already in debt to Li Hongzhang to the tune of 100,000 silver taels and he secured the grand building for an extra, very modest, sum of 310,000 silver taels. And this is where another fable begins. It is generally documented that China Merchants were the first Chinese company to have a presence on the Bund from that date on. In fact, they had already had their headquarters on the Bund for the last eight years at No. 9 the Bund (see page 132).

Li Hongzhang had other plans for No. 6. The building's first new occupant, under the new regime in 1893, was the China Land & Finance Company—a company formerly operated by Russell & Co. themselves. Their agent in the building, Mr. G. H. Wheeler, had been a signatory for Russell from 1882 until its collapse, and he was also director of the Yangtsze Insurance Association.

Sheng Xuanhuai, the director general of China Merchants, was behind the foundation of the Imperial Bank of China, which took over the premises in 1897. The bank, which is regarded as China's first modern Chinese banking institution, had been set up to finance the building of the Beijing to Hankou railway. Around one-third of the registered capital was in the name of China Merchants and, in keeping with their modernist tradition, the bank was organised as a merchant undertaking endowed with

*Advert, 1920s*

government protection. Like China Merchants, the bank employed foreign staff and its first manager, Mr. A. Maitland, was formerly an employee of the Hongkong and Shanghai Bank. Despite its foreign manners, the bank was hindered by over-interfering Qing officials, but matters improved following their downfall in the 1911 Revolution when the bank's English name was changed to the Commercial Bank of China. Following the relocation of the telegraph companies from No. 7, next door, the bank took over their premises in 1922.

*The building, before and after renovation*

*Artist's conception of the exterior renovation at 6 Bund*

Another financial institution, the P & O Banking Corporation, occupied the building for most of the 1920s and 1930s. They temporarily vacated their premises in 1936 and 1937 to allow extensive renovation work to take place on the building—inside and out. As part of the scheme, its red brick face, which had become unfashionable in a period of Art Deco inspired modernism, was smothered with a plain coating. Today, no interior trace is left of its Victorian heritage or of its 1930s makeover and the building's exterior has a brand-new icing cake finish. At today's 6 Bund, the upper three floors of the building are devoted to fine cuisine and high living.

# THE DAVID SUNG VISION

When David came to Shanghai in 1999 he was heartened by the vast changes in the city that had taken place since his first visit to the Bund in 1986, in the grey and sombre days of austerity. He had the feeling that the Bund would be resurrected as the city's main landmark for the world to view, and fell in love with the 'tutorial style' of the former bank building. Whilst he was growing up in Hong Kong, David's parents, who were raised in Shanghai, were forever telling him evocative and colourful stories about the progressiveness of old Shanghai, and when he saw the building he was struck with a vision of bringing back the spirit of those days. Even though the government had no intention of selling or leasing the building, David went through a long and determined process of negotiation to gain his prize of a 20-year lease on the property in 2000.

Describing himself as a 'bean-counter' by trade, Hong Kong-born and US-educated David Sung began his career in banking and public accountancy before establishing his own US-based accounting practice and real estate agency in 1982.

As the Bund was still dominated by the greyness of financial institutions at that time, another task lay ahead in finding suitable occupants who would consider moving in. In the end, the building's new residents were carefully selected and, unlike most other ventures on the Bund, were given charge of their own operations within the building. Another deviation from the norm came with the employment of a local architect to undertake the renovation work. The Shanghai Zhuzong Group Architectural and Interior Design Co. Ltd., which had undertaken renovation work at the nearby Astor House Hotel and Broadway Mansions, were assigned the contract. Originally, the Huangpu District Government wanted to restore the building to its 1897 look, but then proposed a restoration point of 1923. This would have involved a long and expensive removal of the concrete-covered face to reveal the red brick beneath.

Finally, David came up with the bold solution to restore the façade to its 1949 look—a look which would be familiar to most long-term residents of the city. The colonial interior was totally modernised—for, despite considerable efforts to identify any significant historical events that had taken place in the building with an eye to preserving their memory within its interior space, nothing was uncovered. David hopes to establish a Bund Association to uphold his vision of bringing life and energy back to the area and as a way of maintaining a dialogue with relevant government departments.

# No. 7 The Great Northern Telegraph Company Building

A large fire in October 1905, atop the new offices being built for Shanghai's first provider of telegraphs and telephones, took over two hours to extinguish and delayed the completion of the building for a whole year. The roof collapsed and the entire third floor and attic had to be rebuilt. The building, which eventually opened in January 1908, also housed the offices of the British-owned Eastern Extension and the American-owned Commercial Cable telegraph companies. Originally there were three Bund entrances leading to the respective company offices. The Great Northern Telegraphy Company, a Danish concern, had laid a line to Beijing in the early 1880s and had completed the one to Nagasaki before the new offices opened.

*The newly opened building, 1908*

The building, in Renaissance style, designed by Atkinson & Dallas, housed some state-of-the-art equipment, including a pneumatic tube system to handle the telegrams and a lift made by Smith & Stevens of London. Public telephones were found in abundance in the ground floor hall. The Great Northern Telegraphy Company occupied the first floor, and most of the Bund frontage was given over to a series of fine suites for its manager, engineer and accountant. The flags of the three nations present in the building used to fly above the building before the telegraph offices were moved to a new building in East Yan'an Road, behind No. 1 The Bund, at the end of 1921. In the following year the Commercial

*No. 7 in 2006*

Bank of China, which was previously next door at No. 6, moved its business into the building.

The Bangkok Bank took over part of the premises in 1995 and, as in days gone by when numerous consulates occupied the Bund's buildings, the Royal Thai Consulate-General also took up residence.

## No. 9 The China Merchants Steam Navigation Company Building

The history of this building is inextricably linked with that of the former Russell & Co. Building at No. 6 The Bund (see page 122). The China Merchants Steam Navigation Company, the first Chinese company to establish itself on the Bund, had occupied the site of No. 9 and the so-called Stone House buildings to the rear on Fuzhou Road since 1885. The present red brick building, designed by Atkinson & Dallas, was opened in 1901. The company, which was taken over by the Nationalist government

*With Compliments*

**WILLIAM HUNT & COMPANY**
WHARF AND GODOWN ADMINISTRATION

*Flying the American flag again, 1938*

in 1928, was again reorganised in the early 1930s in an effort to improve its efficiency and to stamp out corruption. In a dramatic incident, its general manager, Mr. C. T. Chao, was shot dead in broad daylight by two Chinese assassins at the steps of the building in July 1930. By that time, the Stone House buildings had fallen into such a state of dangerous ill-repair that plans, which were never to materialise, were laid for the reconstruction of the entire site.

Shiatzy Chen

The China Merchants shipping fleet again obtained protection under the American flag in 1937 when William P. Hunt and Co. took a majority stake in the company, in order, as it turned out temporarily, to circumvent its seizure by Japanese interests. Hunt's leased the building out to the Deh Lee Trading Company in September 1939.

*China Merchants building and its shipping interests, 1908*

The building is once again flying the flag as the fashions on display in Shiatzy Chen's flagship store, which opened in October 2005, exhibit a distinctively Chinese heritage amidst the parade of Western fashion marques that now dominate the Bund. The building's Chinese pedigree made it an obvious location for Ms. Shiatzy Chen's ambition to create a strong Chinese presence on the Bund. China Merchant Holdings, which had been back in charge of the building since 2001, were fully in accord with her

*The building, after renovation*

ethos. Work on restoring the original, red brick exterior look and on converting offices into a modern and artistic showplace for Shiatzy Chen's exquisite creations began in late 2001. The interior was fashioned by the renowned Indonesian designer Jaya Ibrahim. Launched in 1978, Shiatzy Chen has 40 stores in her native land, opened her first store in Paris in 2001, the first in Shanghai in 2003, and plans to have 50 mainland outlets by 2010.

*Opening night, October 2005*

Three smaller, independent outlets, housed in the old Stone House buildings to the rear of the building, also parade Chinese inspiration in the form of fine hand-crafted porcelain, modern Chinese art and skilfully hand-embroidered footwear.

*Store interior*

*The bank building, with construction of the Custom House underway next door, 1925*

# No. 12 The Hongkong and Shanghai Bank Building

With India under British rule and given its importance as the centre of the opium trade, most regional financial institutions were to be found in Bombay and London prior to the First Opium War of 1839–1842. It was no surprise that, when Hong Kong and Shanghai were opened up for foreign trade that an influx of British and Indian banking institutions were quick to follow. Sir Thomas Sutherland, Superintendent of P&O, was so shocked by the thought of China being overrun by outside speculation when a group of Bombay merchants attempted to form a Royal Bank of China that he came up with the idea of establishing a cooperative bank based on local knowledge and understanding. And thus the Hongkong and Shanghai Banking Company Limited was born—opening for business in Hong Kong in March, 1865 and one month later on the Bund in Shanghai.

Apart from its extensive activities in financing British-built railways in China, the bank had also, since 1874, been financing the Imperial Chinese Government, amongst others. By the end of the century, after a strong period of growth under the direction of the chief manager Sir Thomas Jackson, the bank was the foremost financial institution in Asia.

As the bank's activities continued to prosper together with Shanghai's rising international status, plans for a magnificent new building were drawn up by Tug Wilson. The manager of the Shanghai branch, Mr. A. G. Stephen, who became the chief manager in Hong Kong in 1920, had made it quite clear that regardless of cost or effort the new building should 'dominate the Bund.' With a 300-foot frontage and a height of 100 feet to the roof and a further 80 feet to the finial of the dome, 'it was to stand out clear to view of the merchant ships of all nations sailing up and down the river in recognition of their courageous industry which has made possible all that this memorial stands for.' Stephen witnessed the realisation of his dream when the bank opened in June 1923, shortly before his death in London a year later. An obituary in the *Far Eastern Review* pointed out that

the building was 'almost entirely due to his advocacy, left to themselves, the court of directors would probably have built something much more modest.'

Mr. G. H. Stitt took over as manager of the Shanghai branch in 1920 and presided over the bank until his retirement in 1926. Stephen and Stitt, like many of the grand taipans were passionate about racing and co-owned a string of successful horses that raced in Shanghai and Hong Kong. Stitt was a tall, affable Irishman who worked hard

*Mr. G. H. Stitt*

and played hard. Not only did he preside over the largest banking institution in the city, he also held the exalted post of chairman of the Shanghai Racing Club at the same time. His successor, Mr. A. B. Lowson, however, was more interested in golf and it wasn't until 1931 that another great racing enthusiast in the person of Mr. A. S. Henchman took over as manager. A keen interest in sports was a prerequisite for prospective foreign recruits.

With the aid of four derrick cranes, each with 90-foot jibs, and the adoption of modern working practices never seen in the city before, the mammoth bank building was astonishingly completed in just over two years. The esteemed London firm of Trollope & Colls came out to supervise the construction and no efforts were spared in sourcing the best materials from around the globe. On arrival, the materials were stored in a yard upriver and transferred to the site by motor truck where they would almost instantly be put in place by the giant cranes. Tug Wilson compared his role to that of a conductor in an orchestra in coordinating the gigantic task of getting everyone to work together. The result he later appraised as being of a 'higher standard than was usually possible in China.' The only glitch arose from the failure of the only Chinese contractor in Hong Kong to deliver the last batch of granite blocks on time, which would have allowed the building to be completed a month earlier.

HONGKONG & SHANGHAI BANK — SHANGHAI

PALMER AND TURNER, *Architects*

HENRY HOPE & SONS' Steel and Bronze Windows supplied and Malthoid-Pabco Concrete Roofing

SUPPLIED AND LAID BY **DUNCAN & CO.**

*The bank's construction was an international enterprise*

The building weighed around 50,000 tons when it was finished. Over 16,000 blocks of fine white Victoria stone granite from the Kowloon side of Hong Kong were used to face the building, with some blocks weighing almost seven tons each. Three and a half million bricks and 140 miles of cable were used and the whole structure was supported by 2,600 Oregon pine piles averaging 25 feet in length. The ground floor was set 12 inches above where it was expected to finally rest, and during the first year the building had sunk into the soft soil of the Bund between four and six and a half inches.

Tug Wilson's original designs for the bank, which were submitted to the SMC in August 1919, and which were rich in sculptural detail inside and out, were later modified to endow the building with a 'neo-Grec' look which relied on line and proportion. The scale of the building was changed and the height of the dome, which was originally to be finished in copper with a large bright band of mosaic, was raised. The bank's landmark, octagonal entrance hall with its magnificent mosaics also didn't feature in Wilson's early design. However, carved heads representing agriculture, industry and shipping once adorned the keystones of the three arches at the entrance of the building. The main sculptural splendour of the building was expressed in the unrivalled quality of its bronzework executed by J. W. Singer & Sons at their factory in the English town of Frome. It all survives and includes the entrance gates, each of the three pairs weighing five tons, which are works of art in themselves.

Singer's were world-renowned for their statuary, their famous castings including the Boadicea Group on the

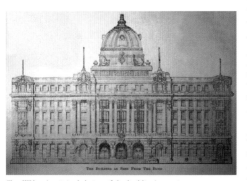
*Tug Wilson's original design of the building's exterior*

Embankment and Justice on the Old Bailey in London. Their castings for the Hongkong and Shanghai Bank's emblematic lions were modelled on a design by Henry Poole. It is often rumoured that the lions were melted down by the Japanese during their occupation of Shanghai in the early 1940s. Whilst it is true that the Japanese forces melted down metal from radiator heating systems and other sources to manufacture munitions, the lions escaped the melt-down and they are now held by the Shanghai Municipal History Museum. Faithful replicas again guard the premises.

The two lions symbolised protection and security and were fondly stroked by almost every Chinese passer-by in days gone by in the belief that power and wealth would rub off on them. The lions are affectionately known after two former managers of the bank—the roaring lion representing A. G. Stephen and the acquiescent one, G. H. Stitt. Another pair of lions was commissioned from the Shanghai-based British sculptor

W. W. Wagstaff, for the bank's new premises in Hong Kong in 1935–which was again designed by Tug Wilson. A third pair now guards the company's new global headquarters at Canary Wharf in London.

*Replica lion guarding the premises today*

The bank's opening ceremony on Saturday, 23rd June 1923 was supposed to be an all ticket affair, but a huge crowd of invited and uninvited guests stormed the building to take a peek at the resplendent interior, which hitherto had been kept a closely guarded secret. In a simple ceremony Sir Ronald Macleay, H. M. Minister to China, drove up at noon and was given a key to open the central gates.

In his speech Macleay remarked that 'reality has outrun anticipation and that this magnificent building not only surpasses the great achievements which the skill of the architects, Messrs. Palmer and Turner, and the art of the designer, Mr. Wilson, but will stand as a lasting tribute to the energy and business capacity of the contractors.' He believed that 'the nobility of its dimensions, the beauty of its decorations, the symmetry of its proportions and the elegance of its appointments, is unsurpassed by any financial or commercial house in Asia and the Far East from Suez to the Behring Sea.'

Tug Wilson declared that 'it is for the community to decide whether the architect has justified the confidence placed in him and produced a building worthy of the opportunity which, as regards the size, site and in other ways, was an exceptional one. It is sufficient for him to say that he has given his best.'

*Sketch by cartoonist Schiff, 1940*

The bank was simply laid out, radiating from its octagonal entrance hall. The main banking hall beyond covered an area of 21,500 square feet (2,000 square metres). The walls and columns in the hall were faced with soft-toned, grey Italian marble, with a seven-arched arcade throughout the length of the west wall in Sienna marble. Apart from the use of Devonshire marble in the

accountant's department, Italian marble was used throughout. Most of the original marble mosaic floor has now gone, apart from that around the entrance hall. As in most other bank buildings along the Bund such flooring not only looked fantastic but was very practical, during periods of heavy rainfall outside, in affording an anti-slip surface. Today, that function has been lost as the mosaics are highly polished.

*The Pudong Development Bank, 2006*

Most of the marble columns in the hall are in three sections. However there are four circular, white marble columns found in pairs at each end of the hall crafted from a single piece of marble, weighing almost seven tons each. The Louvre, in Paris, is the only other building reputed to hold two other marble columns of such a stature. The magnificent double staircase at the south end of the hall is also of white marble and Sienna marble, which once arched over an entrance from Fuzhou Road.

The marble archways at the southwest corner of the main banking hall used to open onto the Chinese banking hall with its blaze of Chinese decoration inspired by the early Ming dynasty and Beijing's Imperial Palaces. It was an extreme departure from the conventional decoration found in Shanghai's modern Western buildings. Bold reds, greens and yellows filled the hall and the adjoining offices were finished in black, dark blue and gold.

Away from the public gaze the bank boasted the most famous private bar in the city. As the renowned American, Shanghai-based journalist and advertising man, Carl Crow, recounted, 'to be invited to enjoy its hospitality was an honour reserved for exchange and bullion brokers and people with heavy overdrafts.'

Another exclusive club was housed in the huge dome on the roof of the bank. The RAFA (Royal Air Force Association) Club, which had been formed in February 1920 by survivors of the Royal Flying Corps, later to become the Royal Air Force, took occupation of their top-flight residence in 1925. Three high-ranking Chinese aviators were admitted to the RAFA Club to great ceremony in August that year, and the premises were later opened to members of the regular forces stationed in Shanghai. The dome's walls were covered with flags donated by visiting aviators, aviation photos, and flying trophies including the first propeller made in China. The club was

*Main banking hall, looking north, 1923*

enlarged, taking in the back portion of the dome, and reopened in January 1933. Sir Victor Sassoon, a former Royal Naval Air Service veteran, served as president from 1939-1941 during which time he hosted numerous 'patriotic lunches' to raise funds for the British war effort. One of his last engagements before he left for India, and his unknowing final departure from Shanghai, was at the club in August 1941 where he was presented with a silver tankard by the new RAFA president, Mr. V. J. B. Holland, in recognition of his sterling work. After the Second World War, the club at the dome had become a

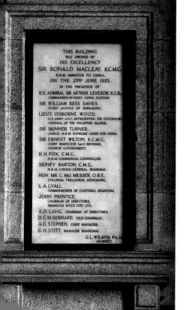

*Surviving plaque commemorating the opening of the bank in 1923*

favourite dining spot for Shanghai's younger set. It was the last foreign outpost in the city where the dwindling number of foreigners could congregate after the Communist takeover, and was still going in 1958, although reserves of spirits were running low. Plans were underway in 2006 to convert the dome into an exclusive club once again.

And on the matter of silver, so much of it was pouring into Shanghai in the uncertain times of the late 1920s that even the bank's vast treasuries couldn't accommodate it all. Mr. James Caldwell, a former cashier, told of how the surplus silver was stored in garages at the back of the bank and in hastily constructed new brick buildings at the rear. He estimated that

between six to seven million pounds' worth of silver was stored in such a fashion when he left the bank in 1932. It was not uncommon for silver arriving from America to be deposited at the bank in old-fashioned, wooden wheelbarrows. There weren't any serious attempts to steal the riches—although in 1924 a cheeky burglar managed to enter the premises through a window and traversed the full extent of the banking halls before smashing his way through another window into the arms of a Chinese constable. He didn't realise that the bank had guards inside as well as out!

*Advert for one of the building's occupants, 1930s*

In more serious times, following the events of August 1937, spiralling inflation resulted in the bank's 250 to 300 employees being paid weekly, receiving one-quarter of their previous month's salary as well as a lump sum, linked to the monthly cost of living index, at the end of the month. Following the requisition of the bank by the Yokohama Specie Bank on 8th December 1941, its doors remained closed for three days before some 2,000 desperate depositors queued up to withdraw what they were allowed in the space of three hours.

SMA

*Photographs of the interior taken in 1956 when
the building was occupied by the Shanghai
Municipal Government*

# SYMBOLS AND SUMS—
# THE BANK'S MOSAIC MAJESTY

*The bank's interior, 1920s*    HSBC

An artistic conception of the Hongkong and Shanghai Bank's philosophy was portrayed in its magnificent entrance hall. Aside from its visual splendour, the domed interior symbolised the high ideals and aspirations of the banking business and represented a scene, both symbolic and corporeal, where commercial activities were propagated and disseminated across the globe. Its octagonal form borrows from Chinese mythology where the number eight symbolises fortune and prosperity. The concept of aspiration, expressed in the form of a dome, is carried upwards through the building to the roof dome 150 feet above to reflect continuity of thought. The once glistening dome exterior was also covered with Italian tiles terminating in a finial of golden mosaic.

The 52-foot-wide octagonal ceiling is supported by eight Sienna marble columns. The outer arcade of the octagon is of the same marble, whilst the bases and capitals of the columns are of English bronze. The banking hall's Venetian mosaics were crafted in Italy from paintings by the London artist George Murray, who according to Tug Wilson had 'spent time and trouble in their preparation.' They were set in position by two Italian craftsmen over a period of several months.

The circular, topmost centre panel displays the mythological figures of Helios, Artemis and Ceres. Helios, the god of the moon and of the gift of sight and the measurement of time is shown traversing the heavens with his horses and chariot. To his right, the partially nude figure of his twin sister Artemis is portrayed in the form of a crescent moon depicting the night. Apart from her association with the moon Artemis was a virgin goddess, the goddess of chastity and the protector of the young. A huge multicoloured sun, depicting the day, forms the centrepiece of the mosaic and, below, the dominant figure of Ceres holds a basket of fruit and vegetables. Ceres, the goddess of plenty or abundance also symbolised motherly love.

The circular panel is surrounded by eight heraldic lions and a variety of geometric symbols set in squares, including the reverse swastika, a Buddhist symbol for good fortune, and Solomon's Seal representing wisdom. Below, the signs of the Zodiac are set in a dark blue background with the first sign, Aries, positioned over the imagery for Shanghai.

The eight principal panels represent the banking centres of the East and West. The four Chinese characters separating each panel, which originally displayed the Hongkong and Shanghai Bank's Chinese name, have been changed to those of the Pudong Development Bank. However, the English translation from the Analects of Confucius, 'Within the four seas all men are brothers,' survives and circles the dome.

Each city depicted, features a central cluster of three symbolic figures in a national setting adorned by heraldic motifs.

## SHANGHAI

The central figure with a steering wheel represents Foresight or Sagacity, symbolising a belief in the future prosperity of the city. To the left is a symbolic figure of the Yangtsze River and to the right, shipping. The background displays the bank building and the Maritime Customs building next door as seen from the river. The Custom House depicted was demolished and rebuilt soon after the bank opened. The heraldry shows the flags of both the British and Chinese Merchant Service and includes the Chinese characters for Shanghai.

## TOKYO

The central figure represents Learning. To the left is a figure of Youth, symbolising progress, with the national emblem on his shield, and to the right sits Science with his scroll and instruments. The background shows the enclosing wall of the Imperial Palace, the Court of Justice, Admiralty and Government Offices. Behind, Mount Fuji appears, separated by a band of clouds. The heraldry includes the national flag, the Imperial flag and the Chinese characters for Tokyo.

## NEW YORK

A figure representing Frederic Bartholdi's Statue of Liberty takes centre stage. To the left is Hermes, the promoter of social intercourse and of commerce among men, with his symbols the winged hat and caduceus. To the right is a figure embracing the arms of the United States. The heraldry shows the flag of the Merchant Service, the arms of New York and the American Eagle.

## LONDON

The figure of Britannia with her trident and the British Lion assumes the central position. To the left is a figure with the arms of London, whilst a symbolic figure of the River Thames with a model of a ship, compass and a rule sits to the right. In the background are the Houses of Parliament and St. Paul's Cathedral. The heraldry represents England, Wales, Ireland and Scotland.

## PARIS

The central figure is The Republic with a tablet inscribed with Liberté, Egalité and Fraternité. To the left is a figure of the arts with the Victory of Samothrace on the prow of a boat, and to the right the arms of the Republic. The ancient Victory statue became a prized possession of the Louvre in the late 19th century. The background shows a view of the Seine and the city, highlighting the Notre Dame Cathedral. The heraldry incorporates the Fleur-de-Lis and the arms of Paris.

## CALCUTTA

With the Star of India on her forehead, the central figure symbolises Mysticism. To the left Philosophy holds a scroll, and to the right are the arms of the city. The Hugli River and the High Court of Justice form the background. The heraldry is the Crest of Calcutta and the supporters of the arms of Calcutta.

## BANGKOK

The central figure symbolises Fertility; the figure to the left represents hewers of timber and the one to the right, agriculture and rice cultivation. The background is a scene of the temple at the mouth of the Chao Phraya River (the Mother of Waters). The heraldry consists of four elements—the national flag, the old and new arms of Siam, and the flag of the royal navy.

## HONG KONG

The central figure with the Union Jack celebrates Hong Kong becoming a British Crown Colony. To the left is a figure depicting history with the date 1842, and to the right, the Canton River. The background is a view of Hong Kong and the Peak from the harbour. The heraldry displays the diplomatic service flag, the Admiralty flag and the Chinese characters for Hong Kong.

The eight spandrels that circle the hall beneath the main panels support a further 16 mosaics of figures symbolising abstract values:

Prudentia (prudence), Probitas (integrity and honesty), Historia (inquiry and learning), Aequitas (fairness), Temperantia (temperance), Justitia (justice), Labor (work and effort), Subtilitas (subtlety), Fortitudo (fortitude), Philosophia (philosophy), Ordinatio (order), Fides (faith), Veritas (truth), Experimentia (experience and skill), Scientia (knowledge and science) and Sapientia (wisdom).

*Images courtesy of Donald Insall Associates*

# UNCOVERING AND RECOVERING THE PAST

D onald Insall Associates (DIA), the renowned London-based specialists in conservation and restoration work, sent a team of experts to Shanghai in 1997 at the invitation of Hong Kong-based architects, American Design Associates, to assist in the restoration of the former Hongkong and Shanghai Bank. DIA's project director, Alan Frost, recalls that when he arrived the building resembled something of a 'time capsule.' He was surprised that 'an amazing amount of the interior had survived from pre-1949, including the manager's private dining room (Edwardian) and sitting room ('Tudorbethan') as well as the more formal reception rooms and service areas such as original lifts and lavatories.'

The team had no idea of what condition the mosaics were in, or even if they had survived at all. As it turned out, the mosaics were only covered with a thin coating of white painted plaster just one to five millimetres thick and, once this was removed, the vibrantly coloured mosaics were

*The interior domed-ceiling as it appeared to the architects on their arrival in 1997*          DIA

*Restoration of the mosaics skirting the dome*          DIA

spectacularly revealed, virtually intact. The team also discovered that the colours of the richly decorated Chinese banking hall had also just been covered with white paint. However, despite, or perhaps in spite of, the Pudong Development Bank's

*Restoration of the Tokyo mosaic panel*    DIA

*Traces of colour in the former Chinese banking hall*    DIA

very Anglophile approach, the Chinese decoration was not restored and today it hides beneath a fresh coat of white paint. The building's new owners encouraged the use and retention of as many British artefacts in the building as possible.

Although much of the interior decoration and fittings had survived, the building had

suffered from neglect. Natural finishes had been painted over, and wall and ceiling partitions had been installed when the building was occupied by the Shanghai Municipal Government. Humidity had also caused considerable damage but the quality of the original fittings, especially the Indian teak and British bronze and steel work, was such that it was possible to retain most of the existing windows, doors and other joinery.

Educating the local workers who were to undertake the cleaning and restoration work was an important task. The Chinese had little experience of currently approved Western restoration techniques and had previously been applying harsh chemicals to bronze and marble surfaces with disastrous results. Specialist cleaning materials were flown in from Scandinavia, the UK, and the USA by specially chartered aircraft. But, as Alan Frost recounts, 'we had difficulty in persuading the Chinese contractors that some items were available locally. A classic example was when they professed that hacksaw blades were not to be found until I revealed that many such blades bought in the UK are marked 'Made in China!'

Though the erection of bamboo scaffolding was initially a shock to their Western sensibilities, the team were much more concerned about the amount of asbestos floating about to the complete nonchalance of the local workers. With a profusion of people power at their disposal some finer details received rare attention including the removal, cleaning and re-fitting of thousands of small screws in the Hope & Sons bronze and steel windows. Although manpower was in abundance, additional machinery had to be flown in, and marble for the restoration of the main banking hall was transported from Italy.

The project also involved advising the Australian lighting

*Restoration of the main banking hall* DIA

consultant and working with foreign contractors in the five-week process of cleaning the exterior granite. DIA noticed a close resemblance between some surviving light fittings and those found in County Hall, London, and in the Bank of England. A section of a very brittle multicoloured linoleum floor below the roof dome and bearing the insignia of the Royal Air Force Association was also uncovered. The architects had originally planned to restore the area as a club and to create a garden courtyard on the roof.

The complete renovation project took just seven months and in the words of DIA was 'one of the most challenging fast-track international projects on record.' The Pudong Development Bank began trading in their impressively restored banking hall in July 1998.

*Screw holes on a door panel reveal that the original HSBC logo had been hidden during the Cultural Revolution*

# CARVED IN STONE—LOST LEGACIES

Today, little evidence is left of where the foundation stones, which marked the ceremonial baptism of most of the Bund's buildings, were placed. Most were destroyed or permanently screened from public view in the 1950s and 1960s. Although only a few marks from the original inscription are visible on the marble slab, which is over six feet in length, under the

*Site of the blank foundation stone*

southernmost of the bank's ground floor windows, it is one of only two spots on the Bund where the existence of such a memorial is apparent (the other being at the Bank of China at No. 23).

No other foundation stone laying ceremony in the history of Shanghai had aroused so much public curiosity as the one held at the Hongkong and Shanghai Bank on 5th May 1921. There was tremendous interest when four tower cranes, the first ever seen in China, arrived on the site, and the foreign community looked forward to the erection of its own 'veritable temple of finance.'

The scene could have been The Mall in London as Sir Beilby Alston, the British Minister to China, drove along the Bund from the British Consulate in torrential rain escorted by Sikh mounted police, whilst the town band played the national anthem, to be greeted at the bank by a salute from a guard of honour composed of local British infantry.

THIS STONE WAS LAID BY
HIS EXCELLENCY SIR BEILBY ALSTON K.C.M.G. C.B.
H.B.M. MINISTER TO CHINA
ON THE FIFTH DAY OF MAY 1921
IN THE PRESENCE OF
H E. VICE-ADMIRAL SIR ALEXANDER DUFF K.C.B. COMMANDER-IN-CHIEF CHINA STATION
H.E. SIR EDWARD STUBBS K.C.M.G. GOVERNOR OF HONGKONG
C.T.M. EDKINS CHAIRMAN OF DIRECTORS
A.C. STEPHEN CHIEF MANAGER                          PALMER & TURNER ARCHITECTS
C.H. STITT    SHANGHAI MANAGER                      TROLLOPE & COLLS CONTRACTORS

*Inscription on the original foundation stone*                                   SMA

Mr. A. G. Stephen announced that 'the building will be an indication of our faith in the future, in the future development of the trade of China, in the future of this port where we expect all nationals will be allowed to trade peacefully for all time, and in the future of the Bank which we trust will always maintain its leading position here.'

Lady Alston then placed some keepsakes in a cell under where the stone was to be laid, including five Hongkong and Shanghai Bank notes from $1 to $100 in value, one $5 Bank of China note, one Mexican Dollar, as well as copies of three Shanghai newspapers and one from Hong Kong and an edition of the British Chamber of Commerce Journal. It was customary practice to place such time capsules beneath the foundation stones of all major buildings. No doubt this historic deposit lies undisturbed, but the gold chiselled inscription on the

marble foundation stone, along with Alston's belief in having his name permanently associated with the building, has been all but wiped away.

One of the few foundation stones to be left undisturbed in the city can be seen on the two-storey Tudor-styled building just to the rear of the bank building

*Macgregor House, 1937*

THIS STONE WAS LAID BY
SIR JOHN BRENAN K.C.M.G.
JANUARY 6TH 1937
SIN JIN KEE                    PALMER & TURNER
CONTRACTORS                    ARCHITECTS

*Macgregor House foundation stone*

优 秀 历 史 建 筑

**HERITAGE ARCHITECTURE**

福州路 4 4 号

原为正广和公司［英］。公和洋行设计，砖木结构，1936年竣工。英国
乡村式。平面凹形、两翼向后。南立面对称，中部架空为过街楼式主
入口，墙面露粗扩的木构架。红色双坡屋面，砖砌高烟囱。

Caldbeck Macgregor & Co. Building. Designed by Palmer & Turner,
Architects and Surveyors. Completed in 1936. Masonry structure.
English country style.

上 海 市 人 民 政 府 1 9 9 4 年 2 月 1 5 日 公 布
Shanghai Municipal Government Issued on 15th Feb. 1994

*The building's heritage plaque*

*Sir John Brenan*

on Fuzhou Road. It was formerly the headquarters for Caldbeck, Macgregor & Co., a British company founded in 1862, which evolved as Asia's leading purveyor of wines, spirits and mineral waters. The stone was laid by Sir John Brenan, H. M. Consul General and a good friend of the Macgregor family, on 6th January 1937. Something of a folly, given its time and place, Macgregor House was erected at the double in a little over five months and completed on 31st March 1937. A witty welcome speech was made by Mr. J. C. 'Jack' Macgregor when the building was christened. He said that the idea for an Elizabethan-style building belonged to his brother Norman, and the work was carried out by Mr. P. O. G. Wakeham of Palmer and Turner —so it could not be considered the 'house that Jack built.' The building's official government heritage plaque, which is just a few feet away from the original foundation stone, is even more of a folly in that it asserts that the building was completed in 1936! It appears that what still remains carved in stone might as well not exist.

Robert Bickers

*Loud speakers flank the redundant original bell*

## No. 13 The Custom House

Visitors in the 1930s could be forgiven for thinking that they were walking along the Embankment in London as the Custom House clock bells suffused the waterfront with the chimes of Westminster's Big Ben. Today, the clock tower plays a different tune. However, its muted CD rendition of *The East is Red,* broadcast from banks of loud speakers on the top of the tower, is hardly audible above the constant drone of traffic noise below.

The Chinese Customs was first housed in a temple-like Chinese compound. The Customs Service was a unique venture in that, since its establishment in 1854, it had been run by foreign, largely British, officials under Chinese administration. Sir Robert Hart charted the course of its development with devout magnanimity for over 40 years until his death in 1911. The early buildings were demolished in 1891 and in early 1892 work started on the foundations of a red brick, Victorian building, resembling an ecclesiastical or scholastic institution, which opened following the Chinese New Year celebrations on 9th February 1894. By the end of the First World War the building was proving far from adequate as a centre for dealing with China's rapidly expanding foreign trade.

As Frederick Maze (later to be knighted), Commissioner of Customs, pointed out when the foundation stone of the new

*The first Custom House on the Bund*　　Wattis Fine Art

building was laid in December 1924, Shanghai was 'the natural distributing centre' for the Yangtsze River basin with an importance based on the fact that it housed around one-tenth of the world's total population. The building was conceived as an outstanding monument to foreign trade and was massive in design, structural detail and size. It was designed by E. Forbes Bothwell of Palmer and Turner and put together by a taskforce of around 1,200 Chinese labourers.

The structure took just 30 months to complete and was opened on 19th December 1927. Despite the importance of the institution, the opening was a very informal affair, celebrated by a select band of bankers, customs officials and consular staff over champagne and sandwiches.

The strong vertical lines of the building offered a sharp contrast to the horizontal lines of Palmer and Turner's neighbouring building for the Hongkong and Shanghai Bank. Much of the ornamentation, inside and out, was symbolic of the sea. Bothwell, who had been practising in Shanghai for ten years, was renowned for his intimate knowledge of ancient Greek arts and architecture. He designed a spectacular frieze featuring ancient cargo boats, with a centrepiece depicting the benediction of the gods of the sea in the five metopes, or panels, above the Parthenon pillars of the main entrance. These, unfortunately, have long gone. The present frieze found on the wall in the portico, a recent fibreglass creation made to resemble bronze, depicts revolutionary scenes from May 1949 when the Communists took the city.

Although the building is out of bounds to the public, some impression of its former grandeur can be glimpsed from the door of the entrance hall. The original, delicately coloured mosaics portraying

*The Custom House, 1868*                    Dennis George Crow

river scenes and junks set in an octagonal rotunda have survived intact. The building itself had over 500 rooms in its three blocks that could be accessed by covered passages across its large courtyard. The extensive general offices of the Chinese Maritime Customs, which once occupied the first floor of the building,

*The 1894 Custom House just before its demolition in 1924*                    SMA

could be approached by no less than five staircases and 12 Otis elevators. They used to boast, at 610 feet, the longest counter in the world, built of marble slabs and teak, running around three sides of the building. Various departments were to be found on the floors above, as was the finest single room in the building on the third floor, reserved for the Commissioner of Customs. On the back block there were four canteens capable of seating over 500 staff.

The upper floors facing the Bund, which originally contained 'palatial and commodious living quarters,' opened a couple of months later than the main building. There were five apartments on the sixth floor—three facing the river, with a large hall, dining and drawing rooms, three bedrooms and two bathrooms and verandas. Actually, in the clock tower itself, there were two furnished apartments, each with four bedrooms and three bathrooms. Up to four floors of more modest accommodation, largely for staff, was provided in other parts of the building and, today, scores of people, in far less palatial surroundings, still call it home.

*The Custom House in 2006*

Palmer and Turner's initial plans for the building's clock tower 'as the very motif of the design,' didn't find favour with Sir Francis Aglen, Inspector General of the Chinese Maritime Customs. A debate followed as to whether the building should have a tower at all. However, following the assertion by the Custom's engineer-in-chief, L. Tweedie-Stoddart, that without a tower 'the building will entirely lose its public character and become merely a building on the Bund,' Palmer and Turner redesigned the structure. Aglen was

*The Custom House in 1934*

in accord with the new design, which featured a clock, but wished 'a striking bell and chimes to be provided' as well.

The new clock and its chimes were affectionately known as 'Big Ching.' The clock was manufactured by J. B. Joyce & Co. Ltd., of Whitchurch, in the English county of Shropshire. Its four faces, 18 feet in diameter, were especially designed with double glass and metal band reinforcements to withstand the punishment of a Shanghai typhoon. The original clock mechanism was operated by a system of weights. The chimes of Westminster, from five large bronze bells manufactured by the Taylor Bell Foundry in Loughborough, England, used to ring out each hour between 7.00 a.m. and 9.00 p.m. There were four chimes on each quarter-hour. The chimes, relayed from a wireless station in the tower, were heard far and wide by fellow Britons in other Chinese treaty ports.

Like its predecessor, the clock was regarded as the most accurate public timepiece in the city. The old clock, which also sounded the Westminster chimes with bells cast by Gillett & Johnson of Croydon, was installed in 1893, prior to the completion of the previous building. It was dismantled in April 1924 as the structure was pulled down. In its absence, the noon-day gun, which was normally fired from Monday to Friday from the Pudong Signal Tower, opposite the Bund, extended its service to weekends. The new clock, which was accurate to within 15 seconds a month when it

*The rejected clock tower design*

*Radio telegraphy has given way to satellite communication*

was installed, was later adjusted and didn't waver more than a second over a two-week test period in August 1928. Commissioner Maze proudly approached Stirling Fessenden, chairman of the SMC, in the hope that a by-law could be introduced requiring all clocks in the Settlement to be synchronised with the Custom House clock. Unfortunately, bereft of the powers to do so, the Council could do no more than issue an official notice requesting the public to do so. The Custom Services reputation for dependability was extended inside the building where electric 'Pulsynetic' clocks made by Gent & Company of Leicester, with an accuracy of two seconds a week, were regulated by time signals relayed by radio from the Xujiahui Observatory to the west of the city.

Whilst Sir Robert Hart's statue opposite the building stood as a statement of Britain's long legacy in China, a sign of the changing times and the diminution of British power was to be found on top of the new building within a week of its opening. The last Soviet consular officials had just been ejected from the city and the flag of the Nationalist Government was hoisted for the first time in the International Settlement above the Custom House.

# MOVING MONUMENTS

The monuments that were built by the British on the Bund to honour the memory of their heroes are today nothing more than memories themselves. Sir Robert Hart's

SMA

*Sir Robert Hart's statue, and a 1908 portrait*

statue was the last bronze symbol of British interests to be removed from its pedestal soon after the dissolution of the International Settlement in September 1943. The importance of his life-time endeavour was marked with the erection of a 13-foot-high statue near Nanjing Road in 1914. It was moved and given a new granite base outside the front of the Custom House, as it was being rebuilt, in May 1926. The SMC's Commissioner of Public

Works considered the site suitable 'provided that care is always taken to prevent the base from being surrounded by idle coolies, chauffeurs and rickshas.'

The statue bore the following inscription:

Sir Robert Hart, Baronet, G.C.M.G. 1835–1911, Inspector General of the Chinese Maritime Customs, Founder of China's Lighthouse Service, Organiser and Administrator of the National Post Office, Trusted Counsellor of the Chinese Government and true friend of the Chinese People. Modest, Patient, Sagacious, Resolute. He overcame formidable obstacles and accomplished a work of great beneficence for China and the world.

Activities at the base of the Bund's principal monument were also a matter of long-term consideration for the SMC. The British Chamber of Commerce in Shanghai first suggested a war memorial to allied soldiers who had fallen in battle in January

1917. Plans for the memorial by Messrs. Spence, Robinson & Partners were finally approved in 1921 and the statue was unveiled on 16th February 1924 by Sir Edward Pearce, Chairman of the War Memorial Committee. The monument, which was positioned at the end of today's East Yan'an Road where the International Settlement met the French Concession, was funded by both their Councils. A substantial donation was also made by the Shanghai Race Club from the proceeds of its New Year's Day meeting in 1922.

By 1939 the monument had fallen into a state of neglect and the SMC was considering moving it to a more suitable location. Unfortunately, its north face had long been utilised as an unofficial public urinal. The first official complaint about this pernicious practice was made by a member of the Shanghai Club in 1922 whilst the monument was under construction. He noted that 'it is one of the principal reasons for the large number of flies which have lately been coming into the Club.' The monument wasn't moved and even though the fine bronzework, including its 'Angel' designed by Henry C. Fehr and executed by J. W. Singer &

*The War Memorial, 1937*

Sons, disappeared in 1943, the monument's granite base survived the Second World War.

A monument of Sir Harry Parkes, G.C.M.G., K.C.B., Envoy Extraordinary and Minister Plenipotentiary to Japan, 1865–1882, and to China, 1882–1885 had occupied the prime position on the Bund facing Nanjing Road since April 1890. The statue was unveiled amidst jubilant celebrations surrounding the visit of the Duke and Duchess of Connaught by the Duchess and Parkes' eldest daughter and wife to James

*The defrocked War Memorial - post World War II*    SMA

Keswick of Jardine, Matheson & Co. The nine-foot-high, bronze statue standing on a four-foot-square pedestal was inscribed on three sides—one in Chinese, one bearing the date of its unveiling and the third quoting Sir Harry Parkes' service in Japan and China. 50 men were employed to move the monument 15 yards nearer the river when the Bund was widened in 1920. A statue of 50-year-old General Chen Yi, the first Communist mayor of Shanghai, which was cast in 1993 occupies this prime spot on the Bund today.

Although it is generally reported, and accepted, that the British monuments on the Bund were torn down by Japanese forces and melted down to make munitions, their real fate is not known with any certainty. According to new findings by Robert Bickers, it appears that the collaborationist Shanghai City Government removed them, either to be stored or otherwise disposed of, in sycophant compliance with the desires of their Japanese and German overlords. Bickers reveals that the Angel was 'discovered in late 1945, minus one arm and part of a wing, by a Russian girl, Nasia Boormistroff, who was looking for a bust of Pushkin in a Japanese metal dump in the Hongkou district. Eventually the (British) United Services Association heard of her find, retrieved the remains and deposited them at the British Consulate-General.' Despite an agreement with the Shanghai mayor in 1947 which would have allowed for the restoration of the War Memorial, the ensuing fate of that bronze icon and its

*General Chen Yi's statue, 2006*

*War Memorial and Semaphore Tower, 1931*

former partners has yet to be uncovered.

Jardine, Matheson & Co. gave their consent for the erection of a monument outside their premises in memory of the crew of the German gunboat *Iltis* who perished off Chinese coastal waters in 1896. The fate of the *Iltis* monument, which took the form of a broken mast in bronze and was unveiled in 1898 by Prince Heinrich of Prussia, became a matter of public debate at the end of the First World War. Many Allies would have liked to have seen it moved to the German Consulate or to a public cemetery. Before any decision had been reached, a group of 30 or 40 French sailors, soldiers and civilians took matters into their own hands and pulled it to the ground in the early hours of 2nd December 1918. The memorial was kept in SMC storage into the 1930s, and was due to be handed back to the German community, although there is little trace of this actually happening.

The former semaphore tower dating from 1907, though not strictly a monument, and actually on the site of the former French Bund, merits a mention as it was moved intact over 70 feet from its original location during the reorganisation of the Bund in 1993.

## No. 14 The Bank of Communications

The original premises occupied by the Bank of Communications on the Bund had been built in 1902 for the German-Asiatic Bank by Heinrich Becker, who also designed the Russo-Chinese Bank next door. Following the denial of German extraterritorial rights in 1917, the bank was closed in August of that year and forced into liquidation by the Nationalist government. A. G. Stephen of the Hongkong and Shanghai Bank was entrusted with

overseeing the dissolution of the institution. The Bank of Communications moved in on 25th February 1920. The second and third floors of their new four-storey, Italian neo-Renaissance-style building had been formerly let out as luxurious apartments. The Bank of Communications, one of China's oldest banking institutions dating from 1908, was created by a special charter allowing it to handle all revenues from the railroads, posts and telegraphs, as well as the administration of ocean and river navigation. A further charter was granted by the Republican government in 1914 that permitted it to deal in government bond issues and treasury notes.

*Occupied by the Shanghai Workers' Union, the building is decorated for National Day, 1950s*    SMA

Whilst work on rebuilding the bank was underway in 1948, a safe, dating back to the years of its original German occupants, was found hidden deep in its walls. Despite speculation that it contained secret German documents or a hoard of gold and gems nothing

*The German-Asiatic Bank, 1908*

of interest was brought to light. The building's architect, C. H. Gonda, who put together designs for the building 11 years earlier, had revolutionised the appearance of bank buildings in Shanghai with his modernist design for the Bank of East Asia on nearby Central Sichuan Road in 1928.

*No. 14 in 2006*

*The home of the Shanghai Gold Exchange, 2006*

## No. 15 The Russo-Chinese Bank

The opening of the Russo-Chinese Bank on 26th October 1902 caused quite a stir amongst Shanghai's foreign community, many of whom thought it looked totally out of place on the Bund. As it turned out the building was to set the trend for modern European-style buildings which would later emerge along the entire waterfront. Heinrich Becker, who had studied in Munich, came to Shanghai in 1899 where he won the open competition for the design of the bank. His design in Italian Renaissance style, using natural stone, was very much in vogue for prestigious European bank buildings of the era. Becker was assisted in the project by British architect Richard Seel, who had previously designed the Government Buildings in Tokyo. Despite some claims that the building was by Becker & Baedeker, including that on the heritage plaque outside, Becker didn't enter into partnership with Mr. C. Baedeker until 1905. The building was successfully completed within two years in spite of numerous hindrances, including the desertion of numerous artisans and labourers during the tumultuous Boxer uprising of 1900.

*Sketch of the Russo-Chinese Bank, 1900*

The building was quite revolutionary in terms of technical sophistication and artistic interpretation. The bank had its own electric generator and, apart from being the first building in China to be equipped with an elevator, it was fully heated with hot air pipes and every single desk was served by two electric fans and two electric lights. Inside the building a beautifully decorated central hall extended through the three-storey structure which was accessed by way of an intricately carved, grand marble staircase. On the interior walls there were sculptures of iron-smelting, agriculture, coal-mining and textile manufacture, as well as of tea, cotton, shipping and electricity. On the third floor two handsome apartments for the managers opened onto the stone veranda and magnificent stained glass ran around the hallway.

Thankfully, much of the original internal decoration still survives though, as the building houses the Shanghai Gold Exchange, it remains well hidden from public view. However, all the outside adornment, including two groups of statues representing industry and commerce and three masks depicting a Chinese flanked by two Russians on keystones above the ground floor windows, has been lost.

The building today provides one of the best illustrations on the Bund of the settling process. There are now two steps down, rather than up, to the entrance hall. An SMC engineer noted in 1923 that this building in particular had 'subsided to a considerable degree,' but went on to note that the pavement level was also much higher than it was when the building was constructed.

When it was first established in Shanghai in 1896, the Russo-Chinese Bank had just five European clerks. When its new building opened its Dutch manager, Michael Speelman, one of only two Dutchmen resident in Shanghai at that time, had charge of over 50 clerks. A new innovation for the bank was the installation, on the ground floor, of 300 safe-deposit boxes for its customers. The Russo-Chinese Bank established the Chinese Eastern Railroad Company and was amalgamated with the Banque du Nord in 1901. It later became the Russo-Asiatic Bank and in 1925, at the time of its liquidation, its property deeds were handed over to the Chinese Maritime Customs who held an extensive credit balance with the institution. A deal was made in 1928 and the Central Bank of China took over the property, with H. H. Kung, later to become the Nationalist Government Minister of Finance, as governor. The building also housed the office of Thomas Cook, travel agents, who had established their first office in China at Shanghai in 1910. The patriarch of the family firm wasn't too impressed by the native elements of the city when he paid a visit on his first round-the-world tour in 1873.

The two, really out of place, Art Deco, three-storey block buildings, which still survive to the south of the main building, were erected in 1930 primarily to provide storage for silver which couldn't be accommodated in the bank's existing vaults. However, much of the silver was shipped abroad when the bank was evacuated during the Sino-Japanese hostilities of 1937. Directly after the evacuation the bank was temporarily used as the offices for the Russian Regiment of the Shanghai Volunteer Corps—a salaried detachment of Shanghai's long established volunteer militia. In 1938, the building provided classrooms for Chinese students from the Ellis Kadoorie School and the Nieh Chih Kuei Public School which had been forced to relocate because of local hostilities. The new Central Bank of China, under the control of the puppet government in Nanjing, took over the premises in November 1940.

In one of the outbuildings, and again looking out of place in its posh neighbourhood setting, the small Three Gun store, a state-run enterprise parading a selection of old-fashioned knitted undergarments, looks as though it has been there for time immemorial. It only took up residence, however, in 1993 and chose the spot purely on commercial grounds. The Three Gun brand was originally established in Shanghai in 1937 by Gan Tinghui in response to the Japanese aggression which had resulted in a boycott of Japanese goods in the city. He combatively named his company

*The Three Gun store*

following three consecutive successes he had scored in shooting competitions. In 1966, the company, among others, was incorporated into the Number 9 Knitted Garment Factory of Shanghai. The Three Gun brand was resurrected in the period of reform following the death of Mao Zedong in 1977, and in 2005, as one of China's largest producers of undergarments, it gained the sole rights to produce and sell children's clothes for the Disney brand. Adjoining the shop are two even smaller spaces housing ATMs for HSBC and the Bank of East Asia—two mammoth banking institutions which now only have a token presence on the waterfront.

## №. 16 The Bank of Taiwan

The Bank of Taiwan, which was a Japanese private joint banking venture, first opened a branch in Shanghai in 1911. The Japanese, who had occupied the island of Taiwan after the Sino-Japanese War in 1895, continued to do so until the end of the Pacific War in 1945.

A couple of startling discoveries were made when foundation work on the new building began in early 1925. A mouldy old coffin, estimated to be 200 years old, was uncovered, as was a section of brick wall four feet wide and twelve feet deep. The wall baffled the experts who later came to the conclusion that some form of river wall had been in existence before the British arrived. This was more than likely the case as the course and dimensions of the

Picture This

Huangpu River had historically been subject to rapid change.

The walls and main entrances of the banking hall were in Italian marble and the floors originally had a rubber tile finish. Today, apart from the intricate marble balustrades on the mezzanine floor, the original marble in the banking hall has been replaced. Presumably the original marble survived only on account of the expense or the difficulty of recreating it. The two floors above the main banking hall were originally rented out, whilst the top floor provided living quarters and recreational rooms for bank staff. Scars on the Japanese granite face of this neo-Grecian building tell of the harsh treatment it received at the hands of workers whilst 'restoring' the surface in 1997.

*Home to China Merchants Bank, 2006*

The bank had temporarily occupied the northern part of the ground floor of the North China Daily News Building next door whilst their new premises were being erected. The architects Lester, Johnson and Morriss moved their offices to the new bank building after it was completed in 1927.

*Sketch of the new bank building, 1925*
*Left: The bank building, 1927*

# No. 17 The North China Daily News Building

The new building for the *North China Daily News* was formally opened in February 1924 to commemorate the diamond jubilee of a newspaper that had begun life as a weekly broadsheet, the *North China Herald*, in 1850 prior to becoming a daily publication in 1864. Its proprietorship had been in the hands of the Morriss family, British Catholics of Jewish descent, since 1880 when Henry Morriss took a controlling interest in the business following his marriage to Una Pickwoad, the daughter of a former proprietor. Henry, who had a great passion for horses, set himself up as a successful bill broker after his arrival in Shanghai from Bombay in 1866. He also accumulated large areas of land in the city, including a large estate to the south of the racecourse (today's People's Square) which became known as Morriss Village or Morrissville. Appositely, his death at the age of 76 in 1911 was attributed to a riding accident a year earlier. Henry senior's passion for horses was adopted by

*Model of the building, 1922*

*Mr. Gordon Morriss*

*Mr. Henry Morriss (junior)*

his son, Henry junior, also known as Harry, chairman of the company when the new building opened, and whose horse *Manna* was the winner of both the Two Thousand Guineas and the English Derby in 1925. Henry was also a greyhound racing

*AIA building, 2006*

*The newspaper's premises, early 20th century*

enthusiast and used to walk his dogs from his substantial estate, today's Ruijin Guest House, to the Canidrome Dog Track next door. Gordon, another of Henry's sons, was also a director of the paper, as well as a partner in the company that erected the new offices.

It wasn't until 1901 that all the papers' offices and presses were moved to the present site on the Bund. At one point, the residents of the Chartered Bank next door obtained a court injunction to stop the hammering noise of the presses' engines that were keeping them awake at nights. The new

*Architect's drawing of the new building*

176

*75th anniversary edition of the newspaper*          *AAU advert, 1930*

building was especially designed in two sections with a rear part, where the presses were placed in the basement, separated from the front part by a hollow wall. The first papers would be gathered from the presses at three in the morning. On the top floor, two luxury flats provided the highest habitable spaces in the city, and the paper's editorial offices were located on the fifth floor. For most British in the city life without the Far East's leading British newspaper and bastion of Empire would have proved unthinkable.

It was Asia's empire builders who were to put a temporary end to the illusion. A local Japanese newspaper, the *Tairuko Shimpo*, remodelled the building and installed their own machinery inside after they took possession in December 1941. However, within a week of the end of the Pacific War, on 21st August 1945, former employees R. W. Davis, the paper's secretary and manager, and assistants Haslam and Yung, who

*C. V. Starr visiting a potential customer near Shanghai, 1922*                    AIG

had all been inmates at the Japanese internment camp in Pudong, walked in and demanded their building back. At first they feared that the newspaper's valuable and voluminous archives had been lost as they were nowhere to be seen. Fortunately, a representative from Jardine, Matheson & Co. phoned from down the Bund to inform them that they were safe in their offices. They were scheduled to have been sent to Tokyo. The newspaper's furniture and equipment was later found scattered all over Shanghai. Remarkably, 'The Old Grandmother or Lady of the Bund,' as she was affectionately known, continued publication after 1949 and was only closed down on 31st March 1951 following its coverage of the Korean War.

Another great institution, the American Asiatic Underwriters (AAU), brainchild of a young American, Cornelius Vander Starr, occupied many floors of the building after 1927. Starr, who established the company in Shanghai in 1919, was to build up the largest insurance empire in Asia, the forerunner of today's leading global insurance company, AIG (American International Group, Inc.).

*Sandbags protect the building in late 1937* SMA

Apart from his insurance interests Starr had a massive hand in Shanghai's realty business and was the owner of Shanghai's only American daily newspaper, the *Shanghai Evening Post & Mercury*.

Like those of the *North China Daily News*, the offices of AIG's forerunner were opened within a week of the end of the Pacific War and, although closed in 1950, they made a grand comeback almost half a century later in 1998.

*AAU's manager's office* AIG

*Rooftop photo celebrating AAU's 30th anniversary, 1949*

A.A.U. 30TH ANNIVERSARY
DECEMBER 19, 1949

SMA

# REINSTATING THE PAST— AIA LEADS THE WAY

AIG (American International Group, Inc.) was the first foreign insurance company to be issued with a licence to operate in China when its business was reinstated in Shanghai in 1992. The company set about regaining its former premises and in 1996 took place in May 1998. Some US$10 million was spent on the restoration process which was undertaken by the renowned New York architects, Jan Hird Pokorny Associates, Inc., under the design build contractor Interact Interiors Limited.

*The interior before restoration*

it signed a 30-year lease agreement on No. 17 The Bund. Through its subsidiary company, AIA, (American International Assurance Company, Limited) it was the first, and remains the only business, to reoccupy a whole building on the Bund. Work on restoring the building began in January 1997 and the formal opening of the new AIA building

The interior of the building was found to be in an extremely poor state with most of the original fittings and decorative features having been destroyed or damaged. There was also extensive water damage and all the interior columns and beams had to be reinforced. However, the restoration of the main corridors on the third and fifth floors, featuring Japanese oak woodwork and green and gold mosaics, was possible. The ground floor main banking hall was also carefully renovated, though none of the original features could be saved.

Around 1,200 tons of Inada granite from near Tokyo was used on the exterior of the building. Although work on cleaning the granite of the AIA building, and that of the building next door at No. 16, took place at the same time, the results were radically different. The former Bank of Taiwan's granite face was basically destroyed by the use of electric grinders in an attempt to make it appear new. Conversely, respectful cleansing techniques were used to conserve the AIA building's exterior, blotches and all. Initially there was some misplaced criticism that the building didn't look as nice as its neighbour!

Apart from the sympathetic cleaning of the exterior, AIA did a fantastic job in repairing and recreating the building's very special and very impressive exterior decorative features.

The images on the three carved panels above the ground floor windows of the building were hidden from passers-by for almost a generation following their obliteration behind a plain concrete façade in the 1950s. Unfortunately, as the original Italian marble panels were so encrusted in concrete, it was to prove impossible to restore them to their former glory and a decision was made to faithfully recreate them, in fibreglass, as we see today. The almost life-size figures in the frieze depict symbols of journalism, the arts, science, literature, commerce, truth and printing.

To the left of the central panel, a group of three figures representing painting, sculpture and architecture, is set apart from a central group called the Source of Inspiration, amongst which a figure representing literature is also resting. Science is represented by a figure sitting on a sphinx. He is supposedly engaged in a diligent search for new discoveries whilst meditating on the higher problems of the Universe. The sphinx symbolises the unresolved mysteries of the world. Trade is represented by two laden horses being driven by Mercury towards the harbour where vessels are waiting for their cargoes. Truth is represented by a cupid holding a mirror, thereby making it impossible for a lie to escape detection.

*The original and the recreated frieze*

On the left panel the world is represented by five symbolic figures, standing for the five continents. All are anxiously waiting and listening for the news, the knowledge and the deeds that journalism brings to them.

The right panel illustrates the printing process. A huge modern machine of the time is featured in the background. One figure is seen composing and another is carrying freshly printed papers. The youthful figure in the foreground, typifying the coming generation, represents education.

The four pairs of Atlas half-figures, which were used as cornice supports near the top of

the building, were also hidden from view in the 1950s. The tops of their heads and their arms were brutally chopped off so that they could neatly be concealed in concrete cases. Fortunately, the building's *pièces de résistance* were able to be restored.

The figures, which are said to be carrying the whole weight of the world on their shoulders, were designed in Italy and crafted in Shanghai over a five-month period by Japanese sculptors. Every single figure was fashioned out of three blocks of granite, each with an average weight of 20 tons. Positioning the figures was itself a task of Herculean proportions, as each piece had to have a man accompanying it when it was hoisted up so as to prevent damage to the sculpture and

*The head and torso of one of the figures being put in place in 1923*

*The extent of the damage to one of the Atlas figures is revealed as its casing is removed, 1997*

the outside of the building. Following an outright refusal by Chinese workers to perform the task, it was left to their Japanese counterparts to put them in place. The Chinese reluctance to undertake the work was probably related to an incident not long before when a Chinese worker dropped six floors to his death

*Restored Atlas figures*

whilst performing a similar operation at the nearby Jardine Matheson building. The Tankai Company, a Japanese concern in charge of the granite work, proved right in their belief that the carving and fixing of such gigantic figures was a task that would never be repeated in Shanghai. The figures can be admired at close range from the terrace of Bar Rouge on the top of Bund 18 next door.

The only sign of the company's former presence to survive in the building was found on one pane of glass, which is still in place today below the central part of the frieze. An ill-defined circle that once carried the original company logo and the lettering below—UNITED STATES...COM... IN THE CITY... ESTB.—is still faintly visible on the pane placed second from the left.

*AIA's entrance vestibule, 2006*

Surprisingly, the fine marble and mosaic work, which is found inside the two almost identical entrance vestibules on either side of the building and is visible from the street, required little more than skilful cleaning. The walls are lined with Italian Potoro marble (a black marble with gold veins) separated by green and gold mosaic strips while the upper part is composed of smaller Breccia Acquafilante (Italian yellow marble) panels divided by bronze enrichments. The barrel ceiling is coated with gold mosaic, outlined in green with a black-bordered rose in the centre.

*First logo for AAU*

*Bund 18–at the centre of things*

## No. 18 The Chartered Bank of India, Australia and China

The Chartered Bank of India, Australia and China was the oldest of the foreign banks in Shanghai. It was established in 1853 and opened its first branch in Shanghai in 1857. Three earlier banks—the Oriental, the Chartered Mercantile and the Agra were to flounder. The site on which the building stands was purchased from the Oriental Bank in 1893.

Lions' heads on handsome bronze lamp brackets, emblematic of the British nationality of the bank, once adorned each side of the entrance gates. Floral motifs from the surviving English-made

*The former Chartered Bank building, 1908*

F. Gabbiani

bronze gates, which despite their Greek detailing had an Oriental feel, were used in the banking hall. Originally, carved keystones, representing India, Australia and China, incorporating rams' heads were set over the ground floor windows.

The entrance vestibule featured four Brecchia marble columns, and the walls were lined with a rich, cream-coloured,

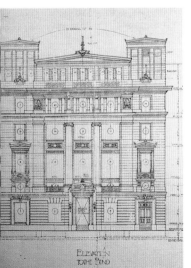

Pavonazzo marble on a black plinth. The original floor was in Roman marble mosaic and the ceiling of fibrous plaster. With the exception of the woodwork, the whole of the wall, floor, coffered ceiling and sculpted Italian marble found on the ground floor was shipped from England. The entire ground floor and the basement were occupied by the bank.

*Architect's drawing*

F. Gabbiani

*Bund 18 awaiting restoration*                                    F. Gabbiani

The steel-framed building, designed by Tug Wilson in a classic neo-Greek style with little ornamentation, rested on two reinforced rafts, one for the main block and one for the back block where the treasuries were situated. The contractors, Trollope & Colls, had erected the head office of the bank in London some years earlier. The Shanghai branch was opened in early May 1923 at a ceremony presided over by Sidney Barton, the British Consul.

Just over 80 years later, in 2004, the building reopened to great acclaim as Bund 18. Its Taiwanese developers had spent considerable effort in restoring as much as possible of the original architectural vision, besides incorporating harmonious modern additions to satisfy present-day needs.

The entrance and banking hall now plays host to a range of luxury emporia, including Cartier and Zegna. Zegna's new headquarters are found on the third floor. The upper floors house the Bund 18 Creative Centre, the Tan Wai Lou Chinese Restaurant, and Sens & Bund with its rooftop Bar Rouge. Sens & Bund is managed by the Michelin 3-star rated Pourcel brothers and Bar Rouge has evolved as the choicest of night-time destinations.

*Sketch of the bank building, 1922*

The restoration was presided over by Filippo Gabbiani of Kokaistudios. Mr. Gabbiani's family, themselves distinguished traditional glass makers, bought Marco Polo's former house in Venice when he was just eight and, from that day on, China was his dream. Filippo fell in love with China on his first visit in 1991. He had his first experience of architectural restoration work at the age of 19. His work on Bund 18, alongside four of his staff, started in 2002 with an intensive three-month critical survey of the building. The restoration phase took one year, during which the Chinese staff were trained in restoration techniques that had long been forgotten. Work went on day after day, 24 hours a day, with the project proving to be one of the most challenging Mr. Gabbiani had ever undertaken.

He ensured that no attempt was made to reproduce or imitate the old design features and style if they could not be restored. 'For me it is important that you leave the fingerprint of what you did in a very readable way—so in the future people can be able to recognise what is original and what was added—when and how.' His work, and that of his team, was rewarded with Bund 18 winning the Award of Excellence in the 2006 UNESCO Asia-Pacific Heritage Awards.

*Restoration of the ground floor*

# THE FILIPPO GABBIANI VISION

Our effort to grasp the identity and authenticity of the Bund 18 building began with both off- and on-site research.

*F. Gabbiani*

With the help of Professor Giuseppe Tonini (from the University Institute of Architecture in Venice), an expert in stone, metal and marble restoration, features of high architectural value were identified and a restoration strategy was formulated.

*Mr. Filippo Gabbiani*

Design features such as the bio-chromatic bronze gates which dominate the imposing front façade, the rare rose-veined mid-18th century Brecchia marble columns which punctuate the entrance hall and ground floor, as well as the Roman-style marble mosaic floor and wooden main staircase balustrade were identified as areas to be cleaned and restored.

Tapping into the high skill of the craftsmen available in China today, the original bronze and copper windows and handles were to be re-engineered and kept, the original window frames were to be cleaned and re-installed, and the unique decorative ornaments on the balcony hand rails, which had been removed by former tenants, were scheduled to be reforged using a mould of the only

F. Gabbiani

remaining ornament left on the building.

The effects of corrosion and carbonization had also taken their toll on the granite exterior of the building, and Professor Tonini adopted a cleaning plan that required that much of the exterior of the building be cleaned slowly by hand using traditional methods developed for Venetian buildings. It took 30 workers two whole months to hand-clean the exterior walls of Bund 18.

*The carefully restored bronze entrance gates and main staircase*

F. Gabbiani

F. Gabbiani

*Signs of the old and the new*

*Restored mosaic flooring*    F. Gabbiani

After having built up a substantial base of historical, technological and sociological information regarding the building, we thus had the necessary perspective to begin to formulate a redevelopment plan that would do justice to the history of the building, while at the same time meeting and exceeding the various levels of protection applicable to this landmark building. During the design process we constantly strove to maintain a balance between our desire to, as much as possible, bring the structure back to its ancient simplicity and splendour, and the need to fulfil the new functional and commerical requirements requested by the client.

In coming up with the functional scheme for the building, the first area of importance was the ground floor. From the original floor plans we knew that the original design had a grand hall with no mezzanine level, the latter having been added during a renovation in the 1980s, and the ceiling height of the whole ground floor had been cut in half, thus shutting off the grandeur of the original design. A decision was taken to open the ceilings to create an inviting space that brought the public into the building and created a dialogue with the city. This allowed us to fulfil the developer's goal of creating a commercial piazza on the Bund while at the same time maintaining the 1980s addition of the mezzanine in order to maximize the available retail space.

The decision was also made to make a clear distinction between the existing structure and the new design features through the use of a thin line of shadows in order to maintain the identity of the work of respective eras. Examples of this can be found where the columns on the ground floor meet with the

*Restored stair balustrade*

F. Gabbiani

*Atrium, Bund 18*

Bund 18

mezzanine, as well as the intersection between the main staircase and the adjacent wall.

In a nod to our Italian roots and the Italian craftsmen who most probably worked on and installed the original mosaics, we employed modern Venetian craftsmen using age-old techniques to create the *marmorino* wall finish as well as the hand-crafted glassware that you find throughout the building.

Our restoration project in Bund 18 is a first in China in many ways, and we hope that it will set the standard and act as an example for future restorations of historical buildings in China.

*Excerpt from an essay by Filippo Gabbiani.*

# No. 19 The Palace Hotel

The Central Stores Company, which was largely financed by Edward Ezra, a representative of one of the three great Sephardic Jewish families that were to dominate the hotel scene in Shanghai, took over the Central Hotel on the southern corner of Nanjing Road and the Bund in 1896. Despite a sharp increase in tariffs, guests were still being turned away and plans for replacing it with the much larger and modern Palace Hotel were drawn up in 1904. The work was to be undertaken in two stages with scheduled completion dates in 1906 and 1908. Building began on the first section of the hotel in late 1904, with its cornerstone being laid by the chairman of the Municipal Council, Mr. F. Anderson, on 21st January 1905. The project, however, was blighted with construction problems from its outset and the western section of the hotel, which was due to be completed in October 1906, wasn't actually opened until April 1907.

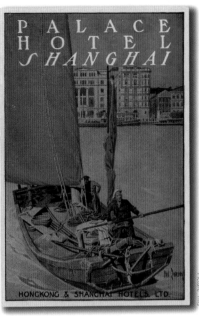

*Stylish luggage label by American artist, Dan Sweeney*

As soon as the first section was completed, the old Central Hotel was pulled down and work on building the front part of the hotel facing the Bund began in August 1907. Again, building work was slower than expected and, with a fire on the roof in December that year, the company had to resort to buying another property a mile away to keep up with the rapidly expanding demand for hotel rooms.

Despite the surviving 1906 inscription over the main entrance, the whole building wasn't fully completed until October 1909. However, the fourth and fifth floors of the front section were opened on 1st February 1909 in time for the landmark meeting of the International Opium Commission, an event that is commemorated by a plaque outside the hotel today.

*Hotel postcard, 1910*

*The completed section of the hotel and its management staff, 1908*

As soon as the hotel was completed, its architects, Messrs. Scott & Carter, came under intense criticism from Moorhead and Halse, architects, in a 23-page report detailing their failures in providing proper plans and guidance for the contractors. The death of Mr. Carter, during the course of its construction, wasn't given any consideration. The building was seen as something of a 'house that Jack built,' as the settling process had left walls, windows and doors askew, and the 'general finish of the bedrooms was the worst we have yet seen in Shanghai in a building of any pretensions.'

Still, the six-storey hotel, with 120 rooms with baths, was the largest and most commodious ever built in China and aimed to compare with the best hotels of Europe and America. The architects placed a strong accent on colour and rendered the building in their locally interpreted 'Victorian Renaissance' design. Most of the ground floor was originally taken over by shops, whilst the whole of the top floor accommodated a dining room, which could seat 300 people, and a 200-seat banqueting hall, which had access to the roof garden. The hotel had its own foreign-managed dairy farm and cultivated a large kitchen garden to supply its fruit and vegetables.

*Premature celebrations for the 100th anniversary of the hotel in 2006*

In line with its attempt at architectural bravura, the early years of the Palace Hotel were beleaguered by management problems, and yet another fire in August 1912 destroyed the hotel's signature roof towers. They were only recreated in 1998. Apart from poor management, overpriced facilities and complaints over the quality of the food, the Palace gained a macabre reputation following a series of guest suicides. For some new arrivals the pressure of finding their feet in Shanghai society proved too much.

*South wing of the Peace Hotel, 1990*

Things began to turn around for the hotel when the Central Stores was reformed as The Shanghai Hotels Ltd. in 1917. Net income more than doubled over the 1918–1920 period and the hotel was again turning hordes of would-be guests away. With the formation of The Hongkong and Shanghai Hotels Ltd. in 1923 plans were set, at an indefinite future date, to replace the Palace Hotel with a more modern structure. However, in the meantime, the whole of the ground floor of the hotel was rid of its shops and the company set about a major remodelling of the hotel, with Palmer and Turner presiding over the conversion. Just

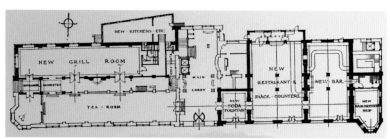

*Plans for remodelling the ground floor of the hotel in the mid-1920s*

*Palace Hotel Tea Lounge, 1931*

*Original multicoloured lights in the ground floor restaurant, 1991*

*Decorative details in the former Palace Hotel Tea Lounge, 1991*

a few years later Tug Wilson remarked that the Palace Hotel 'was never a thing of beauty, it is to be hoped that it will soon give way to something better.'

The highly successful Palace Hotel Tea Lounge, occupying the Nanjing Road frontage left of the lobby, was opened in 1925. It was partnered, in 1927, by an Italian-style grill-room, with an orchestra shell between the two allowing after-dinner dances in the tea lounge. The grill-room was separated from the tea room by silk portières lit by multicoloured lights which remain to this day. To the right of the main lobby, a soda fountain leading into a wood-panelled snack restaurant and a Jacobean-style bar was opened in 1926. New bronze and glass windows were installed, peaked by a canopy of the same materials extending along the entire Nanjing Road frontage. The changes dramatically increased the hotel's profitability.

During the 1930s the Palace Hotel Tea Lounge, with its 18th century style décor, which still survives, albeit with a gaudy brush of colour, simply became known as 'Shanghai's rendezvous.' Meanwhile, the grill-room had adopted a Russian flavour with the appointment of G. Podbelsky, late of the Astoria Hotel, St. Petersburg, and the Hotel de France in Moscow. His famed dishes included Kiev cutlets, Georgian meat orders and the most famous Russian soups.

Whilst all was well on the culinary front, the building itself was feeling the effects of age, and suffering at the hands of modern skyscraper luxury hotels, namely the neighbouring Cathay Hotel and the Park Hotel on today's People's Square. Hotel rates were cut and plans were again laid to demolish and rebuild the hotel in 1939. However the uncertainty brought about by the events in 1937 resulted in a full renovation of the guest rooms instead. Further renovations took place after the Japanese vacated the hotel in 1945, and the top two floors of the

*Palace Hotel restaurant mural, 1930s*

*1930s postcard*

*Palace Hotel boarded up in late 1937*                                          SMA

hotel were requisitioned by the American Navy, who stayed until
October 1946.

Perhaps the Palace's most inconspicuous military guests were
troops from the People's Liberation Army who were billeted at
the hotel in May 1949. The commander of the several hundred
troops first asked if they could be given rooms at half price. The
manager agreed to this. Then the PLA officer explained that the
soldiers were not used to such luxurious surroundings and asked
if it would be too much trouble to remove the furniture from the
rooms. Finally, the troop commander said that perhaps some of
the hotel's permanent guests, particularly foreigners, might be
upset to see a lot of soldiers coming in and out and asked whether
arrangements could be made for his men to use the back door!
The *China Weekly Review* reported that 'the persons working in
the hotel say you would never know the soldiers were living
there.' The quiet Communist revolutionaries closed the door on
Nationalist Party rule in China that had been celebrated in the
very same building on 29th December 1911 when Dr. Sun Yat-sen
entertained over 100 of his boisterous revolutionary followers
after his election as President of the Republic of China. In recent
years a number of potential investors have been eyeing the
building, used as the south wing of the Peace Hotel, with a view
to revolutionising its use yet again.

*Lobby and main staircase of the south wing of the Peace Hotel, 1990s*

*Victorious PLA troops outside the hotel in 1949*

SMA

# AMERICAN EXPRESS—NOT THE BUND!

Al—That's right enough, Elmer, and frankly I'm kicking myself for not acting on your suggestion and staying over in Japan when we had the chance. Too late now, however. We're here for the next five days, so we'd better make the most of it. Look, they've some pretty nice buildings over there any way. That must be the Bund.

Elmer—Just so, but I didn't take this trip to see modern marvels of structural beauty. I can see as many of those as I care at home.

*A sketch on how American visitors see Shanghai, January 1931*

American Express

The average tourist arriving in Shanghai is astonished beyond words that, instead of a Chinese city with perhaps a wall around it … he or she finds a great metropolis built entirely on European and American lines.

*January 1931*

Excerpts from *The American Express Oriental Travelogue*, published by the Shanghai Office, which was first established in 1918.

# BOARDING ON THE BUND

In the very early years there were a number of hostelries, of dubious to modest character, catering for seafarers, new arrivals and visitors to Shanghai. The first establishment on the Bund, the Victoria Hotel, which opened around 1850, quickly became the leading business and social centre. Renamed the Commercial Hotel in 1854, it housed the offices of the Hongkong and Shanghai Bank following their establishment in 1865. The Central Hotel took its place in 1875 and offered sedan chairs for hire, arranged up-country houseboat trips and boasted the best billiard tables and European kitchen in town. However, a visitor to the hotel in 1898 who was preparing an article for *The Hotel World* magazine found the cuisine inferior, and although the bedrooms were 'passable enough the lavatory and sanitary arrangements were not what would be desired.'

With the turn of the 20th century there was a growing demand for large luxury hotels to be introduced to Shanghai. The city was receiving more visitors following the opening of the northern route to Europe on the Trans-Siberian Railway and was besieged by a rapidly growing number of foreign arrivals taking up positions or seeking their fortune in the city. Hotels were, (and still are), a tremendously important part of foreign community life in Shanghai. The institution of the hotel stood for far more than it did in their native lands and provided a refuge where China was cast

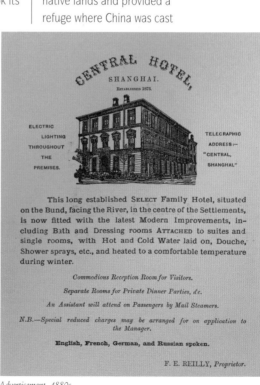

Advertisement, 1880s

*The Bund and Nanjing Road corner in the 1880s, 1930, and today*

into the background. Most 'griffins' or new arrivals to Shanghai, right up until the early 1920s, found permanent abode in the major hotels on, or around, the Bund.

With the 1920s came the giant cruise-liners discharging their hordes, like massive injections of a drug into a fragile body. Local branches of American Express and Thomas Cook ushered the overdressed, curio-crazed visitors over the uneven terrain. More hotels sprang up providing lavish entertainments and bottomless menus. By the early 1920s long-term hotel residents were

*SS Belgenland, cruise-liner*

being increasingly displaced by what became known as the 'four minute guests.' Although Thomas Cook had escorted the first round-the-world tour, taking in Shanghai, in 1872–1873, it wasn't until 1921 that the first of a long stream of round-the-world cruise-liners began to visit the city.

All major shipping lines with their regal vessels, including the *Belgenland*, the *Franconia*, the *Resolute* and the *Empress of Britain*, would call at the city, and by the early 1930s Shanghai was playing host to around 40,000 globetrotters each year! At that time Shanghai boasted the finest hotels in Asia. Two of these, the Palace Hotel and the Cathay Hotel, were found on the Bund itself, whilst the Astor House Hotel was located nearby on what is now referred to as the North Bund. Broadway Mansions, which was principally an apartment hotel, opened next door to the Astor House in 1934. Remarkably, all four hostelries have stood the test of time and are still open for business today. They are likely to be joined by a flurry of new hotel and boutique hotel developments in the near future.

Picture This

*1930s luggage label*

# THE HONGKONG AND SHANGHAI HOTELS LTD.

The union of The Shanghai Hotels Ltd. and The Hongkong Hotel Company in October 1923 revolutionised the nature of hotel-keeping in China. When Edward Ezra, the long-time major shareholder of The Shanghai Hotels Ltd., became managing director in 1920 he added the six-storey Kalee Hotel near the Bund and a major share in Beijing's Grand Hotel des Wagons Lits to the company's hotel portfolio. Plans were set for an ambitious expansion programme which included an intention to build the biggest and best hotel in the Far East. A 14-storey hotel with 650 huge luxury bedrooms including a 1,500-seat dining hall and two ballrooms was proposed for Shanghai.

Unfortunately, Ezra's plans were tragically curtailed by his death in 1922. Soon after another tragedy struck as Sir Ellis Kadoorie, businessman, philanthropist and one of the pillars of the board of directors of The Hongkong Hotel Company, met an untimely death at the age of 57. And that is when James Harper Taggart, a dynamic

*Mr. J. H. Taggart and his millionaire American wife in Hong Kong, 1920*

Hongkong and Shanghai Hotels

Scotsman and former manager of the Hongkong Hotel, assumed control as managing director of the company. The Hongkong Hotel Company, founded in 1866, at that time owned the Hongkong, Peak and Repulse Bay Hotels in the Crown Colony. In May 1922, Taggart, on behalf of the company, acquired an 85% controlling interest in The Shanghai Hotels for the princely sum of two and a half million Mexican dollars. The two companies were amalgamated in the following year when The Hongkong and Shanghai Hotels Ltd. was born.

*A local newspaper lauds the hotel company's achievements, 1935*

M arried to an American millionaire heiress, the diminutive but sharp-minded Taggart immediately set about engineering the creation of new rendezvous and entertainment centres for Shanghai's social and business circles. He dropped his original endorsement of plans for a new, super hotel in favour of converting the palatial McBain residence, the home of the owner of No. 1 The Bund, into the Majestic Hotel in 1924. Its clover-shaped ballroom became a legend. He injected new life into the Astor House and Palace Hotels. Dinner dances and European-style grill-rooms were all the rage in 1920s Shanghai. Meanwhile, in Hong Kong, the legendary Peninsula Hotel was preparing to open its doors.

And today Shanghai expectantly awaits the opening of a new Peninsula hotel at the northern end of the Bund.

# SHANGHAI'S WALDORF-ASTORIA— THE ASTOR HOUSE HOTEL

### ASTOR HOUSE,
THE OLDEST ESTABLISHED HOTEL AT SHANGHAI.

AS a first-class FAMILY HOTEL, this house is unsurpassed, comprising every comfort and convenience, particuiarly for Gentlemen and Families travelling. The Cellar is replete with every description of the choicest Liquors

Elegant open and close Chairs to be had on application at the Office.

Hot and cold Baths always ready. Boats attached to the Hotel.

Terms moderate.

H. W. SMITH,
Proprietor.

tf  Shanghai, 5th April, 1862.

*The new proprietor's notice in the* North China Daily News, *1862*

*Astor House Hotel luggage label*

British-born Mr. Peter F. Richards, one of the earliest arrivals to Shanghai, set up a ship chandler's and commission agent's business, as well as the 'Hotel Richard' in the former French Concession, in 1844. He established the Astor House Hotel, just to the north of Suzhou Creek, on its present site, in 1858. Even though the hotel has also been known by Richards' Chinese name of 'Licha' for almost 150 years, Richards only actually had possession of the original two-storied hostelry until 1st January 1861. His successor, Henry Smith, also had a short tenure with ill-heath forcing him to retire in 1863. Smith's claim to fame was the addition of a perennially popular 12-table billiard room. Other forms of entertainment for the early hotel residents included wildfowl shooting excursions to the plentifully stocked local area and the idle consumption of whisky.

The Astor House developed apace along with the swelling influx of adventurers, missionaries and families forming the new community of Shanghai. The hotel was enlarged in 1876 and a new propriety was offered when it was taken over by the Jansen family in 1884. The Jansen's long residency in China allowed them to offer an information and travel service for visitors wishing to explore other parts of China, as well as offering kitted-out houseboats and dogs and guns for those seeking recreation around Shanghai. Families lived in the hotel whilst their new houses were in the course of construction and 50 rooms were added before the Jansens sold the hotel to Monsieur Auguste Vernon in 1900. He took up the position of managing director of the Astor House Hotel Company, but was forced to retire, again for reasons of ill-health, two years later. He also left a headache for the board as he departed owing the company a considerable amount of money.

The company had taken a 30-year lease on the entire block, of which the old hotel occupied just a part, allowing room for expansion. As demand for hotel space was sky-rocketing, Chinese shops at the back of the original hotel were hastily torn down and a new 120-room hotel emerged. Following an outbreak of cholera in the city, guests were few on the ground when the hotel opened in November 1903. The building survives today as the northern section of the hotel. It was originally managed by an eccentric American called Louis Ladow—whose infamous trio of bartenders Happell, Hill and Bobbett, were reputed to serve the finest cocktails in the Far East. The Russo-Japanese War of 1904–1905 spurred a wave of wealthy Russian guests, who drank the finest champagne and

Dennis George Crow

*The Astor House Hotel, early 20th century*

*Early 20th-century postcard showing main entrance to the hotel*

were always obliging in paying for their shattered glasses. Despite stiff competition from hotels in Hong Kong and Singapore, as well as from the Cathay Hotels in Shanghai, the Astor House's reputation for the best cocktails was still upheld in the 1930s.

In 1907 the company decided to embark on a new hotel, 'fitting of Shanghai's growth and importance' and 'better than any in the Far East.' Work on building the main portion of the hotel in English Renaissance style began in November 1908. Concerns over the public reaction to the employment of a gang of 240 convict labourers to lay out the major new roads surrounding the hotel in early 1909 resulted in a debate within the SMC. Although the Police Department was making very good profits from such activity, it was decided to confine the gangs to lesser thoroughfares, out of sight of the public, in the future. Another criminal who made himself invisible was the unlikely figure of the hotel's Swiss hotel manager, Mr. Walter Brauen. He ran off with a huge chunk of hotel funds just three months before the hotel opened, six months behind schedule, in January 1911. Brauen was spotted shortly after in Nagasaki, but escaped capture.

*Adverts for the recently enlarged hotel, winter 1907, when it was first described as the 'Waldorf-Astoria of the Orient'*

*The bar, billiard room and lobby of the new hotel, 1911*

*The new hotel under construction, 1910*

The building, designed by Messrs. Davies & Thomas, originally had grounds extending to the waterfront. The grounds were taken over, soon after, by the Russian Consulate and its building, which was completed in 1916, is still standing and again houses the Russian Consulate. The hotel's ground floor was taken over by a handsome buffet bar, a huge lounge hall, a billiard room and a reading room. On the first floor was a two-storey dining room with balcony and veranda, capable of seating over 500 guests, as well as a

*Main dining hall, 1911*

Following the hotel's acquisition by Central Stores Ltd. in 1915 plans were laid for a new ballroom and the conversion of part of the double-tiered dining room into luxurious rooms. The ballroom, designed by Lafuente & Wooten, opened at the end of November 1917. Under the directorship of The Hongkong and Shanghai Hotels Ltd. the ballroom was further

Shanghai Construction Archives

*Lafuente's drawing for the remodelled ballroom featuring a new vaulted glass ceiling, 1922*

banqueting room and private dining rooms. From the second floor upwards were to be found 211 rooms and seven suites. The hotel set a stately seal on the city's fast expanding aspirations.

Though the hotel was a magnificent structure, the large public areas were not proving profitable and it wasn't long before calls were made for the building to be redesigned.

remodelled in 1923 to keep up with the Shanghai passion for nightly entertainment. The new ballroom's light blue walls were decorated with dancing sylphs and maidens, and a large peacock shell structure which constantly changed colour provided the backdrop for the Astor orchestra. The ground floor was also remoulded and its new grill-room soon earned distinction.

In the early years of the 20th century the anarchic and flamboyant Astor House played host to a potpourri of regal guests. Various members of the Japanese Imperial family, Czar Nicholas II, the last czar of Russia, Prince Heinrich of Prussia, the Aga Khan, and Prince Pitsannloke of Siam all took up residence. King Kalakaua of the Hawaii Islands

ASTOR HOUSE HOTEL—SHANGHAI

POPULAR GRILL ROOM

**THE HONGKONG & SHANGHAI HOTELS, LTD.**
*(Incorporated in Hongkong)*

*Operating*

The Hongkong Hotel, Hongkong    The Astor House Hotel, Shanghai
The Repulse Bay Hotel, Hongkong  The Palace Hotel, Shanghai
The Peak Hotel, Hongkong         The Majestic Hotel, Shanghai
The Peninsula Hotel, Kowloon     The Italian Garden, Shanghai

**HOTELS of DISTINCTION**

*Advert, 1930*

*Mr. Bershadsky's quintet at the Astor House ballroom*

into his family's round-the-world tour in 1879, he actually didn't—although before he became US President, some 30 years later, William H. Taft did.

Visit The New COCKTAIL LOUNGE

a Popular Innovation

O-NIGHT
DINNER
DANCE

Dinner $4.00

on-Diners No Cover Charge

TEA DANCE DAILY

**Astor House Hotel**
For Reservations:
Tel. 42255

**THE HONGKONG & SHANGHAI HOTELS, LTD.**
*(Incorporated in Hongkong)*

*Advert, 1930*

was one of the earliest and more flamboyant monarchs to stay at the hotel in March 1881. Known as the 'merry monarch' for his love of parties and balls, he was on a round-the-world tour promoting commerce and immigration to Hawaii. And although the present management would have us believe that ex-President Ulysses S. Grant stayed there, two years

The hotel had a long relationship with Shanghai's foreign newspapermen dating back to the arrival of Mr. Edwin Pickwoad from Australia in August 1860. Pickwoad took over the ownership of the *North China Herald*, and oversaw the advent of the *North China Daily News* in 1864. He also acted as secretary of the Municipal Council. Later, the hotel was home to the most important

*Luggage label designed by Dan Sweeney*

*Mr. Thomas Millard*

fraternity of American journalists in China. Thomas F. Millard took up residence in 1900 and his protégé, J. B. Powell, moved in when he was called upon by Millard to help found the *China Weekly Review* in 1917. Edgar Snow, the famous leftist writer, took up residence in 1928. All were graduates of the University of Missouri's journalism school.

American author Emily Hahn was one of the hotel's more illustrious female visitors. She lived beyond the pale of foreigners and her Shanghai stories were opium-enriched and sexually charged. Emily Hahn wrote for the *New Yorker* magazine and worked at the *North China Daily News* offices on the Bund. Eccentric and amoral, she could be spotted around town with her pet gibbon draped over her shoulder and was the concubine of the Cambridge-educated Chinese poet Zao Xinmei. Hahn always asserted that an incident described in Malraux's *Man's Fate*, when a Frenchman in a rage with his Russian mistress fills her room at the Astor House with a menagerie of animals, including a kangaroo, was not an exaggeration. Powell, who stayed in the old 'steerage' section of the hotel where all the rooms were occupied by the 'US young'ens,' was also prey to an unexpected guest. He came to understand why he was told to keep his room locked by a consular clerk when, on one occasion, he returned to his room to find a Japanese lady in his bed.

Aside from its princely, scholarly and fanciful guests the Astor also played host to its fair

*Banquet for W. H. Taft at the Astor House Hotel in October 1908*

*A group of American school teachers visit the ballroom, 1925*

share of fraudsters. Powell was told by an old Shanghailander on his arrival that if one kept one's eyes open in the lobby one could 'see all the crooks who hang out on the China coast.' In 1924, a British woman and her daughter staying at the Astor, posing as the Montgomerys, made a fortune duping Shanghai's foreign community. The daughter, who was supposedly coming into a huge fortune, courted marital proposals and was swift to lose or run off with engagement rings, whilst her mother borrowed many expensive fur coats on the pretence of having them copied, but which were never seen by their owners again. The couple made a safe escape to Hong Kong before the hotel was besieged by their debtors.

Partly on account of its British character, which was frequently compared to that of an English Squire, the Astor was a firm favourite with American

*View of the Bund from near the Astor House, 1934*

Picture This

residents and visitors alike. The American presence came to an abrupt end in August 1937 when the Hongkou district in which the hotel was situated, and which was home to around 20,000 Japanese residents, unofficially became the Japanese Concession. Japanese sentries were posted on the Garden Bridge leading onto the Bund at the front of the property. The Astor was occupied by the Japanese Y.M.C.A. in 1937 and 1938, and remained under some form of Japanese occupation until the end of the Second World War. The hotel fared badly in the war and expensive refurbishment bills were deferred following its requisition by the US Army who remained until June 1946. It was leased soon after to

a Chinese development company and filled with members of organisations involved with the post-war reconstruction of China, including the United Nations Relief and Rehabilitation Association.

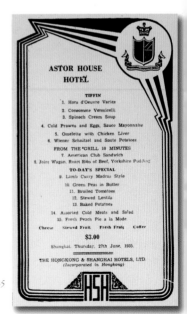

*Menu, 1935*

*The hotel in the mid-1920s*

Picture This

*The hotel, with the Russian Consulate to the right, 2003*

*The third floor hall, before and after restoration, in 2001*

Before reopening as the Pujiang Hotel in 1959, the building had been used by a tea and a textile trading company as offices and dormitories, as well as by the Chinese Navy. In the 1980s and 1990s it was the city's premiere destination for independent travellers seeking dormitory accommodation and became Shanghai's first member of the International Youth Hostel Federation in 1998. Throughout the 1990s its neglected ballroom housed China's first stock exchange of the modern era.

The well-intentioned state-run Hengshan Group, which took the property over in 1994, have grand plans to restore the property to its former glory. Modest restoration has already taken place—the dormitories have disappeared and its glossily restored ballroom was reopened in April 2006. Top hats, as opposed to backpacks, look set to re-establish themselves. However, the ad hoc approach to the building's remodelling in recent years has resulted in an uneasy blend of styles and usage of the property. Such an issue was first raised by the architectural company of Atkinson & Dallas in a letter of May 1918 wherein they commented on the patchwork design of the hotel which had been 'brought about by the various additions having been made without consideration of the final design.' Hopefully, matters will be resolved when, as anticipated, international restoration experts oversee a comprehensive makeover of the hotel.

The Astor House has reinstated its English name and the greater part of the structure still remains relatively unchanged since the 1920s, or even earlier. The third-floor, two-storied, Tudor-style vaulted hall looks much as it did in 1911, whilst the vast arched corridor nearby hasn't changed since it was remodelled in 1918. It is not hard to imagine why the hotel billed itself as the 'Waldorf-Astoria of the Orient.' The hotel can also lay claim to having the oldest surviving hotel room in China—room 103 has many original fittings dating back to the early 20th century. Meanwhile, beautifully carved Shanghai Art Deco furniture, which was manufactured for the Picardie Apartments, opened in 1935, has been placed in some of the rooms. The furniture was able to be rescued from storage by the Hengshan Group as they now operate the former Picardie Apartments as the Hengshan Hotel to the west of the city.

*Room 103*                                    Astor House Hotel

*The voluminous rooms and corridor on the third floor of the hotel was part of a remodelling scheme in 1918*

*Advert announcing the opening of the hotel, winter 1910*

# A DATE FOR AFTERNOON TEA

*Isabel Peake arrived in Shanghai from England in December 1925 to meet her fiancé, Harry. Their union lasted just a short while, and Isabel searched the ballrooms of Shanghai's hotels to make new acquaintances. Her association with an ex-Naval commander came to an abrupt end when his leg was shot off on the Yangtsze River and she eventually married a doctor.*

It was the fashionable Astor House Hotel where I happened to be at the time of the earth tremors (in 1926, during which the walls of the hotel were visibly shaking and swaying), and it was famous for its excellent tea dances which were held everyday—except Sundays. The Paul Whiteman Orchestra played the romantic dance tunes of the period, and all this for the price of One Mexican Dollar: this included sandwiches, cream, and I mean real cream, cakes and other specialities between the hours of 5 and 7 p.m. A number of the younger Europeans were always to be seen enjoying the happy hours with their current boy or girlfriend. The hotel was an exotic setting where we were able to meet new friends and newcomers and have a jolly good time ...

I loved dancing and there was plenty of it at well appointed hotels with their excellent bands. The only thing missing was air-

ASTOR HOUSE HOTEL

TEA DANCE
DAILY

DINNER DANCE
Every Saturday
Night

For Reservations:
Tel. 42255.

The
Hongkong & Shanghai
Hotels, Ltd.
(Incorporated in Hongkong)

*1930s advertising for the Astor House and Palace Hotels*

conditioning, so we had to put up with fans playing from overhead in the summer months augmented by fountains of water which cooled the air as we whizzed past …

The Palace Hotel was a well-known meeting place for almost any foreigner in that area, situated as it was at the corner of the Bund Gardens and Nanking Road; with its vast lounge and plate-glass windows overlooking the street where everything was going on. It was a great attraction to office go-ers and others to partake of tea, meet their friends and generally socialise after the day's work was done. Tea and luscious cakes were served, and there was such an air of warmth and friendliness amongst all who congregated there. It was quite the thing to say to one's old friends 'Let's meet at the Palace for tea,' where one could see the world and his wife, and come across acquaintances who had just arrived back from leave, and hear the latest gossip—how different from the rush and closing hours of the present-day.

From: Mrs. Isabel Duke,
*Victims—All in a Lifetime*,
typewritten memoirs held at the
Imperial War Museum. London.

# CATHAY HOTEL
## THE BUND
### SHANGHAI

"*THE* CATHAY"—the most modern Hotel in China

Cable :—"CATHOTEL, SHANGHAI"

*Cathay Hotel postcard, early 1930s*

# № 20 The Cathay Hotel

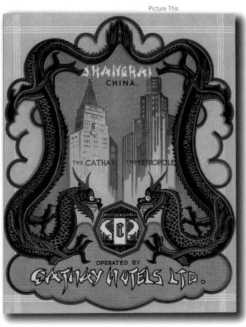

*The Cathay Hotel logo*

L ike an Art Deco rocket ship arising from the impassioned waters of the Huangpu River, the Cathay Hotel of the 1930s was a powerful symbol of thrusting Shanghai society. Sleek and elegant, modest in outward adornment, rich and extravagant in its heart, the mood of Shanghai exuded from its walls. The Cathay was much more than a social institution. It was the body of Shanghai—an anchor of stability and familiarity and a Ferris wheel of novelty and surprise. Embodying a vision of the future, it housed the best of the past in a sublime mélange of reality and fantasy. Though distinct in physical form, the Cathay Hotel was a chameleon being conjured from the minds of a variegated Shanghai society.

Construction of the revolutionary five-million-dollar Sassoon House began in the spring of 1926. Tug Wilson had originally designed the building as a 150-foot-high office and shopping complex with just 20 luxury residential apartments above. The building work, which was underpinned by no less than

*Cathay Hotels luggage label*

1,600 wood and concrete piles, proceeded on schedule until four floors had been completed, when a halt to the operation was called in mid-1928. Victor Sassoon had just established Cathay Hotels, Ltd. in Hong Kong and delivered a new edict to convert the upper part of his building into a luxury hotel. He came up to Shanghai and oversaw Wilson's altered designs, which included

Peace Hotel

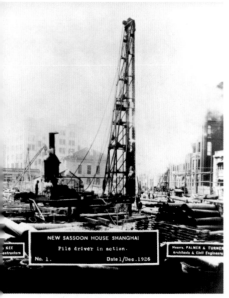

Laying the foundations, 1926

The hotel under construction, 1928

the addition of two extra floors, as well as a rearrangement of the ground floor area. Wilson modelled the hotel's interior around an arsenal of fashionable Lalique lights. They were to be everywhere—even the illuminated bathroom shaving mirrors were of Lalique glass!

Wilson had more than a fanciful interest in the hotel as he was one of the directors of Cathay Hotels, Ltd. alongside others, including William McBain of No. 1 The Bund, Jack Macgregor of Caldbeck, Macgregor & Co., as

H. E. Arnhold

well as H. E. Arnhold who had his offices in Sassoon House and was chairman of the SMC. Sassoon's right-hand man from India, Commander F. R. Davey, previously head of E. D. Sassoon & Co. in Calcutta, followed Sassoon to Shanghai, as a director, as did Mr. E. Carrard, the new hotel's manager. Carrard was formerly manager of the Taj Mahal Hotel in Bombay.

Commander F. R. Davey

*Original design for Sassoon House*

*In the design and construction of this building, Messrs. G. L. WILSON, F.R.I.B.A., P.A.S.I. and F. J. BARROW, A.R.I.B.A., M.I.S.T.E., were the architect and engineer, respectively, for PALMER and TURNER.*

*Revised design for Sassoon House*

All who

visit

Cathay

Hotel

and see its beautifully decorated Ball Room and Lounges will acknowledge that the lighting and other decorations by the gifted old Frenchman, René Lalique, merit the opinion of connoisseurs of art, that he is the world's greatest living artist in glass.

ELECTROLIERS
MOTOR MASCOTS
TABLE LAMPS
TABLE GLASS
VESSELS
VASES

**LALIQUE ART GLASS**

In its many forms is obtainable only from

**The Alexander Clark Co., Ltd.**
Central Sassoon Arcade
Telephone 1002

OTHER DEPARTMENTS
Jewellery
Silverware
Electro Plate
Rolex Watches
Cut Glass, etc.

**SPECIAL WHOLESALE DEPARTMENT FOR SUPPLYING ALL HOTEL AND CLUB REQUIREMENTS**

We offer our expert advice on Lalique Decorating and will make installations for approval.

*Advert, 1929*

229

CATHAY    HOTEL

E. CARRARD
General Manager

TELEPHONE
11240

SHANGHAI, CHINA.

CABLE ADDRESS
"CATHOTEL"

H. M. N
Secre

*Cathay Hotel notepaper*

*A surviving original door handle*

The Cathay Hotel formally opened on 1st August 1929. Many critics and sceptics foretold of failure, arguing that Shanghai already had far too many hotel rooms. Others suggested that it was too large, too lavish and too expensive. They were all proved wrong as the hotel lived up to its epithet as the 'Claridges of the Far East.' The opening of the Cathay heralded a new era for Shanghai and indeed Far Eastern hotels—a pace-setter brimming with the latest amenities and luxuries and a monument to the marriage of art and technology. The advent of the Cathay Hotel also cast a note of optimism for the future of Shanghai in that Victor Sassoon had so wholeheartedly committed himself to such a grandiose and futuristic venture. The first guest to inscribe her name in the register at the Cathay was a rising playwright, Mrs. 'Buddy' Hazel of New Jersey.

# CATHAY HOTEL
### SHANGHAI
## The Most Modern Hotel in the Far East

214 Rooms and Suites, each with Private Bathroom

**Hotel Restaurant**
with Spring Dance-floor opening on Roof Terraces

**"Tower"**
a la Carte Restaurant and Grill Room on 9th Floor

**Banqueting and Private Dining Rooms**
on the Tenth and Eleventh Floors

E. CARRARD, *Manager*

CABLES:
CATHOTEL SHANGHAI

CATHAY HOTEL

*Advert, 1929*

Miss Cathay gives one the impression of being thoroughly at home all over the world and having its choicest offerings at her command. She leads a very gay life during the season and entertains lavishly. Her guests come from all over the world as well as from Shanghai's elite. Many of them do not stay long but she speeds the parting with the same good cheer with which she welcomes newcomers. Her hospitality is so extensive as to meet all tastes, whether one wishes a cup of tea or a dinner for a hundred guests. Somewhat formal in disposition she bows to the wishes of the more Bohemian of her acquaintances and

The Cathay Hotel

"THE TOWER"
9th Floor, Cathay Hotel
Smartest Night Club
in Town

maintains the Tower Night Club for them. One could hardly be said to know Shanghai without meeting Miss Cathay.

*North China Daily News* 15th February 1936

# *A*nother step towards the success of ASIA'S

O F all the visible signs of the recent growth of Shanghai, the most arresting is what is known as the Shanghai Sky Line, the latest and most conspicuous addition to which is the soaring tower of the Cathay Hotel. ¶ The visitor to Shanghai, coming up the river for the first time, little imagines that in this tower, 125 feet above the Bund, is to be found a Restaurant and Grill Room which easily ranks as one of the most modern and luxurious in the World. ¶ It is not necessary to extol the magificent

## Premier Port

views from this Tower—to the East miles and miles of villages and cultivated country and to the North and South, up and down the busy river, a bird's eye view of Greater Shanghai. ¶ With perfection of cuisine directed by French chefs and service supervised by experienced Maitres d'Hotel, the opportunity to lunch or dine in such surroundings is a notable addition to the amenities of Shanghai.

E. CARRARD, MANAGER.

*For table reservations Telephone and ask for "Front Office".*

## CATHAY HOTEL

THE BUND - - SHANGHAI - - TELEPHONE 11240

*Stylish 1929 advert, featuring a drawing of the Tower restaurant*

The Cathay provided the ultimate venue for life's pleasures. On the culinary front M. Victor Boudard, the rotund head chef, presided over the most modern kitchen in China. His 70 Chinese cooks, and one French and one English chef drew upon the best-stocked foreign larder in the city brimming with Californian peaches, Persian figs, Russian caviar, German hams, Italian cheeses, Parisian *foie gras* and Australian butter.

*Advert, 1937*

And whilst the cuisine was legendary, the Cathay was best known for catering to the Shanghailanders in their exhaustive search for amusement. The Cathay thrived on entertainment—from musical folly to classical concerts, from fanciful tea dances and impromptu cocktail parties to pompous balls. There were events for the social elite, the favoured, the opportune, and for the passing world tourist apt to dispense with a stock of dollars in excess of the number of minutes spoiled in Shanghai.

Eric Niderost

Sassoon was renowned for his fancy dress parties, often bordering on the bizarre and perverse, in the Cathay ballroom. At his shipwreck party in 1933 he donned blue trousers, beret and scarlet shirt, and dangled a hot water bottle from his waist. Shanghai's most respected citizens, wearing nightgowns and pyjamas, ambled round the hotel half-clad finding courage in a cocktail glass as well as in the absurdity of their dress. The *North China Daily News* picked out Mary Hayley Bell, for her

**Cathay Hotel**
*Shanghai*

**Dinner**
7:30 P.M TO 9.30 P.M

1. Fruit Cocktail

2. Cream of Tomato
3. Consommé Brunoise Hot or Cold

4. Mandarin Doria
5. Fried Fillet of Sole

6. Veal Steak Schnitzel
   French Beans
   Potatoes Sautées
   Carrots Vichy

7. Baked Duckling with Figs

8. Cold Chicken in Tarragon Jelly
   Salad Russe

9. Cold Pudding Arlequin
10. Pear Cardinal
    Cigarettes - Tuiles

11. Coffee

SUNDAY, 21ST AUGUST 1932

*Menu, 1932*

courage in wearing a flannel nightdress with her hair in curlers, looking 'very much prettier than most girls could in that dress.' Hayley Bell, the daughter of a colonel who worked as a Chinese Maritime Customs official, was to meet her future husband, the late Sir John Mills, whilst he was on tour with the Quaints theatre group in Shanghai.

Despite rumours that Sir Victor was to cut back on his entertaining, the 1934 party season kicked off with a schoolroom frolic where guests were invited to dress for a school and supper party. The Cathay ballroom was transformed into a giant classroom complete with blackboards, maps and other instruments of learning. Old school songs were promenaded by the orchestra with children's games, including musical chairs and Ring a Ring O' Roses adding an element of rough and tumble. Very much at the head, Sir Victor, frocked in a gown with mortar board, wielded a formidable birch cane at all those who came in range! Whilst the school party was strictly for grown-ups, Sassoon also arranged special 'toy parties' for Shanghai's privileged progenies.

A circus party was thrown soon after, with guests appearing as seals, donkeys and circus acts, including one as a tattooed lady. Sir Victor ruled over events in a scarlet ringmaster's coat— this time wielding a whip! It was often remarked that Sassoon would whimsically get his own back on the pillars of the British community at his parties. Whilst he was the most powerful and

*Advert, December 1935*

*Newspaper clippings of Sassoon's circus parties, 1934 and 1935*

*The Ganin sisters appeared at the ballroom in 1935*

wealthy amongst them, his Jewish heritage excluded him from full membership. He was even denied membership of the most exclusive British clubs. His frequent comings and goings to preside over his racing establishment in India, and elsewhere, called for an unceasing round of revelry.

The Cathay ballroom was also popular with Shanghai's young Americans who threw private parties much in the same mould as Sir Victor's affairs. Once a group, who appeared as scavengers, imported a complete roadside Chinese kitchen into the ballroom and set about a treasure hunt featuring live chickens, cockroaches and frogs.

On a more regular basis the Cathay ballroom was Shanghai's premier Saturday night venue. On such nights Sir Victor could usually be found at a long table as host to large groups of friends, being entertained by dancing troupes on their rounds of the world's best hotels and cabarets. Opening nights were gala affairs giving the Shanghai elite a chance to parade their latest Paris fashions. Americans, Harris and Yvonne Ashburn, and the Di Gaetano dancers made a sensational debut, with their mix of classical, tap and acrobatics, in October 1935 when Sir Victor's

100 or so guest-list read like a Who's Who of Shanghai. China's most respected diplomat, Dr. Wellington Koo and his wife, the Countess de Courelles, together with representatives of Shanghai's most established families including the Ezras, Hayims and the McBains, and his friend Emily Hahn were amongst those invited. Sassoon was rarely seen without his camera or cine-camera in hand at such events and Hahn later recounted how he liked to photograph her naked. She was also frequently to be seen with Sassoon at his private box at the race club.

On most evenings Henry Nathan's All American Dance Orchestra took the stage, apart from Monday nights when Mr. Federoff's Cathay Concert Orchestra performed three hours of classical and operatic numbers.

The Cathay Hotel was no stranger to the rich and famous. Noel Coward is popularly credited with having written *Private Lives* whilst staying at the Cathay. Coward had dreamed up the idea for the play in Yokohama, although it took a four-day bout of flu in the final days of 1929 to confine him to his room at the Cathay where he drafted the script. He then went on to Hong Kong where he spent another week typing and revising it. On a return visit in 1936, Mr. Coward, a fan of Chinese talking pictures and personal friend of China's most famous opera star, Mei Lanfang, was working on his autobiography. Coward's last sojourn at the Cathay was totally unplanned when his ship, the *Monterey*, was diverted on its way from California to Australia to pick up foreign evacuees from the city in November 1940. After taking on board many Shanghailanders, including a

*Advert, October 1935*

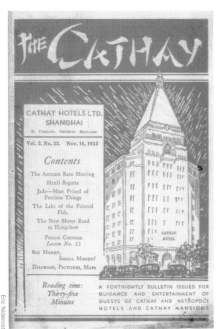

Eric Niderost

*Cover of a 1932 edition of the* Cathay Hotels *magazine*

large contingent of children from the Shanghai American School, Coward, who was on his way to Australia on a goodwill mission, confined himself to his cabin only venturing out for the late dinner call or for coffee and liqueurs in a quiet corner with his group of friends. Among other Hollywood stars, Ronald Coleman, one of Coward's greatest friends, also stayed at the hotel.

Douglas Fairbanks and Mary Pickford, who were frequent visitors to Shanghai, turned up two hours late for a reception at the Cathay in February 1931. Fairbanks, however, found some redemption when he informed his irritated audience that 'to me there are only five prominent cities in the world and Shanghai in my opinion occupies the limelight as the most colourful and interesting and progressive.'

The management today are still eager to point out that Charlie Chaplin once stayed at the Cathay—as are the management of the Astor House Hotel! As Chaplin was a friend of Sir Philip Sassoon, Britain's youngest Member of Parliament and Sir Victor's cousin, there would be little doubt where he stayed in Shanghai. Accompanied by Paulette Goddard, amidst rumours of their engagement and a commotion surrounding his epochal picture *Modern Times*, they made an impromptu trip to the Far

*Charlie Chaplin meets Mei Lanfang on his 1936 visit*

East in 1936. Even though they stayed just one March night at the Cathay, they weren't able to avoid the publicity as 30 journalists besieged them with questions and a curio dealer even managed to sneak into Chaplin's suite. George Vanderbilt and his wife, who were on a roaming honeymoon, stayed in the hotel at the same time.

And when it came to the rich—there was no richer girl in the world than the former Miss Doris Duke, the American tobacco heiress, who stayed at the Cathay in 1935 on the sixth month of her honeymoon tour with her new husband, James H. R. Cromwell. The 22-year-old Mrs. Cromwell had inherited a fortune in excess of US$30,000,000. Their marriage lasted until 1943, and at the time of her death in 1993 her estate was valued well in excess of a billion dollars.

However, all the riches and all the sandbags in the world couldn't ensure the future security of the International Settlement and its landmark hotel. Even though foreign Shanghai society had been witness to scenes of Sino-Japanese hostilities to the north of the International Settlement in early 1932, they were ill-prepared for the upcoming events of 1937. In 1932, parties had rolled through the night in the Cathay ballroom when a six-hour curfew from ten in the evening till four in the morning was imposed as fierce fighting took place in the Zhabei district. Hedonism had developed as an inevitable accessory to war and the battlefields were soon after a must on the hasty agenda of whirling round-the-world tourists.

In early 1937, Shanghai was receiving record numbers of tourists and many were in town in July when Beijing fell to the Japanese, signalling the beginning of the Sino-Japanese War. Shanghai was placed under an unofficial state of emergency—but still wore its impervious social armour. A columnist of the *North China Daily News* surmised that the tourist was in some bizarre sense entertained by the new siege conditions—'the tourist who is not as used to wars as the old resident has proved a very good sport about accepting the annoyances inherent in the situation.

She wishes that she might have seen Peking, not to mention Korea and Manchuria, but she is kind enough to say that she is glad to have had more time to spend in Shanghai.'

By the time that newspaper report was printed on 15th August, no tourist in the city wished to be there. On 14th August two bombs fell at the junction of Shanghai's foremost thoroughfare (see page 86). One bomb curved through the air, penetrated the roof and top floor of the Palace Hotel and caused indescribable carnage. The other glanced off the side of the Cathay Hotel to continue through the canopy covering the entrance to Sassoon House and burst in the street. Shapeless heaps of sheltering refugees lay piled in the main entrances, doorways and arcades of the Palace and Cathay Hotels. The stricken were found far inside the Cathay Hotel arcade. On the street, a visiting cruise party leader, Mr. Robert Reischauer, who was staying at the Palace Hotel, lay lifeless amongst the twisted human fragments. The casualties, both foreign and Chinese, numbered over 400 with around 150 fatalities.

*Devastation outside the hotel, 14th August 1937*       Eric Politzer

It was 4.27 p.m. The Cathay Hotel clock froze as the bombs hit.

Sassoon heard the news in far away Bombay where he was tending his racing establishment. The Cathay and Palace Hotels soon recovered from their superficial tears and wounds and they, like the majority of businesses in Shanghai, put on a brave face as they announced business as usual just five weeks later. However, the Cathay ballroom was still out of operation and the Palace Hotel's gashing wounds on the uppermost floor were only partly sealed by matting. The Cathay acquired a new urgency and exuberance in safeguarding the social obligations of her guests—but her halcyon days were over.

*Advert, late 1937*

Over the following winter season the ballroom was back in action with the all-American Sid's Cathay Syncopators playing fox-trots, blues and waltzes, whilst romantic jazz piano by Waldy was on offer at the Tower Night Club. But, come the summer of 1938, all the Cathay's night spots remained unfamiliarly closed. The hotel played host to numerous unexpected guests and had become a main rendezvous for various military and diplomatic associations. Sir Victor displayed a great and solemn courtesy towards his Japanese guests, and their officers were treated with scrupulous politeness when they dined at the hotel. Such courtesy was not returned when the Japanese eventually seized control of the building in 1941.

However, the neutrality did not extend as far as the Tower Night Club where all profits were donated to the British War Fund in 1940. The Cathay had taken the lead in bowing to a call for more responsibility and sense in a city where elaborate entertainment was viewed either as an unnecessary indulgence or

*Sir Victor Sassoon (centre), with Henry Morriss of the* North China Daily News *to his right, in the Tower Night Club, 1939*

as a drain on the British War effort. The Tower had closed down completely in June, but the management, doing its best to 'infuse a ray of gloom into these gloomy days,' managed to satisfy such opposing needs. The Tower proved that, despite demands for living quietly, lavish entertainment could still add around 4,000 Chinese dollars to the coffers of the British government each month.

To make matters worse, the Cathay Hotel was plagued by two major strikes in 1941. In April the entire Cathay staff walked out in sympathy with sister staff at Cathay Mansions (today's Old Jin Jiang Hotel) where two lift operators had been dismissed. In total 1,000 Cathay Hotels, Ltd. employees left their duties. The management were not unduly concerned as they saw it as an opportunity to solve overstaffing problems. The workers were demanding a 100% pay rise and taunted the management with claims that they were more concerned with their horse racing than settling their grievances. The management retorted with a threat that they would employ Russians and Jewish refugees if they didn't see reason. The workers came back, earning little more than an additional rice allowance for their pains.

A second, more severe strike hit in August with all 2,500 of Sassoon's Chinese employees walking out. The management, once again, threatened to hire a complete staff of European workers and announced an end to the strike within two days when they took on 100 German-Jewish refugees to work in the kitchen and the dining room. The management intended to keep on these foreign workers after the situation had been fully resolved since they were actually cheaper to employ than the local Chinese. Most of the room boys scurried back to work when they realised the management was in earnest, but most other staff stayed away. However, as most guests boycotted the hotel on account of the poor service standards of its European workers, the original Chinese staff were reinstated with improved conditions, including sick leave and a good service bonus. All the foreign refugees were then dismissed. Few staff benefited from the new system as the hotel was requisitioned by Japanese forces on 8th December.

Soon after, the Japanese forces confined all foreign diplomatic staff to the Cathay and Sassoon's other hotels in the city. They continued to receive their salaries, enabling them to maintain their former standard of living and were free to move around the old Settlement area as they wished. Most were repatriated by August 1942. During the war the hotel was converted into spacious godowns and a large number of rooms were rearranged in Japanese style.

When Cathay Hotels, Ltd. resumed control of its properties in late 1945, its representatives returned to an alien city, a city of torment, a city of chaos and a city hanging on to life by a slender thread. Old Shanghailanders looked back on the pre-war days and reminisced that the city was never as bad as it was painted. The SMC and the lines of the International Settlement had vanished forever. The new Shanghai Council with its novice officials, presided over by the Chinese mayor of Shanghai, falteringly took over the running of the new Shanghai—an overworked city, now of some four and a half million residents. The British played little or no part in the city that, just a decade earlier, they considered rightfully theirs.

The management had reconverted and redecorated about half the rooms by the end of 1945 and the ninth floor grill-room was able to offer modest snack lunches. The cost of putting everything back in order came at a high price, and hotel rates were running at some 600 times their pre-war levels! Sir Victor's cousin, Lucien Ovadia, returned as chairman of the Sassoon interests just in time to add the finishing touches to the Christmas celebrations in 1945. The rooms were largely occupied by high-ranking American and British officers and embassy staff. General Wedemeyer, Commanding General of US Forces in China, had taken over Sir Victor's personal suite. Claire Chennault, the former leader of the illustrious 'Flying Tigers,' also stayed in the hotel. Bookings were plentiful for the still requisitioned Cathay, but it was difficult to persuade the Americans to leave.

In early 1946 the newly reopened Tower Night Club tried to exclude the military rank and file by restricting entry on three nights each week to those wearing evening dress, but had to recapitulate and make it Friday nights only 'by special request of

our patrons who are not in possession of evening dress due to the abnormal circumstances.' Evening suits were the last things on the minds of the hordes of American naval personnel on shore leave in what was seen as one of the best liberty ports in the Orient.

*Breakfast at the Peace Hotel, 1978*

But it wasn't long before the uniformed officers of the Nationalist Party were knocking on the door and in April 1949 the Cathay's few remaining guests were moved out as rooms were requisitioned and machine-gun placements installed. In the space of a month the battle was over, although the triumphant Communists didn't allow the Cathay's manager to leave for two long years afterwards. Cathay Hotels, Ltd. disappeared from the Hong Kong Companies Register on 3$^{rd}$ August 1951.

After 1949, the former Sassoon House reverted to its intended original function as an office building. Nevertheless, the ballroom, which was used as a dining hall by the Shanghai Municipal Finance and Economic Commission, still hosted Saturday night

*Tunisian visitors dancing in the ballroom, October 1957*                SMA

dances for local office employees. However, faced with an
increasing number of visiting delegations from the Soviet Union
and Eastern Europe, the Shanghai government decided to convert
the offices back into bedrooms and began re-equipping the
building as a hotel in late 1954.

The formal opening of the Peace Hotel, incorporating the old
Palace Hotel as its south wing, took place on 8th March 1956. Even
though the eighth floor grill-room had been converted into a
lounge and recreation area, there were five restaurants in operation
on the upper floors and the former Tower Night Club was
rechristened as the Nine Heavens Restaurant.

In the 1950s and 1960s the Peace Hotel received guests from
the Soviet Block, and friendship groups from Japan and other
Asian and European countries. They could hardly be described as
tourists. They were a select band of invited writers and artists,
sinologists, sports men and women, politicians and trade-
unionists. Although the billiard tables were back in action and the
hotel shop was stocked with fine arts and crafts at ridiculously
low prices, very little in the way of entertainment was offered.
Obligatory receptions and meetings, alongside outings to acrobatic
shows, operatic performances and kindergarten visits, were strictly
supervised by the Chinese host organisations.

China was proud to show off her achievements under
Communism. The Peace Hotel was one of only two Shanghai

*Nanjing Road entrance, 1990*

hotels permitted to receive such foreign envoys. There were around 80 employees when the hotel opened. Like his comrade colleagues, Mr. Kan, the head chef, viewed his work as political, offering his 'best service so as to encourage the most favourable response from visitors and foreign friends.' 'First-class' cooks, attendants and hairdressers were carefully scrutinised by the Public Security Bureau before being offered employment and most were obliged to learn Russian.

*Luggage sticker, 1980s*

Rarely more than half full, profit was viewed in cultural terms as the hotel was operated on a model of friendship rather than business. Visitors were treated as honoured guests, heaped with official hospitality and shown every courtesy. The guest experience was

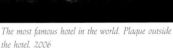

*The most famous hotel in the world. Plaque outside the hotel, 2006*

*Peace Hotel folder, 1980s*

carefully managed and local Chinese required a precious, special permit to gain entry to the hotel.

Whilst the number of visitors fell in the late 1950s, due largely to the hapless devastation of the Great Leap Forward, the number of Peace Hotel employees grew to around 250. In 1964 and 1965 there was a brief opening of China for Communist-sympathiser tourists and Sir Victor's former suite was on offer for a mere 20 yuan, or seven pounds sterling, a night. With the advent of the Cultural Revolution (1966–1976) there were even fewer guests, although staff numbers further increased to around 300. Those employees who were not sent out to the countryside were put on short hours, rolled through political and technical education and endured endless hours cleaning and re-cleaning the hotel. When the hotel became commercial again, under the aegis of the Jin Jiang Hotel Group following the opening of China to foreign tourists in 1978, it was a very pale shadow of its former self.

# THE SASSOON VISION

Born in Baghdad in 1792, David Sassoon, the family patriarch and head of the Mesopotamian Jewish community, fled to Bombay to escape religious persecution in 1832. David Sassoon & Co. Ltd. was essentially a banking institution, though it amassed much of its fortune in the highly lucrative opium trade to southern China. By the time of his death in 1864, David had assumed British citizenship and the House of Sassoon was amongst the most powerful in India. His son, Elias, arrived in China in 1844 and was one of the first merchants to commence trade with Shanghai. He purchased the site on which the north wing of the Peace Hotel now stands and, following his father's death, parted company with the family firm to found E. D. Sassoon & Company.

Elias Sassoon laid the foundation upon which his visionary grandson, Sir Elice Victor Sassoon, was to build a new Shanghai. Sir Victor finally took over the helm of the firm in 1924 and set about transferring his vast fortune from

*Sassoon House at the heart of the business district, 1935*

Eric Niderost

*Sir Victor at Doncaster, England, after winning the St. Leger Stakes in September 1960*

*Eve's, Sassoon's country villa built in 1933, photographed in 1991*

Bombay to Shanghai. His singular vision was to transform Shanghai into a modern cosmopolitan city with a spectacular new skyline. E. D. Sassoon & Company and its banking arm, with branches in Hong Kong, Bombay, Calcutta, Manchester and London, came to dominate the foreign commerce of pre-war Shanghai.

Sir Victor was educated at Harrow School and Trinity College, Cambridge. He was a regal eccentric. With his faintly Eastern appearance, monocle, and distinctive moustache he cut a dashing figure—exaggerated by his partial lameness as a result of a flying accident in the First World War. Victor had a famous passion for horses and built up the largest racing establishment in the Far East. He was reported to have quipped that 'there was only one greater race than the Jews and that was the Derby!' When not at 'Eve's', his rambling Tudor-styled villa in the Hongqiao district or at his hotel suite, Victor was most likely to be found in his private box at the Shanghai Race Club or playing golf at the club near his home.

Sir Victor entered the frame at a most opportune time as building construction in 1929 was forging ahead at unprecedented rates in all parts of the city. Land values were spiralling upwards making it necessary to build skywards to make returns on investments. Over 22,000 new buildings were constructed in 1929 alone, and

Eric Niderost

*Sir Victor Sassoon on holiday at Monte Carlo in August 1960*

many residents were no doubt regretting the loss of the old and expressing doubts over the rapid development of a high-rise city—in much the same way as in modern times. A 1930 census put the population of Shanghai at over 2.7 million, some 700,000 more than was popularly estimated, making it the world's sixth largest city.

Apart from the Cathay Hotel, which symbolised the modernity of 1930s Shanghai, Sassoon constructed two other huge, state-of-the-art hotels, as well as a multitude of apartment blocks, office buildings, theatres, stores and residences around the city. He purchased the influential Arnold & Co. as his vehicle to gain entry to the city, organised the Cathay Land Company, and controlled the Yangtsze Finance Company. From his office at his new headquarters in Sassoon House he saw property values more than treble during the first half of the 1930s.

However, the dream was to be short-lived. Sir Victor didn't make Shanghai his personal base until October 1931, and opportunely left the city just ten years later, months before the Japanese occupation. He didn't return after the Second World War apart from brief visits in December 1947 and April 1948 to divest some of his business interests. He stood as silent witness as his dreams were perverted and destroyed by the Japanese invasion, the dissolution of the International Settlement and the Communist takeover. The final downfall caused him to remark that 'I gave up on India and China gave me up.' In 1959 he married, and passed on his name and his wealth, to his Texan-born nurse and companion, Evelyn Barnes. He died, aged 80, in the Bahamas on 12th August 1961. Sir Victor Sassoon has left an indelible mark on the character of Shanghai, his name remains familiar, and his legacy lives on in the magnificent architecture of the city.

# THE JOURNEY TO THE CATHAY TOWER

*Eighth floor window overlooking the Huangpu River, 1990*

Situated at one of the busiest intersections in Shanghai, the Cathay Hotel provided a peaceful haven from the rush and heat of city life. Most of the hotel's facilities were situated on the upper floors of the building, distancing guests from the hectic street activity below. The calmness and dignity of the Cathay was reflected in its décor and furnishings. No gaudy colours, no heavy mouldings or coarse ornaments, just quiet unobtrusive luxury, marble, bronze, velvet and tapestry.

Originally there were four entrances to the ground floor lounge. It could be reached from East Nanjing Road, Dianchi Road and from the adjoining shopping arcades, as well as from its stately Bund entrance.

The Sassoon House shopping centre originally housed a series of mosaic-floored arcades with 20 shops that was dubbed 'Shanghai's Bond Street and Burlington Arcade under one roof.' At the intersection of the arcades was a great rotunda, covered with a metal and glass

*Vestibule near the original entrance to the arcades from the hotel lobby, 1978*

and georgette handkerchiefs with lace appliqués. There were also two banks—one being the Netherlands Trading Society, which was the first foreign bank to return to the Bund, and to the hotel, in its modern guise of ABN Amro in the early 1990s.

The large and impressive glass rotunda above where the arcades used to meet has survived, even if it is hidden in a modern shopping centre, with an entrance just to the north of the main hotel entrance at 24 East Nanjing Road. The north arcade is still open at 30 East Nanjing Road, running all the way through to Dianchi Road, although its glamour has long gone.

The principal and most imposing entrance was from the Bund where, on entering, guests would be instantly exposed to the gallant splendour of the hotel.

roof. The 'shops deluxe' had huge frontages of marble, bronze, plate glass and electro-glazing. The owners of Shanghai's most prestigious emporia vied for prime space. One could shop for Lalique glass, Rolex watches or pore over the most fashionable and expensive dresses in town at an outlet owned by a flamboyant White Russian, Madame Garnet. Visiting tourists would throng to Gray's Yellow Lantern Shop with its charming collection of lingerie, linens, sports clothes and curios, including silver swizzle sticks with jade handles

*Where the arcades used to meet, 1930*

The entrance hall, with its richly coloured coffered ceiling and marble walls led to a black marble staircase with a heavy bronze balustrade. On the first landing two stained-glass panels, one depicting industry and commerce, the other agriculture, sat either side of a huge central panel depicting East and West. Many fittings in this hall remain intact, including the original Scottish rose-mottled marble, although the central window panel has been lost.

*Artist's impression of the new arcade and rotunda, 1925*

The stairs led up to the three office floors of Sassoon House. Most of the third floor was occupied by E. D. Sassoon & Co. Ltd. and their associate firm, Arnhold & Co. Ltd. The front part of the fourth floor was let to the American Women's Club as club premises with accommodation attached.

Passing under the stairs the inner corridor lounge was subtly lit through magnificent stained-glass ceiling panels, which were unfortunately replaced, rather than restored, in the 1990s. The corridor used to be lined with palms and small tables for cocktails in the 1930s. Above the marble walls colourful paintings depicting the industries of all nations stretched along the corridor. Like the paintings in the adjoining lounge, they disappeared long ago, whilst the beautiful

*The hotel tower, 1990*

*The Bund entrance hall in the 1930s (left) and in 1990 (above)*

original marble facing was torn out in the 1990s.

Light grey and rose-mottled marble panels, edged by dove grey marble strips once encased the main lounge and lobby area giving it an air of dignity usually associated with the very best of European and American hotels. Arising from the marble panels there were depictions of imaginary cities in various architectural styles. Furnishing clothed in tapestry picked out colours from the marble floors, the ceiling and from the royal blue velvet curtains. The balcony in the lobby over the current reception desk was reserved for ladies, whilst opposite there was a barber's to the rear of the gentleman's balcony. The central balcony above the clock on the Dianchi Road entrance was reserved for one of the Cathay's three resident orchestras. Joseph Ullstein's Concert Orchestra performed classical selections daily to accompany the Thé Dansant and the Dinner Dansant in the lounge. Incidentally, the marble around the entrance is still the original.

Ullstein's orchestra countered the prevalent Shanghai jazz mood of the early 1930s, which is today back in fashion in the adjoining bar. The inimitable, almost octogenarian, Peace Hotel Jazz Band was still performing pre-war swing on a regular basis in 2007. The Tudor-styled Cathay Bar used to open on to the arcades behind and was used as a storeroom for hotel furniture in the 1980s.

*Surviving stained-glass windows at the top of the entrance hall stairs*

The fourth to seventh floors were devoted to 214 hotel rooms and suites. The intricate attention given to the décor and colour scheme did not halt at the ground floor. Each floor had its own colour scheme, carpets, curtains and bed covers. Buff, brown and green carpets layered the softly lit, stone-walled corridors punctuated by walnut doors.

There were originally nine 'suites deluxe' depicting a variety of national and historical styles. There were two English suites, one in old English style and one Georgian in style. The former had oak-panelled walls, stone and brick fireplaces and model plaster ceilings. The Georgian suite, with panelled walls finished in cream, had a handsome brass hob grate. The Indian suite, with filigree plaster work on the walls and ceilings, was littered with rich coloured Indian carpets. Reputable Chinese and Japanese craftsmen were employed to ensure that the suites accredited to their respective countries were resplendent to the finest detail. A moon gate separated the sitting room and dining room of the Chinese suite, with an Imperial dragon design on the ruddy red ceiling complemented by red lacquer furniture, and offset by gold-coloured walls.

*Detail of the entrance hall's bronze stair balustrade*

*The balconies adjoining the lounge, 1930s*

Peace Hotel

*Lounge light, 1990*

The Japanese suite had a sitting and dining room of natural wood with plaster panels, some treated with gold leaf. Two modern French suites exemplified a style currently fashionable in both Europe and America, whilst an ultramodern suite paraded a lifestyle of the future. Each suite had two luxurious bathrooms with purified spring water from the Bubbling Well flowing from silver taps into vast marble baths. The hotel still has nine suites and many original features are still evident in the British, Indian and Chinese suites, whilst some of the others have been converted to reflect other national styles, including German, American, Spanish and Italian.

As it is today, the eighth floor was the main area for relaxation and pleasure. Emerging from the lift the visitor crossed a landing speckled with Lalique glass into an upper lounge that overlooked the Huangpu River and Nanjing Road. Inside, Lalique figures set in niches, and wall plaques in opalescent

*Ground floor lounge, 1930s*

Peace Hotel

glass, softly illuminated the dull silver and gold room. To the left of the lounge a stunning reading and writing room, lined with bird's-eye maple and teak, was illuminated by Lalique ceiling fittings composed of many sections held together by silver rings.

The entire frontage of the eighth floor facing the Bund, including these rooms, was entirely remodelled in 1933 to make way for the new Cathay grill-room—an architectural extravaganza in purely Chinese style. The grill-room, which was originally known as the Peking Room, and is now known as the Dragon-Phoenix Hall, retains many of its original decorative features. This was where foreign, predominantly American, tourists were escorted to take in China over 'tiffin' (an Indian term for a light meal or lunch). The room embraced a treasure-laden vision of China in a comfortable air-conditioned environment. Carrard, the hotel manager, worked closely with Palmer and Turner in modelling the new grill-room. Based on designs from Beijing's temples and palaces, the architects decided to create an attraction that was 'pure and true to Chinese tradition.'

Indeed, it wasn't long before the hoteliers of the world came to the Cathay Hotel in search of inspiration. Major Black of the Grosvenor House in London, the largest luxury hotel in the British Empire, was particularly impressed by the hotel on his 1934 visit. He wished to recreate

*Peace Hotel bar, 1990s*

*The murals that once adorned the ground floor lounge*

the grill-room in London, but conceded that without the cheerful Chinese waiters it would lose a great deal of its charm.

The dragon assumes a central position in the design of the restaurant's ceiling panels. Being the chief figure of Chinese mythology, with an ability to control the rains (symbolising peace and prosperity) and a power to rise from earth to heaven, the dragon came to represent the Emperor. The Empress is symbolised in the design through the figure of a phoenix. These figures, surrounded by rain clouds, are arranged around a flaming pearl—a symbol of perfection.

Towards the outer edge of the rain clouds, a bat enters the design, typifying happiness and luck. The ceiling panels were adopted from door panels of the Hall of Blending the Great Creative Forces in Beijing's Forbidden City.

The beams and metal grille-work are decorated with the conventionalised lotus—daughter of the rains, and the sacred flower of Buddhism—a symbol of Buddhist paradise. Features on the beams were also taken from the Forbidden City, namely the Palace of Heavenly Purity and the Gate of Supreme Harmony, as well as from the Temple of Heaven. The motif found on the

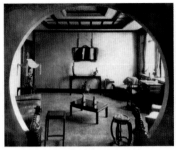  

*The original suites (from left to right): Chinese, Jacobean, Indian and Japanese*

columns was taken from a western gallery in the Forbidden City.

The latticed grilles over the windows incorporate the characters of long life and happiness in their many conventionalised forms and were adapted from a grille in the Yi-Yuen Hall, again in the Forbidden City. The air-duct grilles are based on the characters for longevity and the 'endless knot'—one of the eight Buddhist emblems of happy

*The Chinese suite, 1991*

augury. All of the decorative plaster and metal work was executed by one of Shanghai's most famous sculptors, Mr. W. W. Wagstaff. Wagstaff would soon after cast the second pair of bronze lions to be placed outside of the Hongkong and Shanghai Bank's headquarters in Hong Kong. His son's paintings of a Yangtsze village, the Great Wall and Hong Kong on the west wall of the room have long since disappeared.

The Peace Hotel did not suffer at the hands of the Red Guards during the Cultural Revolution and the survival of the dragon and phoenix designs can be put down to a band of loyal

Peace Hotel

*The eighth floor reading and writing room before it was converted into the Peking Room in 1933*

*The Jacobean suite, 1980s*

*The Indian suite, with its filigree ceiling intact, 1980s*

Many original Lalique wall plaques, and some replicas with flat surfaces, adorn the adjoining mirrored corridor leading on to the ballroom.

The ballroom was regarded as among the most beautiful on Earth. It was decorated with rose-tinted curtains and carpets splashed with gold, dull silver and gold walls, white birch furniture, a white maple dance floor and a liberal show of Lalique lighting. From the Lalique studio, ten individually sculpted, draped female figures in glass, the Ladies of the Fountain, were set in niches and illuminated while numerous ceiling lights, sparrow wall plaques and half-bowls graced the lofty hall. A dining room occupied the south facing part of the ballroom and opened on to three terraces. The ballroom itself underwent a series of facelifts and transformations in

hotel staff who concealed them by constructing a plain, false ceiling below. Similar designs at the only other such room in town at the Pacific Hotel on today's People's Square, which were created in 1940, were destroyed.

The restaurant used to open, to the west, on to a large lounge in a similar style. The room has been converted into a Western dining room in modern times, but displays an array of original Lalique wall plaques and maintains a period ambience.

*Lalique plaque featuring sparrows on the eighth floor*

*Surviving decorative grille-work*

the 1930s. In 1931 the dance floor was moved to the middle of the room and given a new oval shape, and a terrace facing the Nanjing Road was opened containing a small cocktail bar. The ballroom was redecorated and further remodelled in 1935.

The ballroom's main illumination was by indirect lighting through rose-tinted fanlight panels adorned with a pair of the hotel's emblematic greyhounds, which still survive but are rarely used. Special dimmers were used to regulate subtle colour changes—one colour melting into another to produce effects of sunrise and sunset, blazing daylight and moonlight. Other lighting was concealed in the cornices and

pyramidal glass lanterns were mounted in the ceiling. Incongruous, gaudy glass chandeliers, which appear to occupy so many hotel ballrooms and lobbies around town regardless of period or style, were added in the 1980s.

*Advertisement, 1936*

*The Dragon and Phoenix Room ceiling, 1991*

*Period features, including a Lalique glass door panel, found on the ninth floor of the hotel, 1990*

Ascending to the ninth floor visitors were transported to another fairy-tale palace, this time in a Chinese style. On the wall of the staircase landing a large Chinese landscape painting was brushed with light from butterfly-patterned lights of Korean design and an illuminated Lalique golden carp. Ahead, two blackwood doors, each set with circular Lalique glass panels with a gold fish design, which still remain, opened on to the Chinese styled Tower Restaurant. The restaurant was richly decorated in green and gold relieved by black and red lacquer, with gilded panels of Chinese carving set in

the pilasters and piers. The restaurant's coffered ceiling, incorporating symbols of good augury and good luck, was painted by Chinese temple artists. Antique bronze Buddhas and yet another Lalique illuminated golden carp crowned the hoard of treasures. Bold inscriptions in Chinese characters appeared on three vermilion boards:

*The hall is filled with
honourable guests*

*As the fish loves water
so love I pleasure*

*Fine wines from
the four seasons*

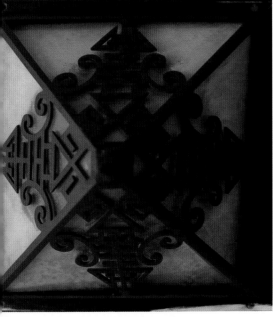

The Tower was the place for curry luncheon in the early 1930s, but was transformed into the Tower Night Club, Shanghai's most chic and fashionable night spot in 1935. Today its riches have been lost and it largely plays host to government functions.

Climbing again, the upper floors of the Cathay Hotel tower were of a demonstratively English character taking visitors back to the best period of English medieval architecture. The tenth floor Jacobean-styled banqueting hall, with its modelled ceiling,

*The lounge that used to link the Chinese restaurant to the ballroom, photographed in 1978. It was converted into the Peace Grill in the early 1990s*

*The ballroom, 1934*

carved panelling and mammoth mantelpiece, has recently been erroneously rechristened as the 'Sassoon Room.' The eleventh floor above was originally a series of private dining rooms, but, following Sassoon's 1931 full-time move to Shanghai, it was there that he kept his personal suite. In recent times its original interior

hosted karaoke parties and banquets. However, in the short-lived belief that the banking fraternity would return to the Bund it was ignobly knocked apart, piece by piece, in 1995 to create a 'banker's club.' Unfortunately, the bankers didn't return.

*The Tower Restaurant, early 1930s*

*The former Tower Night Club, now a function room, 1991*

*Sassoon's former suite used as a karaoke lounge, 1993*

# BALLROOM REVIVAL—THE CHINA COAST BALL AT THE PEACE HOTEL

When the Mandarin Oriental took over the classic Hotel Bela Vista in Macau in 1990, Ted Marr, the inimitable Hong Kong-based Australian lawyer and socialite, was forced to look for a new venue for the society ball he had hitherto organised amidst its colonial splendour. His thoughts drifted northwards to Shanghai and to the Peace Hotel. He'd never been to Shanghai before but he knew, 'as everybody did,' about the Peace Hotel as the 'de facto poste-restante for European backpackers.' It was with some sentimentality that he took to the seas on the *Jin Jiang* bound for Shanghai in August 1990. The ship, formerly the *SS Mariposa*, used to carry Australians of his parent's generation on their way to Europe by way of the US overland route, and it was also the well-known namesake of the state-run group who owned the Peace Hotel.

Ted checked in at the newly opened Portman Shangri-La before heading down to the waterfront and his first foretaste of the Peace Hotel. He strolled in and announced 'look I'm from Hong Kong and I want to do a party for 500 people here...and they looked at me quite strangely, because no one had ever said those words in their living memory.' The timing and delivery of his request couldn't have been better. Shanghai was freshly open for business again and the hotel's executives were eager to indulge in their new-found sense of importance. It was the beginning of a relationship that would extend over nine years and bear deliverance of three humungous parties—in 1991, 1992 and 1997, as well as several smaller ones—the likes of which the city had been starved of for almost a lifetime.

The management preferred to chew over Ted's proposals in what they believed to be the most fitting venue—that of the old Tudor bar on the ground floor of the hotel. Ted recalls his parleys over a beer and peanuts 'sitting almost cold and shivering

*'Shanghai-Yaaah!' Cover of the* South China Morning Post *magazine, 24th March 1991*

in the middle of the day in the thick darkness' of its stone-clad confines. The management's response, however, was much warmer in tone and from their first nibble they 'liked the idea though they didn't know what it was going to be.' But, the order for the go-ahead had to come from the lips of the city mayor himself.

Ted 'found ways of doing things' in his dealings with the veteran architects of diplomacy and was forthright in his desire to set a precedent in bringing foreign entertainers up to Shanghai for the party. Cutely, he had introduced the idea by suggesting that 'some of the people in the group would provide entertainment for the others...almost like someone getting up at a wedding and singing something.' The entertainers he had in mind were referred to as 'the special Australian dancers who were members of our group' and Ted saw no need to complicate matters by seeking any special permission. The term 'special dancers' soon became a matter of common parlance, as if everybody knew what they were, though nobody really thought to ask. The first clue as to just what Shanghai was letting itself in for came at the airport 'when three boys turned up from Sydney with their bags stuffed with frocks, wigs and

*Popular Shanghai dancer, Nellie Farren,
photographed in 1929*

false boobs.' Officials quizzing over what was, no doubt, their first ever sighting of such bulbous prosthetics were informed that they were plain old shoulder pads!

It wasn't until the rehearsals, in 'civvies', on the day of the ball that anybody had an inkling as to what was in store. The event was such a sell-out affair that Ted had commandeered the whole of the eighth floor, and in one room a traditional Chinese ensemble, which 'everybody hated,' played a dull prelude to a phenomenal finale. Just as the drag queens had got fully kitted up, photographer David Thurston took them downstairs and immortalised their presence on the Bund. His sensational picture was splashed on the cover of Hong Kong's *South China Morning Post* magazine. Ted went downstairs to witness a 'mob thing going on as hundreds and hundreds of people appeared out of nowhere.' The ball itself wound up in a more solemn and typically Chinese fashion with a series of speeches on China's opening up to the outside world—and wow, what a flamboyant opening it proved to be. By the time of the next ball the management had become very blasé about the whole affair and they, and particularly their old-time staff, recognised that the days of glitz, glamour and cabaret were right back where they belonged.

*From an interview with
Ted Marr*

# LIGHTS ON BROADWAY

SHANGHAI    CHINA

*1930s luggage label*

The 19-storey Broadway Mansions, along with the Park Hotel, were the tallest buildings in the city when they opened in 1934. Situated at the crossroads of the Suzhou Creek, with its south-facing aspect taking in a full panorama of the Bund, the building had an eye on contemporary needs, as well as those of the future. Although principally a high-quality apartment block, it was partly run on the lines of a hotel as its luxury apartments, containing up to seven suites, came fully fitted and fully serviced. With the needs of the young, single professional in mind, 99 apartments were laid out as 'bachelor pads' comprising a sitting room with a fold-up bed,

*Broadway Mansions and the Garden Bridge, 1935*

*Curvaceous concept drawing of the building, December 1931*

The fifth floor dining room, with a colour scheme of shades of tan and gold chairs with brown leather upholstery, spread across the whole of the building's frontage. When the adjoining lounge was moved down to the

*Mr. Bright Fraser*

which fitted into a recess in the wall, and a luxuriously appointed bathroom of cream porcelain with a dressing room attached. The bathrooms in the larger suites came in a range of colours. The building was owned by the Shanghai Land and Investment Company and, whilst Palmer and Turner acted as consulting architects, Mr. Bright Fraser, from Liverpool, carried out the work on the building. Fraser came to Shanghai in 1922 to work for Atkinson & Dallas before taking up the post of chief architect of the Shanghai Land and Investment Company in 1926.

ground floor in time for Christmas 1935, the vacated space was converted into extra bedrooms. The new lounge's strident modernist blue and gold colour scheme was relieved by the intricate patterns displayed on a scatter of Persian rugs. A four-storey structure at the back of the building, which is largely used today as offices, was originally Shanghai's most modern car park with places for 163 cars. Ramps allowed vehicles to be driven into their lock-ups and a lift was installed to convey drivers up and down.

Strengthening the Japanese stranglehold in the Hongkou district, Broadway Mansions was sold in 1939 to the Shanghai Real Estate Company, a subsidiary of the Japanese Central Development Company. The deal was the single largest property transaction in Shanghai's history. The Japanese flag was raised on the building just 45 minutes after a cheque for $5,100,000 was handed over on the morning of 28th March.

After 1945, the lower nine floors of the building were occupied by the US Military Advisory Group. In keeping with the tradition established before the war when Hallett Abend of *The New York Times* had occupied a huge 15th floor apartment, six upper floors of the building were taken over by members of the foreign press corps and the headquarters of the Foreign Correspondents Club of China was based there. Abend

*Aerial view, 1935*

*Broadway Mansions, 1990s*

of the *North China Daily News*, occupied part of the penthouse. The journalists had the perfect vantage point to report on the events of May 1949 as the Communist forces fought, and eventually claimed victory, on the Bund. The building was renamed on May Day 1951 and equipped with a new neon sign, *Shanghai Mansions*, to announce its new identity. The hotel, 'modernised' like most others, continues to operate and has even adopted its original name, although the only form of neon now to be seen is that of a sign of the times—a huge advertising emblem on its rooftop.

*Broadway Mansions, 2006*

had reluctantly vacated his apartment and returned to the US in late 1941, amidst official concerns for his life following an incident there when he was brutally attacked by Japanese agents. He feared that he might have been thrown to his death, 16 floors below. After the Japanese surrender, George Vine, the British assistant editor

# №. 23 **The Bank of China**

The Bank of China had occupied the former premises of the Club Concordia, or German Club, for over 12 years before they decided to build anew on the site. With China's announcement of war with Germany diplomatic ties between the two countries were severed and German extraterritorial rights were renounced in March 1917. The life of the gingerbread-like club building, which had long been a playground for Anglo-Saxon camaraderie, where nationality was a matter of circumstance, came to an abrupt end on the sunny afternoon of 17th August 1917. Just before 5.00 p.m. a posse from the Shanghai Municipal Police, under the charge of Captain Edward Ivo Medhurst Barrett, surrounded the building. Irish-born Inspector Bourke and Mr. S. K. Chen from the Bureau of Foreign Affairs entered the club to inform its members that it was time to drink up for the last time. The Germans were allowed to finish their last drink in peace and one

*The Club Concordia, 1908*

requested that the Inspector join them for old time's sake. He was reported to have replied that 'I've had many a one with you at the Recreation Club, and it's my sincere hope that we'll have more together when this damned war is over, but today, excuse me, for I'm on duty and if it was reported that I'd had a drink with you, I'd be sure to get into trouble.' The Germans shook the hand of the officer in understanding, drank up and burst into an impromptu rendition of *Deutschland, Deutschland Uber Alles* as they abandoned their past haunt. The club's residents were allowed a further eight days to vacate the building.

*Club Concordia bar*

Despite its new Chinese ownership, some of the foreign community made calls for it to be reopened as some form of club, perhaps for the enjoyment of the Allies, or as a cultural centre. Others pointed out that Shanghai was primarily a place for making money rather than merrymaking and that the building should be put to commercial use. In the end, the Bank of China took over control of the property in 1920, and, following extensive renovations, opened their offices there on the 20th February 1923. They also erected a new building, next door on Dianchi Road, which was used as a vault capable of storing 80 million dollars worth of silver. Atkinson & Dallas presided over the building work.

The Club Concordia was founded in 1865 and work on its new Bund premises, to the designs of Heinrich Becker, began in 1904. Unlike the Shanghai Club, the palatial Club Concordia, which opened in February 1907, was not averse to boisterous entertainment on its premises. Initiated in 1910, the club's annual masquerade ball soon became the greatest event in Shanghai's social calendar. The club found its way into the record books in 1913 when a capacity crowd of 1,000 party-going masqueraders consumed 1,010 bottles of champagne.

*Original design for the Bank of China*

The Bank of China had little to celebrate over its attempt to get into the record books. The definition and execution of the plans for one of the Far East's most costly and ambitious buildings were to be fraught with difficulties. By late 1934 initial plans to build a 33-storey, 380-foot skyscraper, 11 storeys higher than the monumental Park Hotel which had just been completed, were scrapped. A new scheme, featuring twin towers reaching up 24 storeys on the Bund and 26 storeys on Dianchi Road, was proposed but in the end a building of much more modest stature actually materialised. Even though the completed building was 17 storeys high, it still fell one foot short of Sassoon House next door.

The precise reasons for the drastic reduction in the building's height remain shrouded in mystery. It is still popularly believed that Sir Victor Sassoon had a large part to play in dwarfing the Nationalist government's landmark edifice. The Peace Hotel, the present occupiers of part of the old Sassoon House, even retold the story in a 2004 edition of their newsletter. They quoted 'Crippled Sassoon' as saying 'here is the British Concession and any house built next to my building is not allowed to be higher.' The story goes on to say that the SMC refused the building's plans on technical grounds as they would have caused damage to the neighbouring buildings. Sassoon, albeit indirectly, certainly had influence within the upper realms of governance in the form of H. E. Arnhold, a director of his Cathay Hotels Company and Chairman of the SMC at the time. Moreover, Sassoon owned Arnhold's company and they acted as general managers for Cathay Hotels, Ltd. Sassoon also had the ear of the Minister of Finance, H. H. Kung, who personally awarded Sir Victor with a 'Gold Medal of the First Class' for his charitable work in 1935.

Whilst Sassoon may have had some influence, it is more than likely that greater events, further afield, had more impact. Shanghai's armour had been punctured by the effects of the Great Depression and by the adoption of the silver standard by the US in 1933. Silver flooded out of China and reserves in Shanghai fell by half. That, combined with extravagant military expenditure to suppress an increasing Communist threat, resulted in a series of political manoeuvres, engineered by H. H. Kung, culminating in the nationalisation of the Bank of China in 1935. Its new board of directors included the financial genius, Song Ziwen (T. V. Soong) and the infamous Green Gang boss, Du Yuesheng—widely known as 'big-eared' Du.

*Du Yuesheng*

Work on the building, which was designed by Tug Wilson of Palmer and Turner and Mr. H. S. Luke (Lu Qianshou), a British-trained Chinese architect who worked for the bank, commenced following the demolition of the former club building in November 1935. By February 1936, 2,000 Oregon pine piles had been driven into the soil to the great annoyance of guests of the neighbouring Cathay Hotel. The piles, which were up to 100 feet in length, required up to 3,000 blows

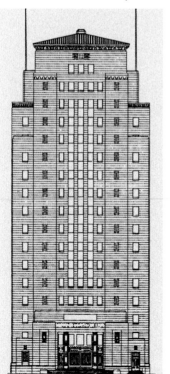

from a three-ton steam hammer to set them in place. It was anticipated that the building would take just 18 months to complete.

Even though the foundation work on the building had not been completed, an elaborate ceremony for laying the foundation stone took place on the requisite and auspicious date of 10th October 1936—the 'Double Tenth' and the silver jubilee of the founding of the Republic of China. The chairman of the board of directors, Song Ziwen, presided over the affair. The new building was designed to be a symbol of progress, as well as stability. Song remarked that 'our board of directors has adopted as a keynote of the new building practical utility combined with dignity without

*Revised elevation for the building*

ostentation.' Tug Wilson handed over a silver trowel to start the proceedings and H. S. Luke handed Madame Song a bronze casket containing newspapers of the day, plans of the building, and an assortment of items, including bank notes and a photo of the Bund, to be placed under the stone. The stone, with its mutilated Chinese inscription, which is to be found on the southernmost front of the building, is one of only two such memorials to survive on the Bund today (see page 152).

*Pile driving operations, December 1935* SMA

*The surviving foundation stone*

*Song Ziwen*

With its modern face of Suzhou granite embellished with motifs representing longevity, the building was to rise to a height of 277 feet, to stretch along Dianchi Road for 550 feet and to weigh a mammoth 70,000 tons. 'Chromador Steel,' known for its properties of strength and lightness and manufactured by Dorman, Long & Co. of Middlesbrough in England, provided the backbone for the structure. The bank's premises were to be fully air-conditioned and 13 elevators were to be installed. It was planned to house the bank's departments on the second and third floors, and the fourth floor was to be set up as a welfare centre for its employees to include dining rooms, lounges and a large lecture room. The remainder of the building was to be leased out. Huge vaults were to extend through the larger part of the basement, in which the first underground car park to be installed in any building along the Bund was also located. The bank's American-made vault door, weighing over 30 tons, was installed in June 1937. Lined with costly marble from floor to ceiling the bank's main, 25-foot-high, hall was to be found on the ground floor. The dignified, original Italian marble was ignobly cast aside in favour of the new during the bank's renovation in 2006. However, the original marble-lined entrance hall has thankfully been saved.

In 1935, when construction work got underway, the bank moved back into its former premises at nearby 50 Hankou Road. The Bank of China, which had succeeded the Ta Ching Bank after the 1911 Revolution, had previously established their offices there in February 1912.

Most sources record that the building was completed, or at least 'flattened off,' by the end of 1937, and the *Shanghai Sunday Times* noted that the bank was 'practically complete' in December of that year. One year later, however, they reported that 'the bank still stood in a state of semi-completion' and that work was 'progressing slowly.' It was anticipated that the bank building would be finally completed in 1939. However, it wasn't to be, as new priorities forced by the Sino-Japanese War had left the building in a state of limbo. Moreover, any suppositions and fears over the damage that the weight of the building might cause proved to be well-founded, as the roads around the building had actually sunk. The SMC

*Model of the new bank building, 1936*

P&T Group

*The completed building, undated source*

sent the bank a costly repair bill in August 1938. Palmer and Turner, who replied on the bank's behalf, suggested that the road work be postponed as 'the building is still in an unfinished state and likely to be so for some time.'

And it was for some time, with the *North China Daily News* reporting in November 1940 that the bank building was the only one to be 'unmolested' on the Bund and that its construction still hadn't been completed. Under the Japanese puppet government based in Nanjing, led by Wang Jingwei, the Bank of China was allowed to resume operations under the direction of the reformed Central Bank of China in 1942. In September, the Bank of China reopened its office in Shanghai—again in their old premises and not on the Bund. The Bank of China officially records that the building, or at least part of it, was first occupied in 1941 by the new regime's reserve bank and that they did not actually move into their building until early 1946—some ten years after they had moved from the Bund.

One of the most notorious episodes in the bank's history took place in May 1949 when the Nationalist government emptied the bank's vaults of its currency and gold reserves, and shipped them to Taiwan on the eve of the Communist victory. George Vine, assistant editor of the *North China Daily News*, watched from his suite at Broadway Mansions as 'all the gold in China was being carried away in the traditional manner—by coolies.'

# No. 24 The Yokohama Specie Bank

This Japanese bank's Shanghai branch, which opened in 1893, had two former homes on the Bund before settling on the site of the former David Sassoon Building in 1911. The foundation stone of the present bank building was laid on 11th February 1923 by its president, Mr. Penji Kodama, and it was formally opened in July 1924 by its general manager, Mr. Gengo Hashidzume. The Yokohama Specie Bank was an extremely important institution as the major portion of Japan's trade to China was transacted through its doors. The bank earned a reputation as 'the listening bank' of its time, without whose help thousands of businesses would not have got off the ground.

*The ICBC building, 2006*

Even though Palmer and Turner's Tug Wilson listed the bank as one of his buildings, much of the design work was undertaken by his colleague, Frank Collard. Collard carefully crafted and successfully adapted many Japanese features to his general neo-Grecian exterior design. Remarkably, some have survived. The building is one of the few along the Bund, and certainly the most illustrative, to exhibit evidence of the vandalism that destroyed so much beautiful statuary and decorative adornment that once graced its buildings.

The most striking examples can be found on the keystones above the building's two ground floor windows. The original, sculpted granite heads, although severely disfigured, are still in place. When the bank opened, a commentator, on seeing the downcast eyes of the figures, remarked that they may 'seem to

*The Yokohama Specie Bank, shortly after its completion*

*One of the granite keystones which was carved in Shanghai, as it was and as it appears today*

echo the placidity of Buddha but which mayhap express only the calm resignation of the modern banker!' The features of similar figures, wearing helmets originally found on the fluted capitals of the two classic Iconic columns running up the centre of the building, have been completely erased, though evidence of their existence still remains. No such evidence is left above the oriel windows to the sides of the building on the first floor where beautifully sculpted copper canopies used to rest.

*Main banking hall, 1920s*

Although the vast, black iron entrance gates set in bronze and cast by Critall-Freeman Bronze of London are still in place, their three magnificent central panels have been replaced. The original bronze panels depicted the mask and arms of the ancient Japanese warrior as guardians of the institution, and had a rather 'Viking' appearance. Two small replicas of the originals have been recently recreated in a small lobby off the north side of the entrance hall. The pair of lamp standards outside the bank today are poor replicas of the originals, which featured finely cast figures modelling ancient Egyptian and

*The original entrance gates alongside those of the present-day, showing where the Japanese warrior panels have been replaced*

contemporary Taiwanese aboriginal costumes. It is little surprise that the new lamps feature four, more appropriate, to the Chinese mind, nude Herculean figures in their place.

The other major change to the outward decoration of the building is on the crest where the original shell-shaped, bronze backdrop, adorned with the Japanese sunburst, flanked by an Imperial Phoenix on each side, has been modified to a plain design.

Inside the bank the main hall differed from many others of its time in that it had few traces of grille-work or ornamental brass. Most of the business was conducted over open, broad, polished hardwood counters punctuated by large square columns of variegated marble. The original grey and white veined marble which was shipped in from England has been totally replaced in the banking hall, but some remnants are to be found in the entrance hall. The sculpted, black bronze caps on the marble columns are now painted over in glitzy gold. Many original motifs on the ceiling have survived, as does the central feature of a domed light by the British Luxfer Prism Syndicate. The company also produced a similar ceiling feature for the Hongkong and Shanghai Bank. British manufacturers figured largely in the building although the protective carborundum blocks covering the vaults were made in the great electric furnaces at Niagara Falls.

# No. 26 The Yangtsze Insurance Association Building

Sir Havilland de Sausmarez, an official of the British Supreme Court in Shanghai, who presided over the formal opening of the building on 29th April 1918, commented that the 'wonderful' new building reflected the giant strength of the Yangtsze Insurance Association which had 'piled storey on storey until on a rainy day the top of the building is lost in the mists of Shanghai.' The company was founded in 1862 by the American firm of Russell & Co. to insure the cargoes and boats of its Shanghai Steam Navigation Company (see page 123). It was reorganised as an independent concern, with a board composed largely of British directors, after the collapse of Russell & Co. in 1891. The Yangtsze Insurance Association's Renaissance-style, seven-storey building, faced with specially imported grey Japanese granite, was designed by Tug Wilson and E. Forbes Bothwell of Palmer and Turner.

*Architect's drawing, 1916*

Apart from the entrance hall, the ground floor was especially designed for the Mercantile Bank of India, which had opened its offices there in March 1918. The bank was originally formed as the Chartered Mercantile Bank and had established premises on the Bund in the 1850s. The new bank was founded in 1917, following a long period of closure during which its affairs were maintained by Jardine, Matheson & Co.

The Insurance Association's entrance hall to the southeast of the building was lined from floor to ceiling with marble and had a

*The present home of the Agricultural Bank of China lists heavily to the left*

*The company's former premises in 1908*    *The Yangtsze Insurance Building, 1918*

white marble balcony halfway up, to their general offices on the
first floor. The general manager's room and boardroom were
located on the second and third floors, whilst the rest of the
building was let out as apartments. The Senior British Naval
Officer kept his office on the fourth floor. Each of the two upper
floors provided an expansive single residence for the bank's
directors, with a roof garden above at a height of 115 feet.

The Union Insurance Society of Canton, which was amalgamated
with the Yangtsze Insurance Association in 1926, transferred its
offices from No. 3 the Bund to No. 26 in 1935. In the late 1930s
the Danish Consulate and the Italian Chamber of Commerce had
premises in the building. Presently occupied by the China
Everbright Bank, the main banking hall is lined with crudely
sculpted Romanesque friezes and the building itself is
conspicuously leaning from the vertical. However, the original
heraldic carvings above the central first floor window outside the
building have survived, although the Yangtsze Insurance
Association's seal in the centre has been obliterated. Granite
brackets, which were carved to represent the bows of a Viking
ship, are also still to be found flanking the lintels over the two
entrances to the building.

# No. 27 The EWO Building

It was justly fitting that Jardine, Matheson & Company were the first to register a building lot on the Bund in 1843. Their first premises on the Bund were completed in 1851. Opium trader and partner William Jardine, known as the 'iron-headed rat,' who died in that year, had been instrumental in influencing the British government to launch the First Opium War. The Jardine interests,

*EWO's 19th century premises*

however, grew to encompass much more than trading activity. They acted as joint agents for the development of railways in China until 1911, and amongst other activities founded enormous cotton mills, developed extensive shipping interests, established an engineering corporation and pioneered cold storage facilities in the city. Arguably the finest beer in Asia, using imported hops, flowed from their EWO Brewery, founded in 1935. Whilst Jardines were best known by their Chinese hong name of EWO, meaning happy harmony, they were known to the Scottish in China as the 'Muckle House' (muckle signifying greatness).

The Rev. C. E. Darwent, in the second edition of his Shanghai handbook (1920), estimated that the cost of the land on which the company's first building was completed in 1851 had risen phenomenally from £500 to £1,000,000 in 1900. The original plans for a new building, which were drawn up in London at great expense, were rejected by Mr. John Johnstone, long-term general

Advertisement, 1930s

manager of the firm in Shanghai and Hong Kong, as being unattractive and unsuitable. In the end, the design work fell to Mr. A. W. Graham Brown of local architects Stewardson & Spence. Work on the modern, Renaissance-style, five-storey building began in early 1920 and was completed in November 1922. The reinforced concrete structure, faced with granite, was designed to permit the addition of an extra storey, which was added at a later date. As was a common practice of the time, the servants' quarters were placed over the garages at the back of the building and the offices themselves had separate stairs and toilet facilities for Chinese workers.

Continuing its traditional worldwide trade in tea and silk, a specially designed silk room, with exceptional lighting, was created for its silk inspectors who were usually of Swiss or Italian descent. Inside the main entrance at the centre of the Bund

*Artist's impression of the building, 1920*

*EWO Building, mid-1920s*

*The building in 2006*

frontage, two boards, which used to list the buildings' occupants have been wiped clean, but remain as a reminder of the past. Although public entry is not permitted, the grandeur of the 16-foot-wide marble and bronze staircase, original woodwork and marble panelling can be viewed from just inside the entrance portico.

The seeds of the EWO institution germinated from a small number of families in, or around, the Scottish county of Dumfriesshire. One family name, which was never to wither, that of the Keswicks, has been indelibly linked with the company from its earliest days right up to the present. The Keswick dynasty in Shanghai extended over four generations and, at one point or another, a representative from each generation acted as chairman of the SMC. The Keswicks had always had more than a keen interest in racing and it was William Keswick who bailed out the fledgling Shanghai Race Club to avoid financial ruin in 1862. Big company rivalries were fought out on the racecourse at its spring and autumn meetings. The first, fought in the 1860s, was between

Jardines and Dent & Co., another influential British trading firm based on the Bund. By 1922, the private EWO stables, which were located next to the Shanghai Race Club, housed 46 ponies and the company had 21 gentlemen riders on its payroll.

Paradoxically, the race club became an arena where much graver national rivalries were to be fought following a failed Japanese attempt to gain ascendancy in the SMC elections of 1940. Mr. William J. Keswick, the recently elected chairman of the SMC, was shot twice by a Japanese assailant at a ratepayers' meeting there in January 1941. Cambridge-educated William, better known as Tony, baronial doyen of business, social and civic life, escaped major injury and was thereafter to travel around the city in a 1925 seven-seater armoured car that had been custom-made for Al Capone. Whilst his company's building was occupied by the Japanese Navy as the base for their intelligence department after December 1941, Tony himself became the London-based director of British Intelligence's Special Operations Executive for the Far East during the war. The building's clandestine history has now come to a close. It, along with two adjacent buildings, is set to be inhabited by high-class eateries and stores, spearheaded by Saks of Fifth Avenue to its rear (see page 342). Luxury residences are also planned as part of this scheme.

*Sandbags protect the premises during the Sino-Japanese hostilities of 1937*

*The building in 1926*

# No. 28 The Glen Line Building

The Glen Line Ltd., a shipping line of Scottish pedigree going back to the 1850s, opened their new premises on the Bund in modest style on 28th February 1922. The building, designed by Tug Wilson of Palmer and Turner in a 'free' Renaissance style, was generally regarded as one of the finest ever to be built in the International Settlement.

The ground floor was occupied by the offices of the Glen Line Eastern Agencies, with the entrance in the centre of the Bund frontage, consisting of an imposing portico with two granite columns on either side. The upper floors were rented out, whilst the tower of the building above the roofline provided accommodation for the Glen Line manager. Another imposing entrance, which was found on Beijing Road, led on to one of the largest single office spaces, of

*The building in 2006*

around 8,000 square feet, to be found in the city. Separate stairs were provided for the Chinese 'coolie' class where foreign feet would dare not tread except in the case of an emergency or a fire.

The Glen Line was acquired by Blue Funnel Lines in 1935, and although the building continued to be known by its former name, its local office closed in March 1936. The German Consulate moved into the building in April 1937 after their old premises were demolished.

The building was propitiously sold by Jardine, Matheson & Co., who were acting as agents, to Japanese interests just four months before the Japanese occupation of the city. Following the war, it was taken over by the American Navy and housed the Fleet Post Office and Shore Patrol. The navy undertook a renovation of the building and one floor was converted into two apartments for visitors. Following their departure, the American Consulate moved in. The consulate, which had not had its own permanent premises since 1931, had previously rented space in various hotel and office buildings near the Bund.

*The building in 2006*

# No. 29. The Banque de L'Indo-Chine

The building for the Banque de L'Indo-Chine was designed by Atkinson & Dallas in Italian Renaissance style and was opened for business in June 1914. It is faced with granite from the nearby city of Suzhou and the two polished granite pillars that run between the upper windows are from the seaside town of Qingdao in northern China. The centre windows of the first floor are flanked by Doric style columns while the two at the end are in Ionic style. The main entrance, again in Doric style, has polished Qingdao granite columns on either side.

Inside the entrance hall the original handsome and massive teak doors still open on to the main banking hall, but the hall itself exhibits little of its original grandeur. There is no evidence of the teakwood that was used to floor the hall and to provide the bases and decoration on the marble columns, and the large glass-domed ceiling has gone. The original marble has routinely been replaced with that of an inferior kind. The banking hall, which used to be four feet above pavement level and reached by a flight of marble steps, is now less than one foot above the pavement. On either side of the entrance hall the rooms occupied by the manager and sub-manager are still identifiable, but their doors are missing. The entire two floors above the ground level were originally laid out to accommodate four voluminous residential apartments.

*1930s poster*

Yang Peiming

# MISSIONARIES AND MILLIONAIRES— THE BUND'S NEW GARDEN OF EDEN

Two of the oldest buildings on the Bund, those of the former British Consulate and neighbouring consular residence, have been quietly abandoned and no longer take prime position at its head. An awkward overpass placed right in front of their grounds hides them from the waterfront and the demolition of two adjacent buildings has dislocated them from the contiguous sweep of buildings along the waterfront.

The former premises of the Japanese shipping line **Nippon Yusen Kaisha** (NYK), which were rebuilt in 1926, became the first victim of change on the Bund in the modern era when they were demolished in late 2004. The other building, which was to its north, the former **Masonic Hall**, was demolished

*1930s NYK pamphlet*

long ago in 1927. The Northern Lodge of China, which was established in 1849, first occupied a Chinese building on Jiangxi Road and had made several moves before the opening of the

*View from the former Friendship store, now the site of the Peninsula hotel, over Pudong in 1995. The former 19th century premises of NYK are in the right foreground*

299

*The former consular grounds looking north, with the new elevated highway to the right, 1995*

Masonic Hall in 1867, for which they shared the cost with two other local lodges. As with the building of the nearby Shanghai Club, it was a cost that the impoverished Shanghai community could ill afford in the aftermath of the Taiping Rebellion. The building, designed by Mr. J. Clark, featured a fine hall replete with a magnificent organ and a lofty Masonic Temple. However, it wasn't particularly well constructed and it had to be rebuilt to a design by Mr. J. Chambers just 30 years later. The new building only survived another 30 years before it was demolished in 1927, following its sale to NYK. The company's intention to rebuild there soon afterwards was never realised.

*The Duke of Connaught delivers a Masonic address in 1890*

Melbourne Chinese Museum Collection

*The Masonic Hall (second right), photographed in 1886*

Operations are now underway on the site of where the NYK offices and the nearby modern Shanghai Friendship Store once stood to build a new Peninsula hotel marking the return of The Hongkong and Shanghai Hotels Ltd. to the city after

*Laying the foundation stone of the Masonic Hall, November 1883*

an absence of over 50 years. In addition to the hotel, an apartment hotel, a retail arcade and other facilities are planned for the area. The project, which is a joint venture with Starwaly Properties (Group) Pty Ltd., was the first tangible sign of the extensive redevelopment that is now sweeping the 'Waitanyuan' area ('headstream of the Bund') and will continue to do so for many years to come.

**B**efore The Hongkong and Shanghai Hotels Ltd. publicly declared their intention to build a hotel in late 2004, it was rumoured that the hotel site would engulf the verdant lawns and buildings of the former **British Consulate**, which forms the heart of the plan. This was not, however, to be. At the time of publication, the fate of the garden area and some of its neighbouring buildings, including the former Union Church, remains unclear. The Huangpu District Government held a separate design competition for the area. The American architect Christopher Choa, one of the three contestants—none of whom

*The Friendship Store is demolished to make way for the new Peninsula hotel, April 2004*

actually won, pointed out that the district government's intention to build two storeys below the site was unworkable as the garden contains a number of designated heritage trees which, at least in theory, cannot be moved.

The area is strangely steeped in historical *déjà vu*. Shanghailanders, and even members of the SMC, regretted the removal of 12 magnolia trees, just to the east of the consular site, in 1921. The precious trees had been given to the city in the 1840s by Sir Robert Fortune, botanical collector to the Horticultural Society of London. Furthermore, the original development of the area by the British in the 1860s revolved around the surrender of British consular grounds. And to top it off, the major part of the current project centres on refashioning two city blocks which were almost totally transformed in a short burst of development in the 1920s and 1930s.

Captain George Balfour, the first British consul, and his successor, Rutherford Alcock, endured protracted and difficult negotiations with the Chinese and British governments, as well as with numerous Chinese landowners, in order to allow their first consular offices to be opened there in July 1849. The marshy land that they acquired was colloquially known as 'the city of reeds.' As the area in question was originally outside the British Settlement, its northernmost boundary being marked by today's East Beijing Road, the consuls had previously taken up residence within the native city. The site they secured covered an area of 20 acres and extended all the way westwards towards a ditch, today's Huqiu Road, and it was not until 1852 that the first consulate building was completed there.

*The 'Waitanyuan' area in 1930 and in 2006*

A decision by the British government to sell off nine lots on its consular grounds by public auction in September 1862 opened the way for the development of today's Yuanmingyuan Road, which was then referred to as the 'New Road,' as well as the present-day Huqiu Road, which was still a ditch at that point. The auction, held in the Court Room, was presided over by Barnes Dallas, the father of the architect Arthur Dallas. After being filled in, the ditch was originally named C N Aomen Road, but around 1873 its name was changed to Upper Yuanmingyuan Road, and the 'New Road,' which had been originally named Yuanmingyuan

*Early 20th century postcard of the British Consulate*

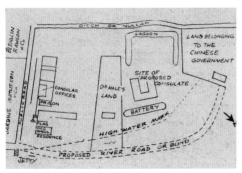

*First plan of British consular buildings and grounds*

Road, was renamed as Lower Yuanmingyuan Road. To avoid confusion, the road reverted to its former name, dropping the prefix 'Lower,' at which time Upper Yuanmingyuan Road was sensibly renamed as Museum Road in 1886. Yuanmingyuan Road, with its proximity to H.B.M.'s Supreme Court, was a popular domicile for the denizens of the legal profession and was alternatively known as 'Lawyers Row.' The thoroughfare took its name from Beijing's magnificent Summer Palace, which was burned to the ground by the British in 1860.

The consulate's first building was tragically destroyed by fire in 1870 with the loss of many valuable records; but some, including the indispensable title deeds of foreign-owned property, were rescued by Consul Medhurst at great personal risk. Its successor, designed by Grossman & Boyce, was completed in

March 1873 and the adjoining Consul-General's house was finished in 1882. Some people have proposed turning the consular site into a swanky private club, whilst others have called for a more civic approach and its conversion into some form of cultural attraction. It seems certain, however, that the unsightly overpass at its gates will be demolished, when traffic is re-routed elsewhere.

The neighbouring **Union Church** has been allowed to degenerate into a very poor state of repair and its octagonal spire, like those of most churches around town, was supposedly removed during the Cultural Revolution. Its roots go back to the earliest days of a foreign presence when the Rev. Dr. W. H. Medhurst of the London Missionary Society delivered the first public sermons at the British Consulate in the Chinese city. Medhurst, in his role as an interpreter, accompanied Captain Balfour to Shanghai in November 1843. He was one of the founding members of the first foreign Municipal Council in 1854 and, treading in father's footsteps, his son later took up the post of British Consul. The London Missionary Society established premises on Shandong Road, five blocks from the Bund, in 1845, and the first Union Church was built there in 1864. The church,

Picture This

*The British Consulate and buildings on Yuanmingyuan Road to the rear, 1928*

*The ruins of the Union Church and the neighbouring hall, June 2006*

which had reformed as an independent multi-denominational body, was forced to look for a new location when the Society wanted their land back for their own purposes. Despite the church's indignant protests, the Society refused to give them any compensation for their loss, and public fund-raising for the new church began in 1881. The site chosen, which was formerly owned by the Chinese government before its sale to the British government, was one of the lots that the consulate disposed of in 1862.

The early English Gothic-style church, designed by the prominent British architect William Dowdall, was opened for services in July 1886 and was enlarged in 1901. At the turn of the 20th century it was under the direction of another Shanghai ecclesiastical giant, the Rev. C. E. Darwent. Next door on the corner of Yuanmingyuan Road, a hall, with classrooms, was opened in December 1899. It hosted the Christian Endeavour Society on Friday evenings, the Literary and Social Guild every other Wednesday, the Boys Brigade on Tuesday evenings and was

*View from the top of the Capitol Building in 1930 and in 2006, with the former Rowing Club in the centre*

the venue for singing classes on Wednesday evenings. The hall was partly demolished in 2006, whilst hopes for the church's revival were put in jeopardy following, yet another, tragic fire in January 2007.

Though the features of the buildings opposite the church facing Suzhou Creek were also radically transformed, some evidence of their century-old history survived, up until 2007. The lower part of the third-generation buildings for the **Shanghai Rowing Club**, which was built on the site in 1904, had provided a base for more recent structural additions. The club was formed

*A surviving entrance to the former Rowing Club, 2006*    *The Fire Brigade in front of the Rowing Club, 1908*

by a quorum of British and American members in 1863, with the aim 'to promote rowing regattas and swimming galas and to provide and maintain a club-house, boat house, swimming bath, and a fleet of rowing boats, for the use of members of the Club.' Designed by Scott and Carter, the two-storey building, which was originally built in red brick, contained a large ballroom, dressing rooms and bathrooms, as well as a large roof garden over the neighbouring boathouse. A swimming bath was added in 1905 and part of the building was converted into a gymnasium in 1916.

For Shanghailanders, the club's autumn regatta was one of the sporting and social highlights of the year. They would crowd on to special trains provided by the Shanghai and Nanking Railway for the 30-mile trip to Kunshan district in neighbouring Jiangsu province. The club committee searched hard to find a suitable and appropriate spot to hold the event, and what place could have been better than the town of Henli. From its inauguration in 1908 the Henli Regatta was the object of strong protests from local Chinese gentry and the Chinese authorities. However, it proved to be a popular spectator sport for the Chinese as much as for foreigners. Despite intercessions by successive British Consuls to keep the event going, the Chinese authorities finally put their oar in and banished the event to the local waters of the Huangpu River in 1929. The Henli event did, however, resurface for a short period in the early 1930s as Chinese attentions were steered towards the course of Japanese expansionism in China.

Outside this area, plans for the greater part of the Waitanyuan project have already been laid covering two large blocks west, and the best part of two blocks south of the garden area. Achieving a resolution between investors, various arms of the city and local governments, and prospective architects was a long and tangled

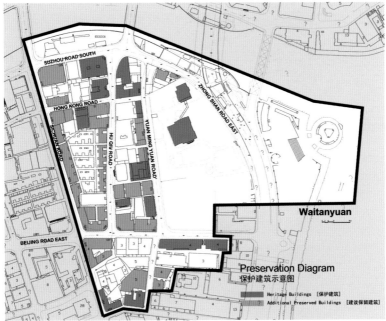

*Architect's drawing detailing the heritage and preservation status of buildings in the area*

Ben Wood

*The first building to be demolished in 2006 was the former Ben Godown on Huqiu Road*

*Conceptual plan for the area*

process. A major breakthrough came in November 2005, however, when Rockefeller Group International, Inc. and NHP, a quasi-governmental agency, announced the official launch of the project with the establishment of the joint-venture Shanghai Bund de Rockefeller Group Master Development Co. Ltd. The Rockefeller Group, who are acting as the master developer, also formed a partnership with Sinolink Worldwide Holdings Ltd. and the Waitanyuan project for that area was officially rechristened the 'Shanghai Bund de Rockefeller Group Project.'

The Rockefeller name has a long connection with the locality. The Laura Spelman Rockefeller Memorial, founded in her memory in 1918 by her husband, John D. Rockefeller Sr., made a large contribution to the cost of the Missions Building on Yuanmingyuan Road. Whilst the name may be the same, the Rockefeller Group International has little relation to those forbears

and is, in fact, a wholly owned subsidiary of the Japanese Mitsubishi Estate Company Ltd.

Four master plans, with radically differing approaches to the commercial and residential complexion of the area and to the treatment of its 14 heritage buildings, were eventually submitted, prior to Ben Wood, of benwood STUDIO SHANGHAI, being selected to execute the project. The work on construction is to be carried out in three phases, most of the business occupants in phase one of the development having vacated their premises by the end of 2005. Phase one of the project, which began with the demolition of some buildings along the Huqiu Road in early 2006, includes luxury residential housing, high-end retail outlets, an hotel, office space and facilities for cultural attractions, as well as public squares and an underground parking area. It is anticipated that this part of the scheme will be completed before Shanghai's hosting of the World Expo in 2010.

*Looking west along Suzhou Creek, with the Rowing Club and the Union Church to the left and, beyond the old Zhapu Road Bridge, the new Head Post Office, 1924*

*The new Zhapu Road Bridge, with the buildings of the Capitol Theatre and B.A.T. to the left, 1932*

*Designed elevation in Yuanmingyuan Road*

Ben Wood

*Aerial view with the projected scheme to the fore*

The area covers one whole block bounded by Yuanmingyuan Road facing the Bund, Huqiu Road to the rear, South Suzhou Road and East Beijing Road. The existing buildings largely date from 1924 to 1933 when the site was extensively and impressively redeveloped to allow the widening of Huqiu Road (formerly Museum Road) up to 50 feet. As part of the development, the Zhapu Road Bridge at the northern end of the road crossing the Suzhou Creek, was rebuilt and opened to traffic on 1st December 1926. Although a couple of buildings dating back to the early 20th century were allowed to remain on the block at that time, with at least one of them hopefully being renovated as part of the present scheme, the last old buildings left in the area from when it was first developed in the 1860s were razed in 1930 to make way for the new Y.W.C.A. building.

Damaging fires to buildings on important road intersections often ignited calls within the SMC for them to be replaced by taller and more slender structures to allow road widening. Such was the case with the rebuilding of Museum Road. Whilst calls

Ben Wood

for road widening after a fire in 1905 were quickly extinguished—a
fire to a property on the eastern corner near Suzhou Creek in
March 1924, where the Capitol Building was to later emerge,
provided the SMC with a well-timed and not to be missed
opportunity to shave off a piece of ground absolutely essential to
its grand remodelling plan. Although there were no reports of
skulduggery, the circumstances surrounding the blaze, which was
reported to be 'one of the worst fires that had ever occurred in
Shanghai,' were suspicious. The warehouses on the upper floors
of the building above the offices of the local newspaper, the
*Shanghai Times*, had just been plentifully stocked with silks
which were responsible for causing noxious gases to explode high
in the sky above, and the fire brigade's float, which might have
saved the building from total destruction, just happened to be out
of action on the night of the fire. Started by a fire in the Hall &
Holtz bakery, a former building on the site had been totally
gutted just nine years earlier.

Picture This

The newly built Beth Aharon Synagogue, 1927

Demolition work underway on the Wen
Hui Bao building in 2006

U p until the present phase of development, all the earlier
structures, apart from the **Beth Aharon Synagogue**, had hardly
been touched. The magnificent synagogue building, designed by Tug
Wilson and E. F. Bothwell, of Palmer & Turner, in 1927 and funded
by the fabulously wealthy Silas Hardoon, was taken over as the
printing workshop for the *Wen
Hui Bao*, an intellectually inclined
national newspaper, in the 1960s.
Regrettably the synagogue was
demolished in 1985 to make way
for the paper's new offices in a
ghastly 25-storey tower. The
building, one of the earliest
modern high-rises in the city, was
fittingly demolished in 2006.

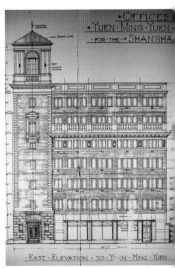

*Architect's elevation and floor plan for the Lyceum Building*

*The Lyceum Building in 2006*

Many buildings in this fascinating area were created by Shanghai's most prominent contemporary architects and were well ahead of their time in terms of design and usage. The heart of the area was occupied by three massive 'godowns' that were developed by the Shanghai Land Investment Company. The seven-storey **Lyceum Godown** or **Lyceum Building** in Italian Renaissance style at No. 185 Yuanmingyuan Road,

*The towers of the Lyceum Building and the neighbouring China Baptist Publication Society Building*

which was completed in 1927, was the largest and finest amongst them and is to be preserved as part of the current project. These godowns were revolutionary in that they afforded commodious office space, cavernous warehousing facilities and huge ground floor exhibition windows for stock display all in the same place. The area also found distinction in that a large number of missionary societies and religious organisations established their China headquarters there, and let out parts of their premises to commercial tenants. On account of its past extraordinary mix of Christian endeavour and commercial enterprise I have come to know the district as the 'saints and sinners quarter.'

The core of the new plan involves getting people to come back to live, work and enjoy themselves in the area. Slender, moderately high-rise buildings accommodating around 100 super-luxury apartments, each of approximately 350 square metres, are planned to be erected behind the façades of the former godowns and

*Former warehouse and office buildings on Huqiu Road that are making way for the new residential development, 2006*

offices facing Yuanmingyuan Road. And whilst the millionaire class may enjoy a lofty panoramic view of Shanghai, it is very much part of the plan to enliven the neighbourhood by keeping 90 percent of the retail activity firmly at street level. Internal atriums with labyrinths of escalators won't be seen, as most restaurants and other facilities are planned for the second floors of the buildings.

*Capitol Theatre interior, 1928*

Apart from the Lyceum Building, other historically significant buildings imbued with 'heritage status' that are to be preserved as part of phase one of the scheme include the Capitol Building (which housed the Capitol Theatre), a building which used to accommodate the China Baptist Publication Society and the Christian Literature Society, the Royal Asiatic Society Building and the Y.W.C.A. Building.

*Gonda's plan of the theatre*

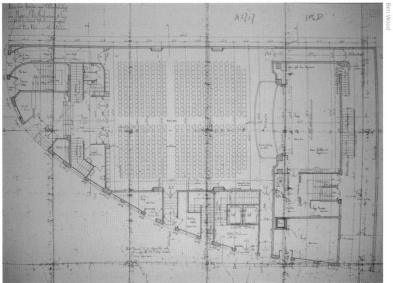

Ben Wood

The thoroughly modern Art Deco **Capitol Building**, also known after its owner as the Shahmoon Building, was the first edifice in the city to accommodate offices and apartments over a theatre. Its magnificently decorated 1,000-seat theatre, devoid of any obstructive columns, had a roof of huge, steel-reinforced concrete beams supporting the floors above. Building regulations had to be totally rewritten to allow such a precedent and the theatre was also the first to be air-conditioned in the city.

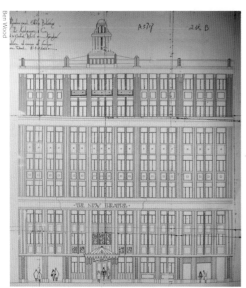

Gonda's drawing of the new theatre building

That fateful fire of March 1924 played no small part in the advent of this unusual and imposing structure. Its modernist, sail-shaped ground plan was determined rather by the SMC's need to have a wide road curvature at that point, than by the architect's design proclivities. And in return for their great prize, the SMC approved Mr. Solomon Elia Shahmoon's radical proposals for the new building in 1925, five months before the new building regulations were to take effect, 'at the express request of the owner...to enable him to erect the type

*Letter from architect, C. H. Gonda, to the SMC seeking to clarify the boundaries of the new building, October 1925*

of building he desires.' Unlike its predecessors, the new building
was constructed of fire-resistant reinforced concrete.

A *North China Daily News* columnist commented that the
'building is an expression of all modern tendencies. It may be
noted that the classical architectural style borrowed from a
bygone period has been abandoned for the sake of adopting a
style which corresponds entirely with present-day constructional
methods in regard to building
materials used and also in
regard to the purpose of the
building.' Mr. C. H. Gonda, its
architect, who later installed
his offices in the building, used
coloured concrete and glass in
its wine- and amber-toned
interior and employed Russian
artists to produce murals and
sculptures featuring thespian
themes. Although such features
are nowhere in evidence today,
much decorative relief has
survived in parts of the theatre
and on its unusual concrete
stairways. The theatre's
original balconies, with their
fine wrought ironwork, have
also withstood the test of time.
Its highly decorated octagonal
foyer, however, has long since
disappeared. The building's

*The former Capitol Building, with the Jinmao building
in the background, 2004*

decorative embellishments were undertaken by Mr. Podgoursky,
a renowned locally based artist, who had recently completed
murals for the Palace Hotel and the French Club and who
was to undertake a commission for the Cathay Hotel in the
following year.

*The corner of Huqiu Road and Suzhou Creek in 1928*

Picture This

*Conceptual drawing of the Capitol Building*

The Capitol, on the corner of Huqiu Road and South Suzhou Road, which opened on 25th February 1928, also employed a fine orchestra under the direction of Mr. Bakaleinikoff, another Russian. The major Hollywood studios, among them United Artists, Columbia Films, Twentieth Century Fox and Paramount Films, made their headquarters in the building. Although the theatre featured a film vault on its roof, a large group of armed Italian marines stormed the theatre in January 1929 and forcibly took the first reel of the film *The Street Angel* from the projection room during an evening performance. Mussolini had personally taken offence at the movie and the marines set fire to the celluloid outside the entrance of the theatre. Shanghai's Censorship Board responded by cutting a few clips from the film in deference to Italian susceptibilities, including one scene where Naples was described as 'sordid' and another showing monkeys assaulting the Neapolitan police. Later, in its guise as the Culture News Theatre, Japanese propagandist newsreels and documentaries were screened to a less than indifferent audience between 1943 and 1945. As part of the present scheme, the theatre will be reopened and the rest of the building, with its prime roof space, is scheduled to be reinvented as a fashionable boutique hotel.

One of Shanghai's most celebrated architects, Ladislas (Laszlo) Hudec, who, like Gonda, was born of the Austro-Hungarian Empire, created the imposing, jagged-edged, ecclesiastically styled tower next door to the Capitol. Hudec's buildings are noted for their intricate and artistic brick finishes. However, much of the detailed work was left in the hands of Mr. G. G. Hudec, who had practised architecture in New York before joining his elder brother in Shanghai. The new building occupied the site of the 700-capacity **Lyceum Theatre**, which was designed by William Kidner and opened in January 1874. The theatre was home to the Amateur Dramatic Corps (ADC), a predominantly British association dating back to 1866, who kept the foreign community entertained with an inimitable blend of Shanghai-grown British farce.

The ADC grew out of the union of two former thespian societies, the *Footpads* and the *Rangers*, with their histories going back to 1853. At its very first performance, in 1867, of a farce called *Whitebait in Greenwich*, the audience was curiously advised that 'persons not having carriages can sleep in the Theatre on application to the Harbour Master (at a fee) and they must find their own gas!' Gilbert and Sullivan operas were particularly popular with the Shanghai public and were complemented by performances from international companies such as the Royal Italian Opera as far back as 1879. An earlier Lyceum Theatre, which was built nearby in 1867, burned to the ground in 1871. The New Lyceum, as it was first known, aged quickly and demolition was considered in 1905. Eventually the SMC forced its temporary closure on safety grounds in 1922. Facing severe financial difficulties, the theatre was unsuccessfully put up for auction in June 1928. In due course the ADC managed to find a buyer in January 1929 and their 223rd and last performance at the old theatre, *And so to Bed*, was staged on 27th April 1929.

The A.D.C. "Pirates of Penzance"

*Sapajou cartoon of an ADC Gilbert & Sullivan performance*

The building which took its place opened in May 1932, straddled the block and housed the headquarters of the **Christian Literature Society** on Huqiu Road and the headquarters of the **China Baptist Publication Society** on Yuanmingyuan Road. Spreading the word of the gospel now took centre-stage. Apart from accommodating many other missionary societies' libraries and commercial offices, Hudec moved his own architectural practice to its eighth floor. The premises of the Christian Literature Society had been given an unexpected baptism of service, as, for some

*The former premises of the Christian Literature Society, 2006*

weeks before their opening, they were employed as a miniature refugee camp housing families dislocated by the Sino-Japanese hostilities to the north of the area.

The Christian Literature Society, which was founded in 1887 as 'The Society for Diffusion of Christian Knowledge among the Chinese', had numerous members of the foreign business community on its board. Sir Robert Hart, Inspector General of Customs, was its president before his death in 1911. The Society's most infamous early 20th century director was Edward Selby Little, whose secular and competing aspirations were expressed in his roles as missionary, businessman, administrator, diplomat, agitator and social commentator. British-born Little came to China with the South California Methodist Episcopal Conference in 1886 and, amongst other activities, went on to become: the first China manager for Brunner Mond, ICI's founding company in China in 1900; an SMC Councillor in 1905; and the Australian Trade Commissioner in China in 1921. He was renowned for his less than transparent dealings in the development of Kuling, China's largest hill resort for missionaries, which he established in 1895.

The eastern portion of the building, on which building work had started in

*The Chinese characters for 'True Light Building' were still above its entrance in 2006*

September 1930, was occupied by the China Baptist Publication
Society. It was more familiarly known as the True Light Building—
the title of the Society's journal, which was printed on the
premises. Sunday school lessons, bible tracts and other Baptist
literature were printed on presses that had been brought up from
Guangzhou in southern China. The Society itself had a much
shorter journey as its offices were previously in the Missions
Building, just a few doors away. The building also housed the
downtown School of Commerce of Shanghai College.

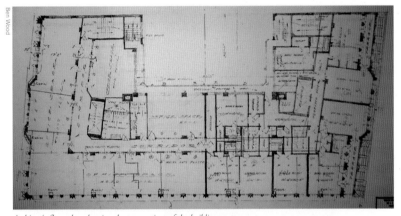

*Architect's floor plan showing the two sections of the building*

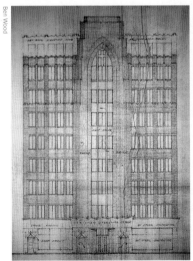

*Architect's drawing of the elevation of the Christian
Literature Society Building*

*Architect's drawing of the elevation of the True Light
Building*

*The former True Light Building in rags, 2006*

*The former RAS building, 2006*

Faint print marks of where the letters 'RAS' used to adorn the crest of the former **Royal Asiatic Society Building** at No. 20 Huqiu Road are still visible today. The Shanghai branch of the RAS was founded in 1857 under the name of the 'Shanghai Literary and Scientific Society' until its affiliation with the RAS of Great Britain in 1858 when it became the Royal Asiatic Society (North China Branch). Their first permanent building, completed in 1871, housed the Shanghai Museum with its collection of wildlife and birds that had been initiated by local sportsmen in 1874. The collection soon outgrew its confines, but plans to erect a new building on the site were stalled by the outbreak of World War I. When he was appointed as honorary curator in 1922, Mr. Arthur de C. Sowerby pushed the cause further by asking the SMC to support a real museum and 'not just a stuffed-bird show.' He wanted to have an art gallery, museum and library all under the same roof. The SMC, however, didn't like his proposal to use the former premises of the French Club as a home for such a British institution.

By 1928, the Society's premises, which were on a site given in perpetuity by the British government, had been so molested by white ants that Tug Wilson, its architect and an RAS Council member, and Ellis Hayim, the building's sub-contractor, began a campaign to raise funds for a new building. It was only the third time in the Society's history that it called on the public for support. Previously they had largely funded the original building, as well as the purchase of a fine collection of books from Dr. Alexander Wylie, a famous missionary scholar. On this

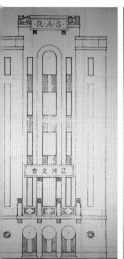
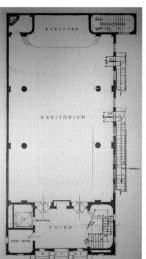
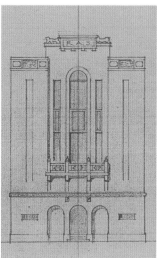

*Wilson's alternative designs for the RAS building*

occasion they weren't so giving and it took a donation from the SMC of 50 percent of the estimated building costs to allow the foundation stone to be laid by Sir John Brenan, H.M. Consul General, on 20th October 1931. The SMC's funding allowed Wilson's plans, which were drawn up in December 1927, for the building as we see it today, to go ahead. For fear of being unable to secure the necessary funding, Wilson had submitted plans to the SMC, in April 1930, for a scaled-down version of the building, with only three floors.

The effects of the Sino-Japanese hostilities and the falling price of silver in 1932 resulted in the building falling behind schedule and, when it opened in February 1933, the Society was

P&T Group    *The RAS building, 1932*    *The foreign personnel of the Shanghai Museum, 1933*

heavily in debt. The building had ended up 50 percent over budget. Further calls to the community for extra funds largely fell on deaf ears and in his magazine the *China Journal*, Mr. Arthur de C. Sowerby, who was director of the museum at that time, made it known that, in a city where huge fortunes had been made, there were very few publicly spirited citizens around. The fabulously wealthy Henry Morriss, of the *North China Daily News* contributed just a small fraction of the modest sum needed to equip the library with bookshelves. Previously, Sir Victor Sassoon had made the largest individual donation from Shanghai's foreign community—but it was still only enough to cover one-thirtieth of

*Cover of a special museum edition of the* China Journal, *1933*

the building's eventual cost. On the face of it, the most sizeable anonymous donation came in the form of a ten billion ten million mark banknote of 1923 from the Reichsbank in Berlin. The bill, however, was practically worthless and would only afford the addition of a couple of books to the library. The shortage of funds for equipping the museum, on the fourth and fifth floors of the building, delayed its opening until November 1933.

*Balustrade, featuring the name seal motif, above the entrance of the former RAS building, 2006*

If it were not for the fact that Mr. A. S. Henchman, the manager of the Hongkong and Shanghai Bank, was their honorary treasurer things could have been considerably worse. Although the immediate shortfall in funds was helped by a further substantial donation from Dr. Wu Lien-the, the head of the Chinese Government Quarantine Service, the Society was plagued with financial problems throughout the 1930s. Its greatest, but ill-timed, hope of financial stability came in late 1941 when the American financed International Institute of China rented part of the building and moved in their library. Ironically, during the Japanese occupation, in its guise as a Sino-Japanese cultural centre, the museum received more visitors than ever before in 1942. The visitors, however, were largely made up of organised school parties, who could not refuse the invitation, rather than interested individuals.

Tug Wilson combined a highly successful mixture of ancient Chinese ornament with modern Western architectural design in the RAS building. The motif on the central bronze panel on the exterior originates from a native bronze of the Zhou dynasty. Wrought iron grilles, inside and outside, were adopted from Chinese seals. Although the building's elaborately decorated entrance doors have unfortunately been lost in recent years, the original grilles featuring the yin-yang symbol have survived on their flanking octagonal windows. The interior had a Chinese theme. Its auditorium, which was named after Dr. Wu Lien-the, the building's financial saviour, featured jet-black structural

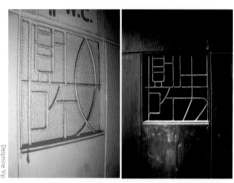

Delphine Yip

*Surviving grilles set in the bathroom doors*

columns set against starkly contrasting 'old silk' beige walls, highlighted with notes of green and vermillion. Designs from Chinese seals were embodied in the wrought-iron grilles of the doors in the public halls and lobbies. None of these appear to have survived, although some highly stylised grilles with Chinese characters in the form of 'man' and 'woman' were found to have survived on some bathroom doors in the building.

*The Shanghai Museum, 1933*

The building housed the Shanghai Museum, as well the magnificent RAS library with its collection of around 15,000 volumes. Some museum exhibits have been preserved and are open to public view today at the Shanghai Natural History Museum. The major part, if not all, of the library collection, which was shipped to Japan during the Second World War, was recovered by the Nationalist government after hostilities ceased. The core of the collection, as well as hundreds of thousands of other books, periodicals and newspapers from other foreign libraries and archives established before the end of the 1930s, miraculously survived the Japanese occupation and the perils of the Cultural Revolution and can still be consulted today at the Shanghai Library's Bibliotheca, in Xujiahui, to the west of the city.

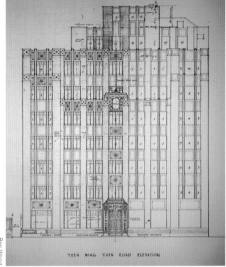

YUEN MING YUEN ROAD ELEVATION

*The entrance to the former Y.W.C.A. Building, 2006*    *Architect's drawing of the Y.W.C.A. Building*

*Mr. Poy Gum Lee*

The nearby **Y.W.C.A. Building** at No. 133 Yuanmingyuan Road, again epitomises a fine modern synthesis of Western and Chinese design which can be found no place other than Shanghai. Its architect, Poy Gum Lee, who was born to Cantonese parents in New York in 1900, trained in the US before coming to China. He left his work with the Y.M.C.A. Building Bureau in 1927 to help design Dr. Sun Yat-sen's mausoleum in Nanjing and by the tender age of 30 he had been appointed president of the Society of Chinese Architects. In accordance with the organisation's ethos, and in something of a first for Shanghai, Chinese women made up the larger part of its building committee. They were adamant in demanding the construction of a gracefully designed structure that incorporated Chinese architectural features.

The brick exterior of the building is finished in Suzhou granite carved with symbolic Chinese designs. The designs around the door frame incorporate the triangular symbol of the association on each corner, and the original Chinese name of the building survives intact. Apart from the ground floor entrance and auditorium, which were in Chinese temple style, using reds, golds and greens for the terrazzo flooring and painted ceiling designs,

the rest of the building was fitted out as functional, modern office space. The only other trace of China was to be found in the temple-like hall, at the northwest corner of the building, built as a memorial to the former general secretary Grace L. Coppock. It was popularly known as the 'women's building' on account of its modest and dignified design.

*The former Y.W.C.A. Building awaits a new beginning, 2006*

The site for the new building, which included three structures from 1863 known as the Balfour Buildings, was acquired by the National Board of the Y.W.C.A. of the USA in 1919 and later passed into the hands of the National Committee of the Y.W.C.A. of China in 1927. The old buildings provided temporary accommodation before a decision was made in October 1929 to build anew, and they were subsequently demolished in 1930. Funding for the new building largely came from America and substantial individual donations were received from the former United States Minister to China, Mr. Charles R. Crane, and the owner of the Dollar Steamship Lines, Captain Robert Dollar, in memory of his daughter, Bessie Hamilton, who passed away in Shanghai. Dollar, who himself died in May 1932, never saw the completed building as the opening was delayed from March till October 1932 on account of the local hostilities. The building's penthouse was originally occupied by Lady Pringle, whose import-export company used to bring the flavours of HP Sauce and Royal Braemar Whisky to Shanghai.

The Y.W.C.A. had long been recognised as having a civilising influence in Shanghai society. As far back as 1917 a report on a Y.W.C.A. meeting noted that 'ten years ago it was a rare thing to see any Chinese woman in the Shanghai streets, except of the obviously servant class. Now the large number of pleasant-looking, lady-like girls constantly to be seen in trams and richshas is a notable feature of every day. There is no question but that these owe their emancipation and the new interests in life they so clearly evince to the Y.W.C.A. and kindred schools and institutions.' In 1936 the second floor of the building was taken over by the Clarendon Club to provide

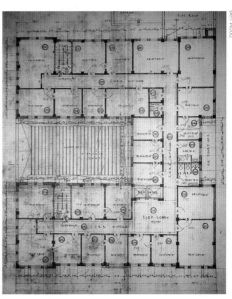

Ben Wood

*Y.W.C.A. building floor plan*

accommodation, Chinese and Western food and recreational activities for Shanghai's aspiring businesswomen of limited means. The building also housed the headquarters of the Rotary Club and the offices of the missionary journal, the *Chinese Recorder*. The journal noted that 'more than being the home of the National Committee and staff, it is the home of the whole movement. Every member even in the remotest part of China can feel a sense of pride in its possession, knowing that it houses the movement's national life of which each local unit is an integral and vital part.' With its origins going back to the 1890s, the Y.W.C.A. of China evolved as a huge, powerful, locally administered organisation that even found acceptance with the Communist authorities after 1949.

**The Missions Building**, two doors north of the Y.W.C.A. at No. 169 Yuanmingyuan Road, was the first building to be completed as part of the 1920s-era redevelopment, being opened in 1924. Erected by the Mission Architects Bureau under the supervision of Mr. Charles A. Gunn, it was built as a symbol to display the unity of the Christian Church in China to the Chinese. Whilst its primary occupant, the National Christian

Council, occupied the third floor, the rest of the building was taken over by a wide range of interdenominational organisations, including the American Bible Society, the National Bible Society of Scotland, the London Missionary Society, the China Council of the Presbyterian Church, and the

*Sketch of the proposed Missions Building, 1917*

American Red Cross. Although this building is designated with the lesser class of 'preservation,' rather than 'heritage' status, it is hoped that its façade will remain intact.

A similar designation is given to a nearby building, which stands out in terms of its architectural statement of commerce, if not of Christianity. It is the grand, six-storey, neo-classical building, which once housed the **Industrial Bank of China**, on the northeastern corner of Huqiu Road and Beijing Road. The site was previously occupied by the British Post Office until its closure and incorporation into the Chinese postal system at the end of 1922. Devoid of any treaty agreements, there were, bewilderingly, post offices representing seven different nationalities in Shanghai at that date. The first building completed on the site, in 1858, was that of the British prison.

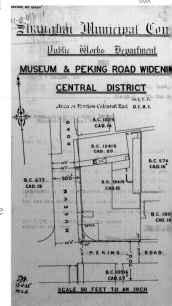

*SMC plan outlining road widening in the area, 1925*

*The British Post Office and the Chinese Post Office to the rear, 1908*

The new bank building, designed by Atkinson & Dallas, with its decorated granite face and beautifully finished marble interior, took two years to build and was opened in April 1930. The bank's exchange department and general offices occupied the ground and first floors, whilst the upper floors were let out. Despite the grandness of the bank building and the novel nature of its enterprise in promoting industrial development throughout China, its own history was not so creditable. The bank was forced to temporarily close down in October 1934 following the arrest of its managing director, Mr. S. H. Loh, on fraud charges. A few months later he was released from custody to face 300 Chinese creditors at a meeting of the Chinese Bankers' Association on Hong Kong Road. During the furore, which followed his announcement that

*Looking south along Huqiu Road, with the phase two project area to the right*

he couldn't afford to pay half his debts back, he escaped from the building, hotly pursued by a seething crowd before being re-arrested.

The second phase of the project covers the block to the west side of Huqiu Road. Its northern section, including the buildings on both sides of Hong Kong Road, was largely completed before 1925. Again it was home to numerous Christian organisations in days of old, though its future development, in line with that of the entire Bund area, will embody a demonstrably secular spirit. Three buildings in this section are to be preserved as part of this phase of development.

The building opposite the Capitol Building was originally erected in 1907 as a godown for the **British American Tobacco Company (B.A.T.)** and **Mustard & Company**. Under the direction of John W. Wilson of Algar & Company, the building was totally transformed and modernised between March 1924 and August 1925. It serves as a fine example of how the conversion of older buildings, an integral feature of the present-

*Looking east with the phase two project area, facing Central Sichuan Road, to the right*

day development, is by no means a new phenomenon. As well as the addition of an extra floor and a mansard roof, new elevations on the road fronts were carried out in Italian style, with red and buff granite and coloured cement as the motif, in preference to the grey granite plaster so pervasively used in the city. The building was of a classical design with two light courts, or 'sky wells,' allowing daylight to penetrate the inner structure.

The interior was fitted and decorated in a classical manner with black and white mosaic floors, a main staircase finished with white marble terrezze, walls lined with Sienna, marble effect,

*B.A.T.'s new offices, 1926*

glazed tiles, as well as an abundance of bronze work and teak joinery. The principal B.A.T. entrance was at the west end of the South Suzhou Road front. The main part of the ground floor was taken over by Mustard & Company, a British import and manufacturing concern established in 1862, which occupied ten out of the 11 large show windows on the ground floor.

Next door at No. 131 Huqiu Road, the original occupant's name, carved in English above its main entrance, remains visible. **The National Committee of the Y.M.C.A.** first occupied the site, previously owned by the International Race Club, in 1910, although their origins in Shanghai go back to 1896. The movement was incorporated by the Ministry of the Interior in Beijing when China became a republic in 1911 and its board of directors, known as the National Executive Committee, were exclusively Chinese. The Y.M.C.A. was another hugely successful Christian enterprise. The number of secretaries it employed had grown from just two in 1897 to over 350 at the time that the new building's corner stone was laid in June 1919. By 1921 the organisation's Chinese membership had grown to over 50,000 in 31 city associations and 184 student associations scattered across China.

*The former B.A.T. building, 2006*

The building itself was a monument to the brotherhood of commerce and Christianity relying on two American donors for its existence. Charles M. Stimson, a Los Angeles real estate magnate, and a lifelong bachelor who resided in a suite of rooms at his local Y.M.C.A., donated the money to purchase the site and Helen Gould provided the funds for the building itself. Helen Gould was the philanthropist daughter of Jay Gould, America's most infamous late 19th century businessmen. He was credited with a collapse of the gold market in 1869, which led to the financial ruin of numerous brokerage houses, banks and hundreds of private investors. Helen inherited part of her father's colossal US$125 million estate when he died in 1892, and donated countless millions to the Red Cross, to the Salvation Army and to the Y.M.C.A.

*The former building of the National Committee of the Y.M.C.A. was used as a residential building in 2006*

The building, designed by Shattuck & Hussey architects, was completed in January 1921 and fitted with the most modern equipment, including an elevator. The United States Minister to China, Charles R. Crane, who later made a substantial donation to the nearby Y.W.C.A., presided over the building's dedication ceremony in April of that year. The Y.M.C.A. Committee, who had their offices on the ground floor, let the rest of the building out to commercial enterprise.

The final building given protection status can be found at No. 59 Hong Kong Road. The Grecian colonnaded building stands in stark contrast to others around and is a neighbour to the red brick, American colonial structure of the Navy Y.M.C.A., which was completed around the same time. The building to be preserved was the home of the **Chinese Bankers' Association**, which had been formed in 1909 to provide mutual assistance

*The swimming pool inside the former Navy Y.M.C.A. on Hong Kong Road*

for its ten member banks including the Communication Bank and the Ningbo Bank. Their general offices were located on the lower floors and their club-rooms above. The design for the six-storey building, which was thrown open to competition, was executed by a Chinese architectural partnership between Y. M. Kuo and H. C. Chiu, known as the South Eastern Engineering and Construction Company, and completed in 1923.

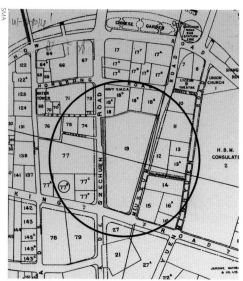

SMC plan outlining lot 19, owned by Jardine, Matheson & Co.

The entire southern portion of the block behind the large buildings on Hong Kong Road was formerly owned by Jardine, Matheson & Co. Using the opportunity afforded by another fire, which destroyed a row of ramshackle Chinese shops on Central Sichuan Road on the western perimeter of the current development, the company redeveloped the entire locale in 1925 and 1926. Unlike the surrounding area, however, this section was traditionally devoted to Chinese commercial and residential use—and the new plans set out to upgrade the fabric of the area without transforming its nature. The heart of the area contained a series of *lilongs*, or lanes, so typical of Shanghai's inimitable residential development until recent years. The houses adopted the arrangements of both a

The mid-1920s lilong development, 2006

*Architect's drawing of the new development for Jardine, Matheson & Co, 1925. The road to the left is today's Central Sichuan Road and the one to the right is East Beijing Road*

*The former premises of Gibb, Livingston & Co. in 1908*

British terrace and a Chinese courtyard dwelling—and featured a typical *shikumen* or 'stone-framed door' entrance. Plans involve the creation of luxury high-rise apartments in their place.

Jardines employed the services of Stewardson, Spence & Watson to design a homogeneous, high-quality development of three- and four-storey buildings to flank the residential area from the corner of Yuanmingyuan Road, around East Beijing Road and northwards along a long stretch of Central Sichuan Road. Among other buildings, the old Chinese post office was razed and the handsome new buildings were largely let to Chinese retail and commercial enterprises. They have all survived intact and it is expected that their frontages will be preserved, at least to some extent, as part of the present scheme.

As a prelude to the third phase of the project, Asia's first Saks of Fifth Avenue store is set to occupy the 1908, Queen Anne-style, red brick building opposite the site of the Peninsula hotel on East Beijing Road. The former offices of **Gibb, Livingston & Co.**, on the northwest corner of Yuanmingyuan Road and Dianchi Road, are also included in this phase of the development. Gibb, Livingston & Co. was founded in the 1830s by Thomas Augustus Gibb, formerly of the East India Company. Their headquarters, which were originally in Macau, were later transferred to Shanghai and, by 1908, they also maintained offices in Hong Kong and Fuzhou. The company operated a large general mercantile, shipping and commission business and had a whole host of agencies and insurance companies under their wing. Needless to say, the firm's family members were well represented on the ruling bodies of Shanghai's most prestigious institutions, including the SMC and the Shanghai Race Club, as well as serving as trustees of the nearby Lyceum Theatre.

# THE BEN WOOD VISION

The thing that fascinates Ben Wood most about Shanghai architecture is the thought that foreign architects in the 1920s and 1930s were doing exactly the same things that he is doing today. 'It's all happening over again, history is repeating itself.' Shanghai still conjures up images of a place where anything can be done and foreign architects are currently engaged on very important projects that are changing the face of the city. In the 1920s and 1930s they dealt with the scions of Shanghai commerce such as Sir Victor Sassoon and today they are dealing with billionaire patrons who want to make a name in much the same way as Sassoon did when Sassoon House was completed in 1929.

Shanghai was an important, if not the most important, city in the world in the 1920s and 1930s. Whilst the Sassoon dynasty ruled the East, New York was also booming under the aegis of the Rockefellers. Such dynasties changed the face of the world and Ben feels that one of the most incredible things about architecture is the opportunity to leave a legacy behind.

Ben Wood has already left his mark around the city and in other provinces. His first assignment in China was the ground-breaking Xintiandi project in Shanghai. The Xintiandi area, with its flamboyant mix of shops, restaurants, bars and other entertainment facilities as well as a boutique hotel has proved a huge success and has acquired an international fame like Soho in New York. In contradiction to the Shanghai vogue of building high and pasting the city with redundant huge 'public' green spaces, Wood created intimate, European-style plazas in Xintiandi. He is set to repeat that formula in the Waitanyuan area. Ben Wood is vehemently against the creation of vertically organised cities, which he sees as representative of the tragic demise of community, and maintains that three- and four-storey shikumen-style properties (the traditional Shanghai town house) can achieve the same population density as the present-day spatial arrangement of 30-storey buildings.

For similar reasons he is critical, and sceptical of the success, of some of the recent projects on the Bund itself, pointing out that the buildings were constructed like fortresses to keep the public away from their upper floors. He also believes that buildings of greater architectural innovation and merit, apart from the former Sassoon House, can be found behind the Bund, including many in the Waitanyuan area.

However, Ben Wood is not a preservationist and feels that very few buildings in the world deserve to be preserved, even though from an architectural perspective having old buildings on the site means the new buildings look even more modern. Whilst many classic buildings will survive intact and many others will be modified in the new project, it is the idea of bringing community and life back to the streets that is of paramount importance. People will be living there, entertaining themselves there, and maybe even going to church there again just as they did when the area was originally fully developed in the 1880s.

*Ben Wood is the principal of* benwood STUDIO SHANGHAI

# THE BUND DIRECTORY

## ARTS AND CULTURE

**Bund 18 Creative Centre**
4/F 18 First Zhongshan Road (E.) 中山东一路 18 号
Tel: 6323 7066 www.bund18.com

**Shanghai Gallery of Art**
3/F Three on the Bund 3 First Zhongshan Road (E.)  中山东一路 3 号
Tel: 6323 4549 www.threeonthebund.com

**Studio Rouge** (Contemporary Chinese art gallery)
17 Fuzhou Road  福州路 17 号
Tel: 6323 0833 www.studiorouge.cn

## DINING AND NIGHTLIFE

**Three on the Bund**
3 First Zhongshan Road (E.)  中山东一路 3 号
Access from 17 Guangdong Road  广东路 17 号
www.threeonthebund.com
4/F **Jean Georges** (Contemporary French dining)  Tel: 6321 7733
5/F **Whampoa Club** (Contemporary Chinese cuisine)  Tel: 6321 3737
6/F **Laris** (New World cuisine)  Tel: 6321 9922
7/F **New Heights** (Casual rooftop international dining and drinks)
Tel: 6321 0909
**The Cupola** (The ultimate private dining venue)  6323 0608

**5 The Bund**
5 First Zhongshan Road (E.)  中山东一路 5 号
Access from Guangdong Road  广东路
B1 **number five** (Café and bar)  Tel: 6329 4558  www.numberfive.cn
3/F **Moonsha** (Teppanyaki restaurant and lounge bar)
Tel: 6323 1117  www.moonsha.net
6/F **The Glamour Bar**  (Michelle Garnaut's latest sensational venue)
Tel: 6329 3751 www.m-restaurantgroup.com
7/F **M on the Bund** (Shanghai's most famous restaurant with flavours from
Europe to the Middle East)
Tel: 6350 9988 www.m-restaurantgroup.com

**6 Bund**
6 First Zhongshan Road (E.)  中山东一路 6 号  www.6bund.com
G/F **Dolce & Gabbana & The Martini Bar** Tel: 6339 0268/6339 1200
1/F **Suntory Japanese Dining Sun and Aqua Bar** Tel: 6339 2779
2/F **Tian Di Yi Jia**  (Beijing-style fine dining)
3/F **Visus—Ristorante Da Gio Gio, Savoy Pizza and Sofibar**
(Italian dining and penthouse-style bar)

### 12 The Bund
12 First Zhongshan Road (E.) 中山东一路 12 号
2/F Room 226 **The Bund 12 Café** (coffee shop with veranda in the heart of the former Hongkong and Shanghai Bank building)
Tel: 6329 5896

### Bund 18
18 First Zhongshan Road (E.) 中山东一路 18 号  www.bund18.com
Atrium **Sibilla Boutique Café**  Tel: 6329 9339
5/F **Tanwailou** (Cantonese cuisine)  Tel: 6339 1188  www.resto.18.com
6/F **Sens & Bund** (Contemporary French cuisine)
Tel: 6323 9898 www.resto.18.com
7/F **Bar Rouge** (Chic rooftop venue)  Tel: 6339 1199 www.resto.18.com

### 20 The Bund
**Peace Hotel** Access from 20 East Nanjing Road 和平饭店 南京东路 20 号
G/F **Old Jazz Bar** (Home of the legendary Peace Hotel Jazz Band)
8/F **Dragon and Phoenix Restaurant** (Chinese restaurant in an historic setting)
8/F **Peace Grill** (Western restaurant with Art Deco interior)
Tel: 6321 6888 www.shanghaipeacehotel.com

### Huangpu Park
1/F 500 First Zhongshan Road (E.) 黄浦花园 中山东一路 500 号
**Family Li Imperial Cuisine** (Imperial Chinese cuisine in private banquet rooms)
Tel: 5308 1919

# HOTELS ON, OR NEAR, THE BUND

### Astor House Hotel 浦江饭店
15 Huangpu Road 黄浦路 15 号 Tel 6324 6388  www.pujianghotel.com

### Broadway Mansions 上海大厦
20 North Suzhou Road 苏州北路 20 号 Tel: 6324 6260
www.broadwaymansions.com

### Hyatt on the Bund 上海世茂外滩尊悦酒店
199 Huangpu Road 黄浦路 199 号  Tel: 6393 1234  www.bund.hyatt.com

### Peace Hotel 和平饭店
20 East Nanjing Road 南京东路 20 号  Tel: 6321 6888
www.shanghaipeacehotel.com

### The Westin Shanghai 威斯汀大饭店
88 Central Henan Road 河南中路 88 号 Tel: 6335 2772
www.westin.com/shanghai

Tongji University

1  2  3  5  6  7  9  12

# HOTELS OVERLOOKING THE BUND

**Grand Hyatt Hotel Shanghai** 上海金茂君悦大酒店
Jinmao Building, 88 Century Boulevard 世界大道 88 号 Tel: 5049 1234
www.shanghai.hyatt.com

**Oriental Riverside Hotel Shanghai** 东方滨江大酒店
2727 Riverside Avenue 滨江大道德风尚 2727 号 Tel: 5037 0000
www.showhotel.com/china

**Pudong Shangri-La, Shanghai** 浦东香格里拉大酒店
33 Fucheng Road 富城路 33 号 Tel: 6882 8888 www.shangri-la.com

# SHOPPING

Aside from the array of international goods on offer, a number of outlets stock items
with a distinct Chinese flavour:

**Annabel Lee**
No. 1, Lane 8, First Zhongshan Road (E.) (behind No. 9 the Bund)
中山东一路 8 弄 1 号
Chinese-inspired gifts and home ware. Tel: 6445 8218 www.annabel-lee.com

***Blue* Shanghai *White***
17–103 Fuzhou Road 福州路 17–103 号
Stylish ceramics, furniture and tableware. Tel: 6323 0856

**Shiatzy Chen**
9 First Zhongshan Road (E.) 中山东一路 9 号
Superb neo-Chinese chic fashions.
Tel: 6321 9155 www.shiatzychen.com

**Suzhou Cobblers**
17 Fuzhou Road 福州路 17 号
Hand-embroidered silk shoes, slippers and accessories.
Tel: 6321 7087 www.suzhou-cobblers.com

**Younik**
Bund18 F/2 18 First Zhongshan Road (E.) 中山东一路 18 号
Fashions and jewellery from local designers
Tel: 6323 7066 www.bund18.com

## STREET NUMBERS OF THE BUND

13    14    15    16 17    18    19    20    23    24 26    27    28 29

# WELLBEING

## Barbers by Three
Three on the Bund, 2/F
3 First Zhongshan Road (E.) 中山东一路3号
Tel 6329 0418 www.threeonthebund.com

## BUND FIVE Spa
5/F 5 First Zhongshan Road (E.) 中山东一路5号
Tel: 6321 9135, 6321 9176

## Evian Spa
Three on the Bund, 2/F
3 First Zhongshan Road (E.) 中山东一路3号
Tel: 6321 6622 www.threeonthebund.com

Eric Niderost

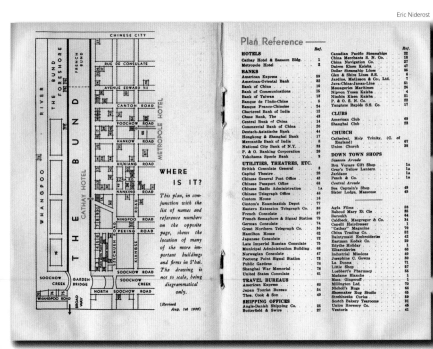

*Bund directory from* The Cathay *magazine, 1932*

# THE BUND—NOW AND THEN

| Address | Date Completed | Original Occupants | Present Occupants |
|---------|----------------|--------------------|--------------------|
| No. 1 | 1915 | The McBain Building | Various company offices |
| No. 2 | 1911 | The Shanghai Club | |
| No. 3 | 1915 | The Union Building | Three on the Bund |
| No. 5 | 1921 | Nisshin Kisen Kaisha Shipping Co. | M on the Bund and others |
| No .6 | 1881 | Russell & Co. | 6 Bund |
| No. 7 | 1908 | Telegraph Offices | Bangkok Bank—Thai Consulate |
| No. 9 | 1901 | China Merchants Steam Navigation Co. | Shiatzy Chen |
| No. 12 | 1923 | Hongkong and Shanghai Bank | Shanghai Pudong Development Bank |
| No. 13 | 1927 | The Custom House | The Custom House |
| No. 14 | 1948 | Bank of Communications | Bank of Shanghai |
| No. 15 | 1902 | Russo-Chinese Bank | China Foreign Exchange Trade System |
| No. 16 | 1927 | Bank of Taiwan | China Merchants Bank |
| No. 17 | 1923 | North China Daily News Building | AIA Building |
| No. 18 | 1923 | Chartered Bank of India, Australia and China | Bund 18 |
| No. 19 | 1909 | The Palace Hotel | Peace Hotel, South Building |
| No. 20 | 1929 | The Cathay Hotel | Peace Hotel, North Building |
| No. 23 | 1940s | Bank of China | Bank of China |
| No. 24 | 1924 | Yokohama Specie Bank | Industrial and Commercial Bank of China |
| No. 26 | 1918 | Yangtsze Insurance Association | Agricultural Bank of China |
| No. 27 | 1922 | EWO Building (Jardine, Matheson & Co.) | Foreign Trade Building |
| No. 28 | 1923 | The Glen Line Building | China Everbright Bank |
| No. 29 | 1914 | Banque De L'Indo-Chine | China Everbright Bank |
| No. 33 | 1873 1882 | The British Consulate The British Consular Residence | |

# WALKING THE BUND— THE WAY TO GO

*A*llow at least two hours for this walk—and more if you want to see and learn more, or stop for a drink or lunch en route. Note that photography is strictly prohibited in bank buildings. Of course, the walk could be done in reverse and, should you wish to omit the walk along the promenade to save time, begun from the Astor House Hotel. With a morning start, regardless of which way you go, lunch could be taken at a spectacular rooftop, or lofty, venue at M on the Bund, at Three on the Bund, or at Bund 18.

To view the main highlights of the Bund area, following the general sequence as outlined in chapters 6 and 7, begin at the corner of East Yan'an Road and the Bund (First Zhongshan Road East). Passing the former **Shanghai Club** ❶ at No. 2 (see page 91), first take a look at **Three on the Bund** ❷ (with its entrance just around the corner on Guangdong Road, see page 103). Walk a little further up Guangdong Road to the intersection with Central Sichuan Road to view the fabulous interior of the former **C.M.L.I. Building** ❸ (No. 93, page 108, open weekdays from 9.00 a.m. to 5.00 p.m. and weekends from 9.00 a.m. to 12.00 noon and 1.00 p.m. to 5.00 p.m.) before returning to the Bund. At the next intersection on Fuzhou Road, take a slight detour to see what was **Macgregor House** ❹ (No. 44, page 152) and walk back to the Bund alongside the former **Hongkong and Shanghai Bank** ❺, looking at its foundation stone and the famed bronze lions just around the corner. Visit the main banking hall with its fantastic mosaics (page 144, open from 9.00 a.m. to 5.30 p.m. daily). Continue northwards past the **Custom House** ❻ (page 155) to No. 17, the **AIA** building ❼, to view its impressive exterior (page 175) and take a look at the interior of **Bund 18** ❽, next door, to see how the past and present meld together (page 186).

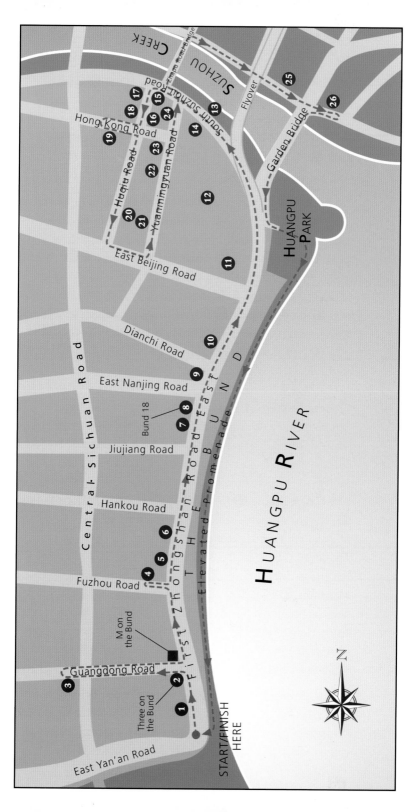

CREEK

SUZHOU

Zhapu Road Bridge

South Suzhou Road

Hong Kong Road

Huqiu Road

Yuanmingyuan Road

East Beijing Road

Dianchi Road

East Nanjing Road

Bund 18

Jiujiang Road

Hankou Road

Central Sichuan Road

Zhongshan Road East

THE BUND

Elevated Promenade

Fuzhou Road

M on the Bund

Guangdong Road

Three on the Bund

First

East Yan'an Road

Flyover

Garden Bridge

HUANGPU PARK

HUANGPU RIVER

START/FINISH HERE

N

① ② ③ ④ ⑤ ⑥ ⑦ ⑧ ⑨ ⑩ ⑪ ⑫ ⑬ ⑭ ⑮ ⑯ ⑰ ⑱ ⑲ ⑳ 21 22 23 24 25 26

The next major highlight is the **Cathay Hotel ❾**, now the north wing of the Peace Hotel, on the northern corner of East Nanjing Road (page 227). Continue northwards passing the mutilated warrior faces and bronze gates of the former **Yokohama Specie Bank ❿** (No. 24, page 283), before crossing East Beijing Road to enter the Waitanyuan area.

Passing the site where the **Peninsula hotel ⓫** is being erected, the grounds and buildings of the **British Consulate ⓬** (page 302) come into view on the left. Following the road around, (now South Suzhou Road) the site of the **Shanghai Rowing Club ⓭** (page 308) is on the right and the **Union Church ⓮** (page 305) on the left. Cross the Yuanmingyuan Road and turn sharp left onto Huqiu Road at the **Capitol Building ⓯** (page 318). Pass the building and the neighbouring premises of the **Christian Literature Society ⓰** (page 323) on the left and the **B.A.T. ⓱** and **Y.M.C.A. ⓲** premises on the right (No. 175 South Suzhou Road and No. 131 Huqiu Road, pages 336, 338), before turning right on Hong Kong Road to see the **Chinese Bankers' Association ⓳** building (No. 59, page 339). Return to Huqiu Road and continue on past the site of the new luxury apartments and the premises of the **Royal Asiatic Society ⓴** (No. 20, page 326) before taking a left on East Beijing Road, and another left, to head northwards on Yuanmingyuan Road passing the **Y.W.C.A. Building ㉑** (No. 133, page 331), the **Missions Building ㉒** (No. 169, page 333), the **Lyceum Building ㉓** (No. 185, page 315) and the **True Light Building ㉔** (page 325) near the corner. Take a slight left at the top of the road and cross the Zhapu Road Bridge over Suzhou Creek. Take a right, passing **Broadway Mansions ㉕** (No. 20 North Suzhou Road, page 271), which has a display of some old photographs in its lobby, before arriving at the **Astor House Hotel ㉖** (No. 15 Huangpu Road, page 212). Apart from the lobby, ensure that you visit the ballroom to the rear and the Tudor-styled hall on the third floor.

On leaving the hotel cross the former **Garden Bridge** on its left-hand side (page 52) and take the first entrance into **Huangpu Park** (the former Public Gardens, page 55). Continue along the elevated promenade at your leisure and at the peril of hawker harassment.

# INDEX

## Note for Users:

The order of index entries is word-by-word.

Page references to the main text are in normal typeface.

Photographs and illustrations and the text of their captions have also been indexed. Page references to these entries are in bold type.

Where the same subject appears in both text and a photograph on the same page, two entries for that page number are given, one for the text, and the other for the photograph, viz: cruise-liners, 208, **208**

# Recent Reviews of other Odyssey Guides...

"Thorough and beautifully illustrated, this book is a comprehensive—and fun—window into Afghan history, culture, and traditions. A must have for travel readers and a gripping read for anyone with even a passing interest in Afghanistan."
—Khaled Hosseini, author of *The Kite Runner*—

"...for coverage of Chongqing and the Gorges, and of the more placid and historically notable sites below Yichang and downriver to Shanghai, it is unrivalled..."
—Simon Winchester—

"It is one of those rare travel guides that is a joy to read whether or not you are planning a trip..."
—*The New York Times*—

"...Essential traveling equipment for anyone planning a journey of this kind..."
—*Asian Wall Street Journal*—

"If travel books came with warnings, the one for AFGHANISTAN: A COMPANION AND GUIDE would read, 'Caution: may inspire actual voyage.' But then, this lavishly produced guide couldn't help do otherwise—especially if you're partial to adventure."
—*TIME*, August 22nd 2005—

"Above all, it is authoritative and as well-informed as only extensive travels inside the country can make it. It is strong on the history. In particular the synopsis at the beginning is a masterly piece of compression."
—*The Spectator* (UK)—

"A gem of a book"
—*The Literary Review* (UK)—

"...Quite excellent. No one should visit Samarkand, Bukhara or Khiva without this meticulously researched guide..."
—Peter Hopkirk, *author of* The Great Game—

"The Yangzi guide is terrific"
—*Longitude Books*—

"...The bible of Bhutan guidebooks..."
—*Travel & Leisure*—

"...It's a superb book, superbly produced, that makes me long to go back to China..."
—*John Julius Norwich*—

"...Odyssey fans tend to be adventurous travelers with a literary bent. If you're lucky enough to find an Odyssey Guide to where you're going, grab it..."
—*National Geographic Traveler*—